Cinematic Encounters with Disaster

Thinking Cinema

Series Editors
David Martin-Jones, University of Glasgow, UK
Sarah Cooper, King's College, University of London, UK

Volume 12

Titles in the Series:
Afterlives: Allegories of Film and Mortality in Early Weimar Germany
by Steve Choe
Deleuze, Japanese Cinema, and the Atom Bomb
by David Deamer
Ex-centric Cinema by Janet Harbord
The Body and the Screen by Kate Ince
The Grace of Destruction by Elena del Rio
Non-Cinema: Global Digital Filmmaking and the Multitude by William Brown
Sensuous Cinema: The Body in Contemporary Maghrebi Film
by Kaya Davies Hayon
European Cinema and Continental Philosophy by Thomas Elsaesser
Limit Cinema: Transgression and the Nonhuman in Contemporary Global Film by Chelsea Birks
The Dark Interval: Film Noir, Iconography, and Affect by Padraic Killeen
Fertile Visions: The Uterus as a Narrative Space in Cinema from the Americas
by Anne Carruthers

Cinematic Encounters with Disaster

Realisms for the Anthropocene

Simon R. Troon

BLOOMSBURY ACADEMIC
NEW YORK • LONDON • OXFORD • NEW DELHI • SYDNEY

BLOOMSBURY ACADEMIC

Bloomsbury Publishing Inc, 1359 Broadway, New York, NY 10018, USA
Bloomsbury Publishing Plc, 50 Bedford Square, London, WC1B 3DP, UK
Bloomsbury Publishing Ireland, 29 Earlsfort Terrace, Dublin 2, D02 AY28, Ireland

BLOOMSBURY, BLOOMSBURY ACADEMIC and the Diana logo are trademarks of Bloomsbury Publishing Plc

First published in the United States of America 2024
Paperback edition published 2026

Copyright © Simon R. Troon, 2024

For legal purposes the Acknowledgements on pp. vi–vii constitute an extension of this copyright page.

Cover design by Eleanor Rose
Cover image: Still from *On an Unknown Beach* (2016), dir. Adam Luxton and Summer Agnew. Photograph courtesy of Adam Luxton

All rights reserved. No part of this publication may be: i) reproduced or transmitted in any form, electronic or mechanical, including photocopying, recording or by means of any information storage or retrieval system without prior permission in writing from the publishers; or ii) used or reproduced in any way for the training, development or operation of artificial intelligence (AI) technologies, including generative AI technologies. The rights holders expressly reserve this publication from the text and data mining exception as per Article 4(3) of the Digital Single Market Directive (EU) 2019/790.

Bloomsbury Publishing Inc does not have any control over, or responsibility for, any third-party websites referred to or in this book. All internet addresses given in this book were correct at the time of going to press. The author and publisher regret any inconvenience caused if addresses have changed or sites have ceased to exist, but can accept no responsibility for any such changes.

A catalog record for this book is available from the Library of Congress.

ISBN: HB: 979-8-7651-0150-6
PB: 979-8-7651-0154-4
ePDF: 979-8-7651-0152-0
eBook: 979-8-7651-0151-3

Series: Thinking Cinema

Typeset by Newgen KnowledgeWorks Pvt. Ltd., Chennai, India

For product safety related questions contact productsafety@bloomsbury.com.

To find out more about our authors and books visit www.bloomsbury.com and sign up for our newsletters.

Contents

Acknowledgements	vi
Introduction: The cinematic imagination of disaster	1
Part I Hollywood and Its Shadow	
1 Hollywood's disaster movies	35
2 Strange disaster in American independent cinema	67
Part II Two Documentary Views of Disaster	
3 The view from above	99
4 The view from a body	119
Part III A Neorealist Legacy for Eco-Catastrophe	
5 Realist auteurs after the disaster	141
Coda: 'The fall of the regular fall of the beat, the disaster again'	173
Bibliography	183
Filmography	197
Index	201

Acknowledgements

For my capacity to do the work that has led to this book, I am indebted to multiple communities and networks of comrades and colleagues. Among many others, I owe special thanks to Michel Rubin, Belinda Glynn, Grace C. Russell, Robert Letizi, Melanie Ashe, Isabella McNeill, Kathrin Bartha-Mitchell, Aneta Podkalicka, Whitney Monaghan, Kirsten Stevens, Janice Loreck, Fincina Hopgood, Killian Quigley, Pansy Duncan, Nicole Seymour and James Leo Cahill for time spent reading my writing; organizing screenings, seminars, conferences, reading groups and writing workshops; assisting with various opportunities; and for solidarity, consolation and advice over years of toil. All have helped me to persevere through, and find joy within, the persistent feeling of disaster that often seems to contour life as a casualized, precariously employed academic.

Much earlier iterations of passages from Chapters 3 and 4 were previously published in the article 'The View from a Body of Water: Representing Flooding and Sea Level Rise in the South Pacific' in *Studies in Documentary Film*, vol. 15, no. 1, 2021. Earlier iterations of passages from Chapters 1 and 2 were also previously published in the article 'The Way the World Has Ended: An Alternative Apocalypse in Richard Kelly's Disaster Movies' in *The Neutral: Graduate Journal of Cinema and Media Studies* (no. 2 (2021), *Period: Media and the Anthropocene*).

Adam Luxton kindly granted the use of an image from his and Summer Agnew's 2016 film *On an Unknown Beach* for the cover of this book.

As series editors, David Martin-Jones and Sarah Cooper have engaged with my thinking and writing attentively, critically and generously. I applaud their efforts with the Thinking Cinema series, which embodies film studies at its most vital best.

At Bloomsbury, Katie Gallof, Alyssa Jordan and Stephanie Grace-Petinos have been mercifully patient, understanding and enormously helpful.

Brett Hutchins has provided much generous counsel and crucial advice during the time of writing and revising this book.

This work would not have even begun without the kind guidance and meticulous care of Therese Davis and Belinda Smaill. Belinda's ongoing suppport and clear-eyed optimism have helped me continue this work through many faltering moments.

Finally, I owe more than can be expressed to Lisa Divissi for her patience, understanding and belief.

Introduction: The cinematic imagination of disaster

How might we imagine life in a disaster zone, a world delimited by disruption, displacement and death? This question was put to me when, in 2010 and 2011, a series of earthquakes shook my hometown of Christchurch in Aotearoa New Zealand. When the first quake struck, I was elsewhere, travelling, and I saw its impact via news footage on a television screen outside a supermarket. Looking at images of familiar streets strewn with wreckage, my reaction echoed the observations of many witnesses and commentators after 9/11: it was like a movie, I thought. The deadliest quake was an aftershock months later that collapsed many buildings and killed 185 people. Life in this disaster zone was more complex than I could have imagined, characterized not only by loss and confusion but also by bravery, altruism and unique moments of communality. People responded to the disaster in a variety of ways, grieving and working to reorient their attachments to the city and to each other. During this time, we received news of another disaster a hemisphere away. We saw and read about 3.11 – the earthquake, the tsunami and the nuclear event in Fukushima – in news media and again, confronted with images of death and destruction, it was like watching a movie.

Cinematic disaster imaginaries have attained a particular cultural ascendance. As questions about how life can proceed in a climate-changed planetary disaster zone are parsed in science and politics, well-known Hollywood disaster movies continually posit a familiar set of tropes: spectacles of explosion and detritus, ruined landscapes and heroes who rise above. A cinematic disaster imaginary was first outlined by Susan Sontag, writing in the 1960s about 'The Imagination of Disaster' in post-Second World War Hollywood science fiction films (*Against Interpretation* 209) and, as I shall discuss in Chapter 1, the disaster genre emerged unto itself during the decades since, cycling into popularity especially in the 1950s, 1970s and the 2010s. These widely viewed genre films gain distinct prominence, functioning as a touchstone to shape our expectations and perhaps even experiences of disastrous events. But outside of Hollywood, too, disaster has expanded as a cinematic theme. Scenarios of extreme weather, post-catastrophe survival and extra-terrestrial invasion have become the territory of independent cinema, world cinema and documentary. Across genres and regions, diverse films reflect issues that are crucial at our planet's present juncture, holding in play complex ideas about history, nature, science, technology and human subjectivity. This book rethinks the cinematic imagination of disaster, including but also moving beyond Hollywood's highly codified disaster genre to trace how different sensibilities of film style make possible the imagination of disaster in distinct ways. By doing so, it seeks to account for some ways that films, with their imaginative force, can posit powerful ethical potentials for life in the disaster zone.

Life on Earth seems to take on an increasingly disastrous flavour. In addition to events like 9/11 and 3.11, we are confronted with uncertainties and potential threats of many kinds: rapid technological advancement, nuclear weapons, resource scarcity, economic precarity, disease. Our time is, as Eva Horn writes, 'seen as marked by an imperceptible process of doom' (7). The effects of disaster – disruption, displacement, death – are inherent in the designation of Earth's present geological epoch as the Anthropocene, a nomenclature intended to acknowledge human activity as the dominant influence on the planet that thus connotes extractivism, pollution, global warming, climate crisis and extinction. This epoch, according to the scientists who propose it, denotes 'a new phase in the history of both humankind and of the Earth, where natural forces and human forces have become intertwined, so that the fate of one determines the fate of the other' (Zalasiewicz et al. 2229). Envisioning life on Earth as these conditions accelerate is a similar proposition to what I faced watching news footage of the earthquake in my hometown: we gaze at our home as it is being upended, but we are yet to fully experience or understand the ways that our inhabitancy of it is disrupted.

There is an added complexity, though, in our relationships with the present pervasive sense of doom, as those of us living in the industrialized world who continue to benefit from resource extraction and carbon-heavy lifestyles are beset by surreally looming disasters of our own making. We are faced with a growing recognition that the world we enjoy and experience as increasingly doomed is built upon centuries of disaster inflicted on others. Various starting points for the Anthropocene are mooted by scientists, philosophers and theorists. Cataloguing these, Mark Bould illustrates how each one ciphers disaster: from

1.6 million years ago when 'Homo erectus first used fire' igniting a history that leads to 'catastrophic consumption of fossil fuels' to July 1945 when the Trinity nuclear test and the conclusion of the Second World War inaugurated the 'global spread of radioactive isotopes' (9–10). Most of these origin stories hinge on some technological advancement that accelerates the burning of fossil fuels, but Bould also highlights two other twinned stories beginning in the 1400s that signal death and destruction even more directly: 'The European "discovery", exploitation, extraction and colonisation of the Americas' and the Atlantic slave trade (11). What is 'euphemistically referred to as "Modernity"', American historian Gerald Horne posits, is 'marked with the indelible stain of what might be termed the Three Horsemen of the Apocalypse: Slavery, White Supremacy, and Capitalism' (9). In the United States and elsewhere, violent histories of settler colonialism characterized by mass displacement and death pervade everyday contemporary life. Writing from New Zealand, Linda Tuhiwai Smith notes the contemporary atmosphere of doom and disaster – constituent of global crises, the devastation of natural environments, and climate impacts on 'low lying atolls in the Pacific Ocean' (109) – only in order to contextualize a discussion of how, while for many people European imperialism seems consigned to history, 'for Indigenous peoples the passage into a new century is really a continuation of a struggle that began five centuries ago' (119). In these ways and others, the anthropos of the Anthropocene face fresh and compounding disasters from uneven and inequitable standpoints, and with varying degrees of complicity.

As we are pushed to reconceive of our world as shaped by disruptive, deathly forces, including those of our own violent inheritances, interrogating cinematic disaster imaginaries can help us rethink our relationships to Earth, history and the burgeoning catastrophes around us. Hollywood's disaster movies are known for their emphasis on spectacular scenarios where heroes face down threats like earthquakes, tidal waves, infernos, invading extraterrestrials and errant technologies. Blockbuster imagery of cities laid to waste, menacing nature and planetary endangerment reflects an understanding of disastrous events as what Franco Berardi, referring to 3.11's earthquake and tsunami, terms 'noisy catastrophes' (10). A moment of impact from a massive destructive force: a sudden and terrible event that, once passed, clears the ground and creates conditions for a rebuild. But disaster is not uniform, nor is it experienced uniformly and attention to only the spectacular aspects of disaster restricts our understanding of it. Disaster ruptures the world in different ways, instituting its own conditions. The invisible fallout at Fukushima, for example, presents a more frightening 'silent apocalypse' for Berardi, which brings with it 'a new framework of social expectation for daily life on the planet' (10). Amidst the rubble in Christchurch, much was made of moments of unanticipated altruism, connection and joy: what Rebecca Solnit has famously framed as *A Paradise Built in Hell*. However, in the aftermath of Hurricane Maria in Puerto Rico, vulnerabilities produced by colonialism and neoliberal governmentality catalysed an 'experience of time, progression, social action, and political possibility' that Yarimar Bonilla terms 'The wait of disaster': 'not progress but delay, deterioration, degradation, and the forced act of waiting' (2–3).

Beyond Hollywood we can locate different ways of imagining disaster cinematically, and addressing how these imaginaries are figured can help us to gain a better understanding of the complex, multifaceted nature of life in the disaster zone. In addition to presenting spectacular catastrophe, cinema can show us the drawn out aftermath of such an event, as in *And Life Goes On* (1992) and *Time of the Wolf* (2003). Some disasters are experienced slowly, gradually, like the sea level rise visualized in *An Inconvenient Truth* (2006). Disaster can also be private and ambiguous, like the inexplicable illness depicted in *Safe* (1995). It can be outright mysterious, as in *Donnie Darko* (2001), where it is an aeroplane engine smashing into a house but also a ghostly anthropomorphic bunny appearing before a teenager. Films that imagine disaster in these more intricate, nuanced ways can offer distinct and ethically charged reflections of our relationships to the Earth we inhabit, signalling particular understandings of our intertwining with it through conceptions of history, science, technology and nature. By exploring a diversity of disaster films, this book brings to attention the different potentials posed by alternate cinematic disaster imaginaries.

Surveying these and other films, this book weaves paths across multiple institutional and geographical contexts and varied understandings of film style, necessitating recourse to multiple aesthetic traditions and a web of critical, theoretical and philosophical paradigms. But many of the traditions and paradigms this book works with and through originate in the same disastrous moment: the Second World War, including the Holocaust and the bombing of Hiroshima and Nagasaki, which remain major reference points for understanding disaster and representing it cinematically. Hollywood's disaster imaginary emerges from a post-war context when, as Sontag argues, a body of science fiction films channel social anxiety about nuclear weaponry. At the same time, realist film theorists André Bazin and Siegfried Kracauer reflect on the capacities of cinematic form in Hollywood and Europe to adequately represent and interpret mass death and trauma, from the specific horrors of the war to traumatic modernity in a more generalized sense. Theories of realism, particularly in a Bazinian frame, offer a method for appraising the potential for films to authentically reflect and respond to the pressures of history and the contingencies of the material world, and the notions of realism and postwar film style articulated by Bazin, much like Hollywood genre convention, continue to resonate across the world, making possible global cartographies of film style.

At the same time as this book analyses disaster scenarios depicted in films from disparate contexts, it explores how disaster constitutes encounter between humans and various forces that exceed them: nature, technology, aliens, spectral entities and more. A framework for understanding encounter as an intersubjective event of immense ethical magnitude emerges from the writing of Emmanuel Levinas, conditioned by his own experience of the Holocaust. In recent years, new awarenesses of the intertwining of human and non-human that characterizes the Anthropocene have provoked reflection on Levinasian thought to account for dynamic intersubjective relations between humans and the non-human. This accounting-for is a deeply interdisciplinary project, undertaken by thinkers across multiple disciplinary configurations including the environmental humanities, the posthumanities, philosophy and critical theory. From its purview within film studies, this book aims to both draw on and contribute to this ongoing conversation, and it connects especially with ideas that circulate among a cohort of thinkers described by Joanna Zylinska in *Minimal Ethics for the Anthropocene* as 'theorists of post-anthropocentric thought' (16). In particular, during the course of my analysis, I frequently refer to echoes and reworkings of Levinasian ethics and related or adjacent notions of ethical encounter that emerge from feminist thought and the environmental humanities, including that of the great feminist philosophers Rosi Braidotti and Donna Haraway, and Australian multispecies ethnographer Deborah Bird Rose. Rose offers the metaphor of a campfire gathering to illustrate the bringing together of disparate threads of story and theory in her own work, with Levinas himself as 'a special guest in the conversation around the fire' (*Wild Dog Dreaming* 15). In this manner, Levinas, alongside his friend and frequent interlocutor Maurice Blanchot, will likewise appear at times in my discussion of films alongside those others who in more recent years push beyond some of the widely acknowledged limits to his own theorizing of ethical relations, as their originary rethinking of ethical responsibility in the face of mass death continues to resonate at our contemporary standpoint, and the Holocaust and the Second World War remain major reference points for cinema.

The bodies of knowledge called on in this book – Hollywood aesthetic tradition, theories of realism, Levinasian and post-anthropocentric ethics – in many ways constitute creative, intellectual and philosophical attempts to reckon with catastrophe on unknowable scales, and this book brings them together as a productive methodology for appraising cinematic engagements with disaster. Conjoining these paradigms is a generative intervention and demonstrates that an ethics of more-than-human encounter has much to offer to film studies, in particular to the realist thought that descends from Bazin and Kracauer, and vice versa. As I shall discuss below, ideas of indexicality and responsibility resonate across them, giving rise to certain aesthetic and ethical sensibilities. Their intermeshing makes it possible to critically approach all kinds of films about traumatic encounter between humans and disastrous non-human forces by considering them as critically engaged aesthetic responses to the emerging histories of this protracted moment now known as the advent of the Anthropocene.

Before embarking on the transversal analytical trajectories that comprise this book's chapters, the remainder of this introduction calibrates some of these essential conceptual, theoretical and philosophical ideas that subsequently enable my analyses. In particular, it explores how the understandings of encounter, and specifically of ethical responsibility in encounter with others, that are articulated in Levinasian ethics and rekindled by theorists of post-anthropocentric thought, can be purposed for scenarios of disaster in which one is likely to come face to face with death. Following this, it configures an according film-analytical approach primed for understanding how films, by staging such encounters between their protagonists and various other forces, conceptualize ethical situations, often also implicating or compelling ethical perspectives for viewers. It is important to acknowledge some ways that though, as Sarah Cooper notes, 'there is no easy bond to be forged' between Levinas and film due to his own 'dismissive' disposition towards aesthetics ('Introduction' i), his ideas have been generatively adopted within film studies. Acknowledging this book's connections and debts to other important film-analytical approaches that emphasize ethics and interrelation is also important, including recent work that can be framed, broadly speaking, as ecocritical – that is, responsive to concerns of the non-human and the environmental, and especially to the contemporary moment of planetary eco-catastrophe. With these baseline understandings in place, each chapter proceeds into distinct territory, nuancing them and introducing further relevant ideas as necessary.

Firstly, at the outset it is useful to establish a definition of disaster, which is a notion both vague and precise, and a word that can describe a range of distinct events: from a terror attack in New York City to an earthquake in an antipodean town. Philosophical attempts to apprehend disaster are fraught with contradictory or paradoxical tensions, similar to the oscillation between silence and noise observed by Berardi after 3.11, and the Holocaust remains a major reference point. Maurice Blanchot writes that *'it is the dark disaster that brings the light'* (7) as he contemplates the absurdity of trying to understand an event of such horrible magnitude. In a far-reaching discussion of Holocaust representation, Michael Rothberg notes 'seemingly irresolvable contradictions' in approaches to understanding: between the event's '"uniqueness" and its "typicality", its "extremity" and its "banality", its "incomprehensibility" and its susceptibility to "normal" understanding' (*Traumatic Realism* 3). Seeking to define disaster in a larger and more abstract way, many theorists, including some working to frame the Anthropocene, highlight the etymological roots of the word: *dis* and *astro* or *astron*. Jennifer Fay notes that this suggests 'planetary misalignment' (*Inhospitable World* 1), while Timothy Morton details 'a fallen, dysfunctional, or dangerous, or evil, star' (*Hyperobjects* 15). Akira Mizuta Lippit posits that an uncanniness inheres in disasters, which 'are always extraterrestrial, even when their elements are deeply terrestrial in nature' ('Between Disaster, Medium 3.11' 3). This not only clarifies the planetary scale of our contemporary disastrous atmosphere, but also distracts from the embedded specificities of events like 3.11 and the Holocaust. Such specificities are highlighted by Berardi, Blanchot and Rothberg, yet their doing so intimates a sense of futility in attempting to comprehend disaster via rational knowledge. It becomes clear that there is something elusive and enigmatic about disaster: it describes multiple events on different scales, and often exceeds our capacities while also being somehow familiar. On a simpler level, however, disaster certainly connotes a feeling of ill impossibility and a mood of great foreboding, auguring irrevocable change in our experience of the world.

A starting point for defining disaster emerges from film studies. When Maurice Yacowar outlines a disaster genre, writing in 1978, he observes that in cinematic representations of disaster, 'a situation of normalcy erupts into a persuasive image of death' (313). In this regard, disaster can be understood as the interruption of apparent normality with the intrusion or threat of death.

Such an understanding remains open to disaster taking different forms sudden and perduring, isolated and pervasive, and signals its ability to reconstitute environmental and ontological conditions. An understanding of disaster based on Yacowar's observation thus opens up discussion of a diverse array of films under the rubric of disaster cinema (and indeed, Yacowar's early formulation of a disaster genre accounts for an impressive multitude of films). It may even be possible to consider most films as pertaining to disaster in some way.

Cinema is an apt media for the imagination of disaster because, as Laura Mulvey asserts, it figures the eruption of death twenty-four times per second (*Death 24× a Second: Stillness and the Moving Image*), effecting a transformation from animated life to inanimate (or mummified) death. As films reflect the material of the world back to viewers, death is never far from the foreground and a sense of encounter with an ultimate alterity is thus at work in our spectatorship. Mulvey's assertion is elaborated by Anna Backman Rogers to suggest that 'death constantly haunts the cinematic image and threatens to rise to its surface as radical other or abject object' (13). The potential of this dynamic is evident in the fabulous story of the first showing of *L'Arrivée d'un train en gare de La Ciotat* (1896) where viewers are said to have leapt from their seats in terror, believing that the train they saw projected would burst forth from the screen and bring disaster careening into the room. This story, of dubious veracity, illustrates cinema's affective power while also highlighting its special relationship with death and disaster.

Tracing the import of Levinasian ethics to film studies, Cooper cites Mulvey's assertion when honing in on a consideration of death as connective tissue that productively conjoins Levinas's ethics with film via 'connection between death and cinematic time' ('Emmanuel Levinas' 96). Cooper notes that 'in Levinas's work on death and time, death enters life through contact with others' and that per 'the terms of Levinas's ethics', this contact 'gives rise to a new subjectivity – a rebirth of the subject' (97). She goes on to posit that although for Levinas the aesthetic is a different register of experience, prohibited from the ethical dimension, 'encounters in the aesthetic dimension are not entirely separated from similar ones that might take place beyond this realm' (98). This book invests in the possibility that encounters with disaster, rendered cinematically, might provoke viewers and help give rise to more hopeful orientations to the death-connoting effects of the Anthropocene. It asks how forces of disaster like earthquakes, alien invasions and more, that are rendered cinematically in encounter with human protagonists, while conceptualizing nature, technology and science, and human subjectivity among other things, also look out from the frame to confront viewers with the threat of death. Accordingly, this book holds that cinema, a product of the Industrial Revolution and modernity that has evolved as the Anthropocene's death-connoting effects have begun to irredeemably afflict the Earth, is particularly well placed to offer sophisticated, reflexive understandings of what disaster means, how it can be imagined and how we might encounter it in the future. Tracing an ethics of encounter grounded in Levinas's understandings of responsibility to the other, honing it with the assistance of thinkers who are invested in what responsibility means for our present era of environmental and climate catastrophe, and configuring it for film analysis, it aims towards expanding understandings of our present historical moment by elaborating the potential that cinema has to reorient how we understand and experience disaster.

Ethics of encounter for a disastrous epoch

Earth's current juncture demands acknowledgement of plurality and complexity. The idea of the Anthropocene has spread far beyond the scientific domains it was first theorized in to provoke a wide-ranging evolution in the humanities, the full consequences of which are yet to be seen. This is, according to Jamie Lorimer, the Anthropo-scene: a scientific proposal, but also an 'intellectual zeitgeist' (121), and an 'ideological provocation' (123), prompting a 'rich cacophony of new and original academic work' marked by 'epistemic and ontological pluralism' (133). A wordplay-heavy 'alternative nomenclature' (Lorimer 124) – Capitalocene, Anthrobscene, Manthropocene and more – evidences how thinkers formulate ways of understanding the disasters erupting across the world from many important critical perspectives.

As this book investigates cinematic disaster imaginaries, it also probes potential implications this cacophony has for film studies. To do so, it highlights various ethical challenges posed by a dispersed body of work that departs from 'prevalent ways of conceiving human–environmental relations' (Lorimer 125–6) to offer 'different conceptions of the Earth and the human subject' (128). Among those undertaking this task of re-conception, including the theorists of post-anthropocentric thought discussed above, there are shared concerns with a brand of ethics as a mode of interrelating and constituting subject-positions that is often underpinned by recourse, both overtly and obliquely, to Levinasian understandings of encounter and intersubjectivity. Amidst these concerns, a feminist perspective that critiques the dominance of universal, rational, masculinist knowledge over the world becomes prominent. Calling on these perspectives is instrumental in facilitating a search beyond Hollywood where, as I shall discuss in Chapter 1, films overwhelmingly foreground male protagonists and pose solutions to disaster that originate in masculinist ways of knowing and encountering the world. Contrariwise, ethics of encounter formulated in the shadow of the Anthropocene frequently pursue notions of subjectivity that are bound up in the reorientation of the human self in encounter with non-human alterity. Beyond Hollywood's codified representations, there are possibilities to see film protagonists, displaced, respond to disaster in differentiated ways that are charged with distinct ethical orientations.

The act of looking or, more precisely, the question of being willing or able to look, is crucial to comprehension of the disastrous nature attributed to the Anthropocene. Donna Haraway writes that 'these times called the Anthropocene are times of multispecies, including human, urgency: of great mass death and extinction; of onrushing disasters', adding that they are also times 'of refusing to know and cultivate the capacity of response-ability; of refusing to be present in and to onrushing catastrophe in time; of unprecedented looking away' (*Staying with the Trouble* 35). As if in reply to Haraway, the writer Haytham El-Wardany offers the concept of disaster-consciousness:

> a consciousness not damaged by disaster, but honed. Disaster-consciousness does not seek to flee from disaster, nor to manage it like a crisis, but instead strives to set it in plain sight. It does not want to mend what is broken or reclaim what has been taken. It does not want to ask for pardon or forgive. It does not want purgatory or punishment. All it desires is to look disaster in the eye. ('Notes on Disaster')

El-Wardany evokes a way of looking that implies ethical response in a Levinasian manner; a processual change in consciousness for the one who looks, a movement towards openness to contingency and unpredictability, the emergence of a new subjectivity. This effectively keys in to how a disastrous event can be understood as a type of intersubjective encounter that cultivates the subject's capacity for responsibility. The imperative to embrace responsibility and look directly and honestly towards disaster resonates powerfully in the context of cinema which, by its acts of representation, can provoke for viewers more complex processes of looking: witnessing, contemplating, searching.

To look disaster in the eye means to enter into an ethical engagement with the forces that constitute it and respond to their demands. With Levinas, the face is understood as the transformative site of ethical encounter, and a profound sense of vulnerability inheres in meeting another face to face: 'To expose myself to the vulnerability of the face is to put my ontological right to exist into question ... the other's right to exist has primacy over my own' (Cohen, *Face to Face with Levinas* 24). The act of looking towards the other is thus a chief concern for ethics, and Levinas asserts repeatedly in *Totality and Infinity* that ethics is an *optics* (23, 29, 78) – a way of looking. Blanchot reflects on Levinas's ethics at length in *The Writing of the Disaster*, parsing the notion of responsibility in a way that meets Haraway's later evocation of response-ability. Noting the banality of more simplistic, moralistic notions of responsibility, Blanchot suggests that Levinas opens the word up and renews it, giving it a deeper significance: '*My responsibility for the Other presupposes an overturning such that it can only be marked by a change in the status of "me", a change in time and perhaps language*' (25, italic in the original). Responsibility requires a capacity for transformation of the self, and the emergence of a new subjectivity necessitates a change in one's consciousness. A glimpse of the other invokes new ontological conditions, and the moment of encounter occasions a potential for new awareness of the self to emerge. Ethical responsibility thoroughly disrupts the self: 'disengages the me from me ... the subjective from the subject' (24). Responsibility in encounter with alterity, perhaps especially in a disastrous context, thus amounts to the setting aside of one's sovereignty, and an acceptance of whatever unpredictability and contingency that alterity may bring.

Blanchot and Levinas shared a personal relationship shaped in part by the Holocaust, and the consciousness of disaster that each of them formulates across their lives' work takes shape under the ill star of that world-changing event. In a contemporary context, the catastrophic conditions of the Anthropocene prompt many scholars and thinkers to elaborate an ethics that deploys notions of responsibility in encounter with the non-human or more-than-human world that are indebted to Levinas. Joanna Zylinska's 'theorists of post-anthropocentric thought' (*Minimal Ethics for the Anthropocene* 16) include Haraway and Braidotti alongside Henri Bergson, Karen Barad, Wendy Brown, Jane Bennett, Claire Colebrook and Gilles Deleuze (17), and there are many more who could be added to this list. The output of these thinkers constitutes an adaptable multidisciplinary theoretical assemblage, useful for thinking through encounters between humans and more-than-human forces in which these forces have great bearing on notions of human subjectivity. For Zylinska, ethics is, in this contemporary context, 'a historically contingent human mode of becoming in the world, of becoming different from the world, and of narrating and taking responsibility for the nature of this difference' (Zylinska 93).

There are many linked approaches to expanding the understanding of responsibility in encounter from Levinas's ethics for this contemporary context, beyond two widely acknowledged limitations: a broadly Eurocentric perspective and the exclusion of the non-human from ethics. John E. Drabinski refers to Levinas's own 'insularity and general indifference to global affairs and suffering' (1) while also noting the apparent utility of his most crucial insight – 'that sense of responsibility to the Other' – for 'thinking in a postcolonial context' (2). Similarly, Katarina Gray-Sharp posits that 'although Levinas's work can inspire, it must be amended for broader application. In order to reinvigorate the ethical, it must be weaved with *mātauranga* [knowledge] of a different sort' (180). Gray-Sharp works with Levinas to develop an 'Indigenous, non-agential conception of responsibility' for the 'ethical problem' of anthropogenic mass extinction (2), contending that responsibility in the disastrous present must be decolonial as well as non-anthropocentric. A predominant strategy, described by Tom Sparrow, for including non-human others in conceptions of ethical encounter 'attempts to take Levinas's concept of "the face" (*le visage*) and impart its ethical significance to nonhuman animals or the natural environment' (73). Thinking in this anthropomorphic method, Deborah Bird Rose notes that 'the one big limit in Levinas's thought is that he confined his ethics to humans', and wonders whether his philosophy can endure 'when the call of the other is a bark or a howl' (*Wild Dog Dreaming* 15). Later she posits that while 'Levinas developed his philosophy in the shadow of the Nazi genocide … today we live in the shadow of the Anthropocene, and the calls that command our ethical responses include those of nonhumans, and of the Earth itself' (*Shimmer* 6). Barbara Jane Davy similarly contends that 'the other need not be able to speak as a human for ethics to pass … nonhuman others can also be met as persons and inspire ethics in oneself' (49–50). Aiming further beyond humanistic limits, Morton more poetically elaborates an ethics of encounter with more expansive notions of non-human alterity: 'The other is fully here, before I am, as Levinas argues. But the other has paws and sharp surfaces, the other is decorated with leaves, the other shines with starlight' (*Hyperobjects* 125). Alterity is understood in similarly vast but more specific terms by Rosi Braidotti, for whom it encapsulates all those who are subjugated beneath the historically dominant subject of the rational, humanist, Eurocentric, masculinist Man: 'the sexualized other (woman), the racialized other (the native) and the naturalized other (animals, the environment or earth)' (*The Posthuman* 27). Braidotti stresses the particular significance of 'nonhuman or "earth" others' (190) for her brand of posthuman ethics.

In film-analytical contexts where representation of alterity takes on specific connotations, similar approaches to rethinking responsibility via the face have also been formulated. Writing on documentary, Cooper poses Levinas's conception of *le visage*, more transcendent than the literal physical face, in 'disruptive association' (*Selfless Cinema?* 22) with cinematic visuality. Conditions for encounter and 'ethical response', she argues, arise wherein the cinematic subject is thus 'always more than his or her image' (23). Libby Saxton similarly focuses on Levinas's broader discussion of the face in a non-literal sense as, rather straightforwardly, 'the way in which the Other presents himself' and thus, 'the face *expresses, signifies* and *speaks*, addressing and commanding me from a position beyond the perceptual field' ('Blinding Visions', *Film and Ethics* 99, italics in the original). Alterity can thus confront viewers in multiple and complex ways from within the cinematic frame. Highlighting the broader significance of these interlinked, expanded ethical approaches for film analysis, David Martin-Jones observes a far-reaching conception of the historicized other as 'a product of the world system which underpins colonial modernity' (45). Such a conception of alterity, Martin-Jones argues, 'is extremely pertinent for today's globalised world and its cinematic constructions of history' (45), as it allows that encounters with diverse films, via representation of multiple forms of alterity, might help decentre dominant stories about ecology and history that underpin framing of the Anthropocene. In these contemporary formulations of ethical responsibility in encounter that follow Levinas, animals, entities, objects, presences and forces of various kinds alongside humans can be recognized as ethical others; entities capable of inviting intersubjective encounter. In cinematic contexts, they can appear in multifarious, complex ways. As they do so, they bring with them histories and worlds of their own that promise upheaval to the ego of the Eurocentric, masculinist, modern self.

One cinematic example of how this brand of expanded Levinasian ethics might operate with regard to the non-human is apparent in Jeff Nichols' 2011 indie thriller *Take Shelter*. The film details a husband and father beset by visions of disastrous events, including oil raining from the sky, that seem to be connected to mental illness and extreme paranoia but ultimately portend real catastrophe. In one scene, he is confronted by a gathering storm and viewers see him gaze towards banking clouds in a shot-reverse-shot pattern. As we identify with his skyward look, the darkest part of the cloud formation almost takes on the contours of a human face: a spiky nose and mouth jutting out from its shadowy mass. The film stages an unsettling moment of literal face-to-face encounter between its protagonist and an extreme weather event, and the apocalyptic weather troubles the protagonist's patriarch status. In his apparitions of thick black rain, 'like fresh motor oil', the fossil fuels that have underpinned modernity's progress return as if seeking personal revenge, mentally destabilizing him and in doing so, dislodging his authority within his family and their wider small town Ohio community.

This framework for understanding ethical encounter with the non-human incorporates a sense of something like El-Wardany's disaster-consciousness: an awareness of how sovereign human subjects can be destabilized, set aside or elsewise negated by various forces that arrive before them. In films, disaster manifests as non-human alterity in elemental nature: storms, earthquakes, tsunami, volcanoes. It inheres in advanced technology such as nuclear devices, other risky instruments and alien weaponry. Forces like these exceed human protagonists, threatening to eradicate any sense of individual empowerment. Encountering disasters like erupting volcanoes, nuclear meltdowns and rampaging monsters, humans are routinely decentred, wounded and traumatized. They are dwarfed by the scale and violence of the entities they encounter.

Looking disaster in the eye means reckoning with the positionality that such an encounter commands. Events like 3.11 and climate change push humans to reconsider our presumed dominance over the world, and occasion forms of intertwining that necessarily include acknowledgement of our own vulnerability. Particularly for theorists of post-anthropocentric ethics, potentials for the self-awareness of human subjects to be transformed in encounter with the non-human frequently include and even hinge on notions of openness to change, especially when it is decentring. An understanding of environmental interconnectedness that aims towards 'radical intimacy, coexisting with other beings, sentient and otherwise' and necessarily involves 'becoming open, radically open' is offered by Morton (*The Ecological Thought* 7). Rose highlights openness to 'the peril of others' as crucial to Levinas's ethics (*Shimmer* 6). She proposes it as an antidote to the problems of the Anthropocene, as 'in open dialogue one holds one's self to be available to be surprised, to be challenged, and to be changed' ('Slowly' 8), and also emphasizes multispecies connections of 'shared vulnerability and shared suffering' (*Wild Dog Dreaming* 91). Understandings of renegotiated intersubjectivity between human and non-human are parsed throughout much of Haraway's writing, and she posits that in Earth's present moment, 'the task is to make kin in lines of inventive connection as a practice of learning to live and die well with each other' (*Staying with the Trouble* 1).

These theorists and others offer a plethora of conceptualizations for how human subjects, within the dynamic frameworks of a given encounter, might become responsible in a disastrous world. Rose optimistically envisions 'a human conscience that is shaped by its responsiveness towards the calls of others – nonhuman as well as human – and by connectivities that loop through organic and inorganic domains'. Such a conscience is 'able to withstand the horrors of contemporary violence. It affirms its opposition to a world of wilful and deathful bloodshed' (*Shimmer* 17). Of particular interest to this project is Stacy Alaimo's elaboration of the 'exposed subject', which reflects the experience of not only violence but also openness, being one who is 'always already penetrated by substances and forces that can never be properly accounted for' (*Exposed* 5). Alaimo's ethical framing of exposure resonates with El-Wardany's disaster-consciousness, as 'performing exposure' means to 'grapple with the particular engagements of vulnerability and complicity that radiate from disasters and their terribly disjunctive connection to everyday life in the industrialized world' (5). Openness or exposure in this sense thus includes reckoning with the eruption of disaster and engaging substantively with the forces it entails. Openness contains an imperative to reappraise the nature of our encounters with the forces of Anthropocene disaster: to trace the contours of those forces and their formation, re-evaluate the self, accept a decentred positionality and embrace contextual bonds with others. A non-anthropocentric ethics for the Anthropocene thus involves looking unflinchingly towards the complex eruption of death. It calls for an openness to the wounding, decentring and changes in consciousness that may be provoked by such an act of witnessing.

Recognizing complicity becomes a key aspect of taking responsibility for the nature of human difference in this context, and is of increasingly extreme importance because the human subject is far from universal. Humans across the world experience different levels of exposure to disaster. It has been widely noted that chief among the problems with conceptualizing the Anthropocene is its flattening out of all of humanity as anthropos, when in fact it is largely a minority of humans living in wealthy, technologically advanced regions like the United States, Europe and Australia whose fossil-fuelled ways of life impact

Earth geologically and, via climate change, precipitate disasters like drought, sea level rise and bushfires. Meanwhile, those who live in other regions are the most vulnerable to such disasters. The posthuman ethics articulated by Braidotti is particularly useful for working to understand this uneven distribution of agency, suffering and complicity. As human subjects of both late capitalism and environmental crises across the world, she writes, 'we are in this together' (*Posthuman Knowledge* 2) and yet 'we are not One and the same'; being 'positioned in embodied and embedded differential but material locations' (153). Disasters always speak to material and historical embodiments that are specific and localized. As Chris Prentice notes of the Christchurch earthquakes, they 'insist on an understanding of place and social formation informed by an ecocritical perspective cognisant of the dynamic materiality of dwelling' (56). This book speaks to, invests in and becomes complicit with the prominence of both Hollywood and European understandings of cinema's possibilities for imagining disaster. It therefore cannot claim to be decolonial in the sense of divestment from the colonial power that often undergirds the experience of climate crisis or redressing catastrophic imperial legacies. However, its movements beyond Hollywood and its oscillations between documentary and fiction film constitute an attempt to account for, in a necessarily partial way, how narratives and images about disaster are informed by different understandings of geographical place and social formation, and can thus testify to different possibilities for ethical subject-formation in encounter with disaster. In this sense, it aspires to 'open up possibilities for understanding and knowing the world differently and offering different solutions to problems caused by colonialism' (Smith xiii).

Post-anthropocentric ethical thinking about responsibility in the Anthropocene has much to offer analysis of films. At different moments and in different ways in the chapters that follow, this book draws on the ideas of Rose, Haraway, Morton, Braidotti, Alaimo and others, probing their utility for reading cinematic images. At times it also makes direct reference to the ethics of Levinas and Blanchot, as the Second World War and the Holocaust continue to resonate in recent disaster imaginaries. As each chapter explores how films index and present the eruption of death in distinct ways, the understandings of ethical encounter and responsibility that I have elaborated here come to the fore in variable ways, allowing for analyses of how films stage intersubjective encounters between humans and forces of disaster that are sensitive to the vantage points from which they emerge. In the films considered, disastrous forces are most often what Braidotti names earth others (*The Posthuman*

27): natural disasters and other environmental, elemental forces. But as we shall see, disaster also manifests as stranger, more enigmatic entities and presences. When these forces, presences and entities threaten human protagonists with displacement or death, they provoke responses that evince protagonists' capacities for ethical responsibility, and questions of their potential complicity also arise in different ways. My analysis thus focuses on depictions of human response to disaster, examining at length the modes of subjectivity that are figured in key characters who encounter disaster and experience its demands as it disturbs their experience of the world. In Chapter 1, I explore how heroic figures are key to Hollywood's disaster movie genre, and the trajectories I subsequently trace beyond Hollywood involve explorations of characters who are called to encounter in other kinds of film. The distinct ways in which some non-Hollywood characters are shown to respond to ethical demands posed by forces of disaster, insinuating distinct subject-positions, facilitate ideas about how we can imagine life in the disaster zones of the Anthropocene in alternate, and perhaps more responsible, ways.

Thus, while this book certainly partakes in an ethical turn in film studies that, as Martin-Jones writes, 'explores how films can prompt ethical change', being situated alongside other recent scholarship on Levinas and cinema, it remains party to the fact that as Martin-Jones also notes, 'the ever-expanding engagement with ethics in film-philosophy has not produced entire agreement as to what a cinematic ethics entails' (48) and its approach to analysing films is somewhat distinct. Much of the most trenchant writing on film and ethics, and especially on film and Levinas's ethics, directs analytical attention towards relations of power between filmmakers and subjects or participants, and towards relations that inhere in viewership, training analysis towards 'a given filming/viewing self' (Cooper, *Selfless Cinema?* 5). It also focuses on either documentary (Cooper, *Selfless Cinema?*; Nash, 'Documentary-for-the-Other'; 'Telling Stories'; Renov, *The Subject of Documentary*) or narrative cinema (Girgus; Martin-Jones; Stadler). This book, however, as it surveys both documentary and narrative cinema, is primarily interested in how films render processes of encounter and, in doing so, conceptualize both non-human alterity and ethical responsibility. Questions about how viewers, in spectatorial encounters, are implicated in and by these renderings, and about the role of filmmakers in eliciting representations of alterity from their subjects remain vital but subsidiary concerns as while films, in their diversity of form, all conceptualize ethics through scenarios of encounter, invitations to viewers to share in ethics and partake in responsibility are inherently partial and not universally extended. I am also mindful that, as Saxton writes, while films certainly expose viewers to alterity, they cannot entirely stage ethical encounters 'between viewers and images of the kind envisaged by Levinas' (104). The understandings of encounter and responsibility outlined here thus inform, in each chapter, analyses of how elements of film style are deployed in different contexts to create distinct cinematic representations of encounter between human and non-human that inhere in disaster, engendering distinct notions of ethical responsibility and inviting different kinds of real-world ethical engagement with the non-human forces, entities and presences that are represented. If, as Linda Williams argues, 'ways of seeing' are structured into films ('Introduction' 1), then the aesthetic and formal structures of films about disaster invoke ways of looking at, engaging with, responding to or turning away from our world at large at its present moment of urgency.

Responsibility and realism

There is another way that response-abilities are involved here: films themselves constitute aesthetic responses to history, and while the Anthropocene is primarily conceived of as a scientific issue, it is also a problem for imaginative faculties, demanding truly visionary responses. It is, according to Adrian Ivakhiv, 'also a crisis of imagery, meaning, and culture' (*Shadowing the Anthropocene* 18) and thus calls for the imagination of new cultural dynamics and innovative forms. Searching Hollywood and beyond, this book looks for films that articulate the ethical dynamics of disaster in ways sufficiently responsive to the crises of our historical juncture, imagining not just alternative futures but also alternative ways of inhabiting the disastrous present. This book is therefore not interested in the global adaptation of Hollywood's disaster genre, but rather in locating alternatives to it. A movement beyond Hollywood in this way might also require moving beyond classificatory notions like genre, seeking new ways of appraising the sensibilities of film style. This is especially true given concerns for ethics in global contexts. Martin-Jones demonstrates how an analytical approach, following Shohat's and Stam's *Unthinking Eurocentrism* and postcolonial cinema studies, honed towards 'new groupings' that include lifting films out of their originary contexts and examining them alongside films from elsewhere (52), can 'shift our focus … towards equality with others within the world we inhabit' (58). Thus, while accounting for genre and other critical and conceptual categories, to enable truly diverse analytical trajectories, this book also thinks about realism. Or realisms.

Realism can be understood as a method of film-aesthetic response to history. In the broadest sense, it is the engaging of stylistic sensibilities, representative techniques and also modes of production that seek authenticity and honesty in their conveyance of the material world and historical events. Realist filmmakers, for Lucia Nagib, are those who 'feel part of, and responsible for' the material world, 'and want to change it for the better' (*Realist Cinema* 15). Realist film style is often critically posed as distinct from or even directly oppositional to Hollywood film style and, though there are guiding notions – slowness, the long take, an emphasis on immediacy – it remains a somewhat ambiguous, amorphous proposition. Bazin writes in 1948 that 'there is not one realism, but several realisms' (*Bazin at Work* 6), and Bazinian approaches often emphasize this kind of plurality. Realism, Daniel Morgan writes, 'is not a particular style, lack of style, or set of stylistic attributes. … It turns out to cover a surprisingly large range of styles, even those that bear little affinity to the perceptual experience of reality' (445–6). This notion of multiple realisms is expanded in a way that emphasizes the imaginative force of films and the power they can have in the world in Nagib's assertion that 'different cinemas of the world can generate their own theories' (*World Cinema and the Ethics of Realism* 1).

This sense of proliferating realist potentials is fitting for the context of the Anthropocene proposal and the ontological and theoretical pluralities it has provoked. Bazinian notions of realism have not always been popular, or even perceived as valid, among film and media theorists. Tom Gunning describes a time when 'displaying a sympathy for, or even a particular interest in, the ideas of André Bazin encountered the objection that he was an "idealist"', his thinking naïve and 'politically retrograde' (119). However, Nagib charts a 'revival of Bazinian film studies in the 2000s' (*Realist Cinema* 19), through an ongoing theoretical preoccupation with spectatorial phenomenology (*Realist Cinema* 21), to a contemporary standpoint where there exists a strong resonance between Bazinian ontology – film's material connection with the real, objective world it documents – and the 'non-anthropocentric and environmentally-minded stance' in recent philosophy (*Realist Cinema* 21). This book contends, further, that any understanding of realism that is adequate to the manifold exigencies of the Anthropocene must remain open to different stylistic potentials. In the manner that neorealist films like *Rome, Open City* (1945) and *Bicycle Thieves* (1948), favoured by Bazin, are perceived as especially responsive to post-war circumstances in Italy, offering an ethical commitment to that historical situation, a diversity of recent films might offer essential theories about disaster in the context of the Anthropocene. Across Earth, at the beginning of the twenty-first century, there exist many cinematic realisms of disaster that powerfully contend with pressing issues concerning the intertwining of human and non-human.

To provide fuller justification for a recourse to realism, and also a framework for understanding its ethical utility, I turn once more to the world-changing disasters of the Second World War, to Bazin and Kracauer and their accounts of how filmmaking reckons with the post-war world. The war had a profound effect on filmmaking in both America and Europe, prompting filmmakers to reflect on the adequacies of their methods. Bazin cites the Hollywood director William Wyler's descriptions of how war-zone experiences affected him, altering his and his colleagues' approach, honing it in a particular direction:

> All three of us (Capra, Stevens, and Wyler) took part in the war … . We have learned to understand the world better … . I know that George Stevens has not been the same since he saw corpses at Dachau. We were forced to realize that Hollywood has rarely reflected the world and the time in which people live. (qtd in *Bazin at Work* 5)

Bazin praises Wyler, suggesting that such confronting experiences prompted these directors to work to translate 'some of the horror, some of the shocking truths' of the war into an 'ethic of realism' (5), and further surmising that war-time experience led to a 'pledge of dramatic honesty' (9). Realism's ethical commitment is cast in opposition to Hollywood, as Wyler intimates Hollywood's inability to create an accurate or adequate reflection of reality, and Bazin implies dishonesty inheres in Hollywood's established methods. Bazin also praises the post-war Italian films of Rossellini, Visconti, De Sica and others for their 'aesthetic of reality' (*What Is Cinema?* II.16). While he takes care to not reduce these neorealist films to 'common, easily definable characteristics' (30), he does note several traits they share as they depict war-time and post-war society: non-professional actors, minimal lighting, a documentary quality. An emphasis on the immediacy of the material world in these films is also noted: 'Man himself is just one fact among others, to whom no pride of place should be given *a priori*' (38). This tellingly reveals an impulse towards observation of the non-human alongside the more often-noted 'social descriptions of everyday life' (18) that neorealism offers; an attention to the matter and the presence of the world in which humans move. In the cases of both Wyler and neorealism then, Bazin articulates realism as a way of cinematically representing reality that is conscious of history. It is understood as an embedded process of striving to sincerely and authentically reflect the material and social realities of the war and its aftermath, at the centre of which is a devastating sense of death and dislocation.

Alongside Bazin, Kracauer also posits an optimistic function for films in the face of overwhelming death. Kracauer's theory of film hinges on his appraisal of the cinematic apparatus of the camera and his detailing of its capacity to 'record and reveal physical reality', which is also referred to as 'material reality', 'physical existence' or simply 'nature' (28). Ian Aitken describes how Kracauer, writing after the war, 'argued that the way to escape from a debilitating modern condition was through transcending abstraction and experiencing the world in its phenomenological richness' ('Introduction' 18–19). This keys in to a charged ethical dynamic apparent throughout Kracauer's theory, apparent in his attention to non-human presence. Film excels in its revelatory capacity because it can 'reveal things normally unseen' by humans (46), bringing us into a feeling of more intimate proximity with nature and the non-human. Realism in this sense thus works towards a sense of vital encounter with the material forces and presences of the world, offering the promise of a new awareness. A resonance with Levinasian ethics is particularly apparent in the position, argued by Jeeshan Gazi, that Kracauer's theory of film 'offers us new ways of seeing' (68), and that film may thus be able to 'effectuate an alternative mode of existence' (66). The redemptive power of film thus holds potential to catalyse a significant change in the consciousness of viewers, perhaps provoking a sharpening of sensibility not unlike El-Wardany's disaster-consciousness.

Disaster is a thematic preoccupation in the writing of both Bazin and Kracauer, tying their thought to ethical dynamics bound up in ideas of witnessing. Bazin sketches the notion of a 'Nero complex' in his discussion of Frank Capra's *Why We Fight* documentaries (1942–5), referring to 'the pleasure experienced at the sight of urban destruction' (*Bazin at Work* 188). The spectatorial experience of witnessing spectacular disaster imagery is particularly seductive. Kracauer's more prolonged interest in disaster is an important component of the legacy of his thought, his reference to the 'disintegration' of the modern world (qtd in Kracauer xi) and his insistence on 'nature' setting the tone for the recent uptake of his theory in an ecocritical context. Advancing Kracauer's interest in film's redemptive capacity, Jessica Mulvogue theorizes catastrophe aesthetics: an 'artistic orientation' that works to 'rearticulate senses and sensibilities about a world characterized by ecological catastrophe' (41–2). Although Mulvogue stresses that catastrophe aesthetics are not limited to any specific medium, she focuses on experimental documentaries distinguished from Hollywood by a comparable lack of spectacle; a declining to 'visualize the effects of climate change' (44). An ethics of encounter becomes apparent, for Mulvogue, in how such films probe entanglements between humanity and Earth's 'ostensibly inert materials', carrying a 'possibility of a renewed politico-ethical encounter' (53). Also generatively drawing on Kracauer, Jennifer Fay reads his post-war writing alongside early cinematic documentations of Antarctica's hostile, then-unknown environments to pose 'postcatastrophic self-alienation as the basis for environmental thought' (168). This thought is aimed at liberating contemporary humanity from foreclosed understandings of nature and natural history by 'redeeming an alien present' (181), and Fay describes this emancipatory possibility and the perspective it enables as 'becoming extraterrestrial' (194). An ethical transformation is connoted that not only involves but also moves beyond the subject: at once a becoming outside of oneself and an embrace of otherness that inheres within the self. Fay's assertion that Kracauer's theory 'is written with the hope that photography and cinema' can 'break habituated ways of seeing' (196) again resonates with Levinasian ethics. Film does not simply conjure a new optics of encounter. It can initiate, for viewers, new conditions under which ethics may proceed, and thus realisms can inaugurate new ways of apprehending the world and our responsibilities to it. Kracauer's realist theory and its association with disintegration, dehumanization and catastrophe thus help to locate emergent understandings of how film can function in the Anthropocene, honing in on the ability of some films (notably documentaries) to facilitate an ethics wherein viewers witness material reality in such a way that we are alienated from our sovereignty, brought closer to the forces of disaster that inhere in our contemporary world.

Encounters with alterity are thus powerfully present in the possibilities that realism poses for film. After the Second World War, Dudley Andrew contends, increasingly 'all films are uncanny evocations' that exploit 'tension between the human and the alien, between the personal and the foreign' (*What Cinema Is!* xix). As they deal in this tension, films of all kinds stage encounters with otherness. Andrew poses François Truffaut's *The 400 Blows* (1959) as a 'prime example' of Bazin's idea of cinema (xix), citing in particular the film's delinquent protagonist who gains a heightened physical experience of the world when spinning in a centrifuge at an amusement park. This scene constitutes a moment of ethical encounter: the boy meets the matter of the world as spinning energy, 'pure sensation' (xix). A joyous reaction is visible on his face, and reverse shots show viewers his perspective of the world in dynamic motion. The other here remains somewhat vague: centrifugal force may not be an ethical entity, even in the most poetic understanding, but its cinematic presence remains potent and is given greater clarity via Andrew's analytical connection of this scene to the film's ending sequence wherein the boy runs towards the beach, 'spun from this ride out to the end of the land' (xx), and the film marks a passage from urban Paris to the vast, unknown and perhaps alien sea. The final image shows a close-up of the boy's face – the site of ethics for Levinas – after he has stepped into the surf, having encountered the world in material fullness and felt the elemental force of the ocean. As the film ends, viewers are not privy to any revelation he may undergo, but Andrew's analysis describes the process of encounter the film details: 'a kid who got his education on the streets, confronting the world' (xx). The film figures an ethical encounter between its young protagonist and the looming world, which is ultimately given the tangible form of the Atlantic Ocean, lapping at the coast of Normandy. Andrew also observes that in this final shot, the film confronts viewers (xx) as the boy looks directly into the camera. This imparts a sense of responsibility onto us as, meeting his gaze, we feel ourselves confronted by the film's rendering of the world.

Locating a human (and humanistic) perspective in this way is a salient feature of Bazinian realism. Kracauer's realism, meanwhile, is largely unconcerned with how humans are presented on-screen and centres on the possibilities of this kind of confrontation for viewers, placing faith in, as Fay asserts, cinema's 'capacity to maintain the alterity of the unseen world before it is domesticated into narrative' (172). Thinking with both theorists, though, realism is foremostly interested in cinema's capacity to render the material of the world in ways that, contra Wyler's observations of Hollywood, reflect the times in which people live. Films that do so can create terms for encounter between humanity and the constituent entities, forces and material presences of the non-human world. They can push viewers towards ethics by compelling us to consider ourselves as implicated in these encounters, making us newly aware of our positionalities and responsibilities. Understood along these lines, as a means for describing the ways that films configure ethical dynamics for given historical exigencies, ideas of realism help us to seek out something like disaster-consciousness in films that represent worlds gone awry. Formulations of realism and the elements of film style that they describe thus offer multivalent avenues for exploring how viewers might come to look disaster in the eye, guiding us as we search for aesthetics of disaster that might prove adequate.

Tracing the fault lines of film form

Thinking about films via theories like Bazinian realism, which generatively emphasize multiple potentials for film style rather than stipulating fixed formal and categorical dispositions, is one way that film studies, as a discipline, can respond to and partake in the flurry of intellectual activity provoked by the Anthropocene. As the problems of the Anthropocene transcend extant strategies and scales, they demand thought that moves beyond orthodox methods. Calls for new approaches to conceptualizing are made by Haraway and Braidotti, with Haraway asserting that the 'urgencies' of our time 'demand that kind of thinking beyond inherited categories and capacities' (*Staying with the Trouble* 7) and proposing 'tentacular thinking', a mode of thought predicated on capacities 'to make attachments and detachments' and 'weave paths and consequences but not determinisms' (31). Braidotti seeks 'conceptual diversity in scholarship' that 'relies on the defamiliarization of our institutional habits of thought' (*Posthuman Knowledge* 28–9). Answering calls like these in a film studies context requires re-evaluating established notions including genres, modes, and regional and industrial alignments to seek new methods for analysing, categorizing and comparing films. Film analysis that is attuned to resonance across categorical boundaries can make unexpected connections and might even signal new and vital consequences for other knowledge practices. The multivalent understanding of realism posed by Bazin and echoed more recently by Nagib and others enables sustained enquiry into how particular aesthetic sensibilities, and the relationships of responsibility (or irresponsibility) to historical and material reality that they invoke, resonate across and beyond familiar categories. Conceiving of realism as variegated in this way makes it a powerful analytic frame that allows for films to be woven together with other films in unconventional or unexpected ways, and for other theories and concepts to be tentacularly attached to films.

There are, of course, film theorists and critics who have worked in this way prior to the arrival of the Anthropo-scene, and such approaches deliver rich and socio-politically potent analysis. One such writer is Lesley Stern, whose evocations of 'the way that cinema works' are open to the intersection and reverberation of texts and memories (*The Scorsese Connection* 6) and account for how in spectatorship 'disparate things and incommensurate things can be bumped up against one another' (Stern and Cox-Stanton, 'Interview'). Stern elaborates an analytical approach by citing Kracauer's position that 'guided by film, then, we approach, if at all, ideas no longer on highways leading through the void but on paths that wind through the thicket of things' ('"Paths"' 317), adding that her own paths are 'akin to grubbing along in the hedgerows, messing about with things in order to understand two or three things about the cinematic image and its capacity for rendering the material dimension of the everyday' (322–3). This methodological metaphor is apt for ecocritical contexts, and Stern's approach echoes a mode of philosophizing for the Anthropocene advanced by Joanna Zylinska, which is 'necessarily fragmented' and 'gives up on any desire to forge systems, ontologies or worlds', being satisfied with minor yet abundant interventions (*Minimal Ethics for the Anthropocene* 14). This amounts to a declining of aspirations towards totalizing knowledge, and a prioritization of attention to contextual specificities, signalling the importance of resonance. Tuning in to resonance makes it possible to navigate critical and theoretical landscapes often characterized by binaries, making use of them (as I have by invoking the opposition of realism to Hollywood) but working towards complexity rather than simplification. More recently, Adrian Ivakhiv has elaborated an ecocritical method that prioritizes resonance, highlighting the importance of 'condensed "hyper-signaletic" or "resonant moments"' in films wherein 'spectacle, narrative, and meaning are brought together' (*Ecologies of the Moving Image* 64), and focusing on 'key moments – motifs, patterns, and instances that carry the core affective impulses that a film passes on to its viewers' (65–6). This type of attention to moments is a fecund way of approaching films. Analysis hinging on resonant moments works outwards, funnelling critical attention through the remainder of films, across other films and theories that connect with them, and out to the cultural and geographical contexts from which they emerge, thus doubling back on the realities that films represent.

At this point, it is useful to begin honing the critical attention to film form that can guide us beyond Hollywood's disaster imaginary, establishing some aesthetic sensibilities and formal tendencies that resonate across cinematic renderings of disastrous events. Highlighting tendencies here in a somewhat generalized way provides a point of departure for tracing more specific realisms of disaster. A sense of conventional realist style, informed by the post-war filmmaking favoured by Bazin, is described by Aitken: 'the film should "flow" and intersect with things in an organic-like manner, emphasising becoming rather than being' (34). Such a film is 'perceptually realistic in terms of the overall structure of the image but also fluid and impressionistic' (34) and embracing the world in this manner – as processual, ambiguous and in flux – suggests an openness to contingency that chimes with the ethics I have described above. Films deploy a range of aesthetic strategies to achieve this type of perceptually open realism: narratives progressing in indeterminate or loosely defined ways, sparse dialogue and a general focus on atmospheres rather than central figures. At the level of production, this also means, as Nagib notes, 'physical engagement on the part of crew and cast' (*Realist Cinema* 27), which may include on-location shooting and improvization. The 'traditional markers of realist aesthetics' include, according to Thomas Elsaesser, 'static shots, fixed frames, deep focus, and the long take' ('World Cinema' 4) although, as shall be discussed in Chapters 4 and 5, the camera's mobility is also crucial. Realism of this sort is largely posed as an oppositional inclination: Aitken notes how realist theorists 'oppose "traditional" conceptions of film art' in which ideology is more readily apparent and the nature of spectatorship is determined ('The European Realist Tradition' 181), and Elsaesser notes that 'European art/auteur cinema (and by extension, world cinema) has always defined itself against Hollywood on the basis of its greater realism' (3). This attests to a sensibility that is at once particular and far-reaching: an aspiration for an expanded idea of how film enables viewers to see and encounter the world, and the diffusion of this aspirational sensibility into different regional and historical contexts outside of Hollywood.

Elsaesser details a 'new realism' (8) apparent in non-Hollywood filmmaking across the world that resonates especially productively with the ethical thought outlined in the previous section, observing several variations on traditional realist style that indicate a particular sensitivity to the proximity of death and ways that death looms in the contemporary world. Firstly, he highlights narrative structures that 'play with indeterminate or non-linear temporalities and privilege memory over chronology' (4). This not only echoes neorealism's favouring of looser narrative structures, but also signals a capacity for film to invoke temporalities that exceed human scales of perception, and hints at the potential confusion of ostensibly distinct pre-, trans- and post-disaster phases of catastrophic events. While, as I shall elaborate in Chapter 1, Hollywood disaster movies deploy narrative formulas that efficiently provide resolution, other approaches focus more exclusively on post-disaster contexts and are open to the intermeshing of pre- and post-disaster phases, accounting for the ways that disaster can perdure, recur and unravel in slow and unspectacular ways. Narrative indeterminacy also allows for memory to be prioritized over chronology, attesting to a privileging of lived experience, and for heightened attention to specificity and embedded perspectives attached to particular subjects. Connected to this, Elsaesser describes the prominence of characters he calls 'post-mortem protagonists' who are unsure if they are alive or dead, or who inhabit a distinct temporal or dimensional realm (9–10). This bears relevance for my analytical focus on characters who come face to face with disaster and embody particular subjective responses to it. Protagonists are described by Elsaesser 'whose view of the world is different ... marked by limits placed on their physical or mental faculties', such as amnesia, paralysis, mental illness, muteness and pathological violence (9). Such protagonists often evince a consciousness of the world that is not just damaged but also sharply honed: *Donnie Darko*, for example, centres on a teenager who is uniquely attuned to the eruption of death but seems to lose touch with the world around him as his mental illness becomes exacerbated. Characters and documentary subjects who are forced to accept displacement by disaster stand in stark contrast to Hollywood heroes whose primacy is reified by disaster. Using Elsaesser's term throughout this book, I consider as post-mortem protagonists people who are traumatized, bruised, scarred, displaced and killed in their experiences of disaster.

Another facet of the new realism observed by Elsaesser is a tendency for material things – 'objects, spaces, houses' – in films to 'take on a particular presence or agency' (10). This tendency sharpens prior emphases placed by both Bazin and Kracauer on the material world, configuring it in a way that relates more distinctly to the manner in which post-anthropocentric theorists have illuminated non-human agencies. Kracauer writes that the human actor is a 'thing amongst things' (xvii), and a similar decentring of the human is performed by the object-oriented ontology that Morton subscribes to as well as new materialist thought that is 'sympathetic to things' (Bennett, 'Systems and Things' 225). These philosophies refute the modern idea of objects or 'matter as passive stuff, as raw, brute, or inert' (Bennett, *Vibrant Matter* vii) to emphasize the capacities of objects and other non-human presences, particularly their power to act upon humans in sometimes indiscernible but profound ways. Analytical attention to the agency of things in cinema is provoked by Stern's questioning, 'When we speak of things in the cinema, do we mean solid things or something more like the force of things?' ('"Paths"' 321), and focus on the presence and agency of non-human things facilitates a clear understanding of cinema's capacity to render encounters between humans and all kinds of alterity. Analysing films in a way that attends to the force of things or, more specifically, considers representations of non-human things *as* agential forces that affect, threaten and decentre human protagonists keys in to the intersubjective dynamics at hand when disaster occurs, allowing for extrapolative speculation about how real forces of disaster are imagined in the world. For example, what might the encounter between Truffaut's delinquent protagonist in *The 400 Blows* and the Atlantic surf allow us to extrapolate about how we conceive of oceans? What might the encounter depicted between the destabilized patriarch of Jeff Nichols' *Take Shelter* and a gathering storm intimate about how we anticipate extreme weather events and, more broadly, how we conceptualize new climactic extremes? And what of the encounter between Donnie Darko's family and the jet engine that crashes into their house? A violent confrontation between regular denizens of suburbia, minding their own business, and a wayward piece of modern technology.

Each chapter of this book asks these kinds of questions about films of different styles, but establishing these realist tendencies described by Bazin, Kracauer, Aitken and Elsaesser here facilitates an overarching analytical trajectory that begins in Hollywood and moves gradually outward, surveying independent cinema, different kinds of documentary from the United States and elsewhere, and finally films by auteurs from Europe, Western Asia and Southeast Asia. Observing these general tendencies establishes an understanding of what it means to dislodge our expectations from Hollywood aesthetics.

In an effort to describe a decentring of Hollywood and enable the tracing of interconnections between other films of disparate geographical origin, the analogy of waves is popularly deployed. Waves like the French New Wave, Andrew argues, 'roll through adjacent cultures whose proximity to one another promotes a propagation', and in this manner tendencies in film style undulate, crest and come ashore at various locations and historical moments ('An Atlas of World Cinema' 12). This analogy fits well with extant literature on Hollywood's disaster genre which, as I shall discuss in Chapter 1, focuses mostly on two crests: cycles of films produced in the 1970s and the 1990s when production motives, socio-political contexts and formal tendencies coalesced. It is tempting to extend Andrew's analogy and argue that the 2010s have seen a third cycle, another deluge of disaster movies, and indeed Chapter 1 explores how tendencies that came to the fore throughout the two prior cycles have been revived in a widespread selection of 2010s blockbusters, and new tendencies have also evolved such that disaster is now a cornerstone of Hollywood films across multiple generic categories.

Alongside the wave, however, I propose another more pertinent analogy to trace films about disaster that opens onto more complex understandings of shifting film styles, better accommodating the Bazinian notion of manifold realisms: that of the earthquake's epicentre and fault lines. Tectonic forces lurk below landscapes, building tension across subterranean trajectories to become apparent when they burst through the Earth. Inasmuch as an earthquake is a shocking, sudden event, it is also the result of gradually accumulating energies and is followed by repeating aftershocks. Earthquakes can transform regions, altering geography and ecosystems. With this analogy, prior disaster movie cycles may be understood as earthquake swarms: each film a spike on a seismograph, but all clustered around the epicentre of Hollywood, overwhelmingly alike in style and in the ways that they provoke viewers to imagine disaster. The build-up to their collective emergence can be charted in prior media – sci-fi B movies, superhero comics and the like – and their influence is clear in subsequent blockbusters. Other epicentres however may also be sites for more isolated shocks of significant magnitude, as critically significant films that represent disaster in unique and powerful ways are produced far from Hollywood and in fewer number. They may occur as aftershocks to historical disasters, as neorealism follows the Second World War, or exist in other kinds of proximity to events or socio-political conditions. *Stalker* (1979), for example, is often considered in relation to the subsequent Chernobyl nuclear disaster of 1986. Such proximities may be key to understanding their significance and, of course, a great many films evince connection to climate change and other conditions of the Anthropocene.

This analogy allows for connections to be drawn between films of distinct, even oppositional, styles. Chapter 2 of this book remains in the United States but examines independent films produced in the shadow of Hollywood's 1990s disaster movies including *Safe* (1995) and *Donnie Darko* (2001). These films refute blockbuster aesthetics to imagine more subtle, mysterious disasters that undergird quotidian modernity rather than rupturing it spectacularly, but still bear clear markers of proximity to Hollywood style and evince an apocalyptic sense of large-scale eco-catastrophe. Their characters are foils to heroic Hollywood protagonists, being post-mortem subjects characterized by a loss of sovereignty. Chapters 3 and 4 raise distinct notions of realism as they pivot to explore documentaries dealing with climate change and anthropogenic disaster. Chapter 3 analyses prominent, far-reaching US documentaries – *An Inconvenient Truth* (2006) and *Before the Flood* (2016) – that offer a realism grounded in argumentation and ostensibly objective scientific knowledge. More contemplative documentaries analysed in Chapter 4 – *There Once Was an Island* (2010) and *On an Unknown Beach* (2016) – offer a counterposed realism tied to subjective experience as they highlight situated perspectives on specific disasters in the South Pacific, including the Christchurch earthquakes. These documentaries are all produced in clear response to burgeoning anthropogenic catastrophe and aim at ethical filmmaking in divergent ways. A traditional realist style is more explicitly foregrounded in Chapter 5, which examines films that have been categorized as world cinema, auteur cinema and slow cinema: *Life, and Nothing More* (1992), *Time of the Wolf* (2003) and *Death in the Land of Encantos* (2007). These three films originate in different regions and at distinct historical moments but all make crucial use of the long take and, posed together, facilitate an imagination of disaster tied to subjective processes of witnessing and an ethics of passivity, of looking rather than acting.

The archive of films about disaster that this book surveys is certainly not exhaustive, and other films and groups of films imagine disaster in unique ways. Other scholars have surveyed situated archives of disaster cinema that are adjacent to this project: Akira Mizuta Lippit, for example, in *Atomic Light (Shadow Optics)*, poses a theory of disaster's remediation with a focus on Japanese science fiction, and David Deamer's *Deleuze, Japanese Cinema, and the Atom Bomb* also explores the nuclear legacy of Japanese films. Additionally, in light of continuing theorizing of and about the Anthropocene and the non-human, much film ecocriticism is attuned to the implications of other diverse films that thematize and elsewise reflect disaster, including Ivakhiv's *Ecologies of the Moving Image* (2013), Jennifer Fay's *Inhospitable World* (2018), Chelsea Birks's *Limit Cinema* (2022) and more. The selection of films I analyse demonstrates how disaster remains a thematic attraction especially for male directors. For example, within Hollywood's disaster genre, Mimi Leder's *Deep Impact* (1998) is the only prominent film directed by a woman across multiple cycles from the 1950s until the 2010s. Though this book surveys mostly films directed by men, issues of gender become a focus for heightened critical attention, especially as Hollywood disaster movies continually foreground male protagonists and invest in masculinist notions of the human self.

In the chapters that follow, I have attempted to pose a trajectory that incorporates Hollywood and moves beyond it in a balanced manner, taking into account regions and styles that are diverse in nature while also paying heed to major movements and tendencies in film form. My research is conditioned by my own situation as a settler in the Southern Hemisphere, and as someone whose pivotal experience of disaster in New Zealand was connected with the force of Hollywood imaginaries but also greatly removed from it. My examination of South Pacific disaster in Chapter 4 especially reflects this situation. This book's arc from Hollywood to a traditionally realist style allows for the consideration of an array of realisms with often surprising resonances, particularly when documentary is taken into consideration. Indeed, my turn to documentary enables a discussion of how different documentary practices can refract the aesthetic sensibilities foregrounded by both Hollywood and realist styles. In this manner, Hollywood traditions and the post-war realist style offer two guiding notions about how disaster can be imagined cinematically: two oppositional apparitions of life in the disaster zone. As Martin-Jones posits, however, 'this is not a case of art cinema vs Hollywood ... but of understanding how transnational histories emerge across the cinemas of the world' (58). While opposing binaries can be useful, as this book investigates possibilities for the cinematic imagination of disaster, it is more acutely concerned with the subtleties of formal resonance and tension that play out in less clearly defined territories. These aesthetic territories can be like disaster zones themselves: as-yet-unknown, engendered by ruptures of form and the collapse of known categories. In the manner that disaster demands, this book seeks to open up the complexities they occasion.

Part I

Hollywood and Its Shadow

1
Hollywood's disaster movies

In *San Andreas* (2015), California is devastated by a series of huge earthquakes, moments of cinematic disaster that resonate along multiple fault lines. Near the end of the film, the hero pilots a boat through the flooded streets of downtown San Francisco. Floating rubble blocks his path and cleaved skyscrapers burn in the background. In a scene just prior, a tsunami has thundered across the Bay Area, carrying a massive container ship into the Golden Gate Bridge, tearing it in two and snapping its cables like rubber bands. This tsunami scene is a version of a sequence that has played out in Hollywood since at least *The Poseidon Adventure* (1972): a massive wave, rendered as a swathe of elemental force, careens across the frame obliterating human presence: people, ships, landmarks, entire city skylines. As the hero and his estranged wife navigate the wreckage searching for their daughter, the film's catastrophic vision of San Francisco also resonates with real disaster in a multitude of ways. Most obviously *San Andreas* relates to the many historical earthquakes along the San Andreas fault that runs through California, including the 1989 Loma Prieta quake that killed sixty-three people and injured thousands in the Bay Area. It also relates to anxieties about a potential future megathrust earthquake striking North America's Pacific Coast. Indirect resonances are apparent too. *San Andreas*'s depictions of collapsing skyscrapers – glissading glass and rubble, clouds of dust and smoke – echo 9/11, its flooded urban environment also appears much like a city devastated by sea level rise and the detritus that blocks the hero's path looks like the Great Pacific Garbage Patch has floated into the Financial District.

These scenes intimate much about the status of disaster imagery and thematics in Hollywood blockbusters of the 2010s. Disasters often erupt in these films as recursions: not only repetitions or remakes of scenes from prior films, especially of Hollywood's 1970s and 1990s disaster movie cycles, but also from elsewhere. The container ship smashing into the Golden Gate Bridge is a scenario repurposed from the Korean film *Haeundae* (2009), for example. As visual effects technologies become increasingly sophisticated, Hollywood films render events like these – earthquakes, floods, collapsing buildings – with ever greater visual verisimilitude and in increasingly spectacular ways. However, as Hollywood's representation of disaster becomes more visually realistic and sentimentally persuasive, relationships between cinematic disasters and disastrous historical events can become increasingly unclear. Many recent blockbusters thematize issues intrinsic to recent and present historical disasters, particularly 9/11 and climate crisis, but they often do so within narrative frames that enact encounters of occlusion wherein possibilities for recognition and responsibility are obfuscated, or even abdicated.

This chapter makes the case that disaster movies are a major force within Hollywood and thus constitute a well-established, culturally dominant way of imagining disaster. In order to do so, it charts their emergence, in relation to socio-historical exigencies, from Sontag's writing on post-war films up to a contemporary standpoint where they are frequently described in light of the Anthropocene. Scholarly writing on disaster movies, while not as widespread or far-reaching as writing on adjacent genres such as horror and science fiction, is comprehensive, especially in relation to the popular cycles of the 1970s and 1990s. Accounting for the history of the genre, and assessing its recent relevance with the aid of Sontag, Yacowar, Nick Roddick's 'Only the Stars Survive: Disaster Movies in the Seventies', Stephen Keane's 2001 book *Disaster Movies*, who all schematize cycles of disaster movies, as well as other key writing by Michael Ryan and Douglas Kellner and Despina Kakoudaki, this chapter surveys a large number of films before consolidating analysis of several 2010s films: *Gravity* (2013), *San Andreas* (2015) and *Avengers: Age of Ultron* (2015), which illustrate the recent reach of the genre in different ways and in light of issues bound up in the Anthropocene. Being attentive to an entire genre, my discussion here is broader in scope than in the chapters that follow, but establishing historical context allows a more granular analysis of these recent films, particularly insofar as they thematize issues pertinent to the Anthropocene.

The evolution of Hollywood's disaster genre up to its present state can be mapped by tracing the consolidation of narrative and visual formulas that codify, in remarkably formulaic ways, processes of encounter between human protagonists and forces of alterity that usually invoke elemental nature, extraterrestrial invasion or a combination of both. The films discussed in this chapter feature non-human entities with faces like aliens, animalistic mutants and robots, as well as more expansive earthly presences like earthquakes and tidal waves, and also more absolute forces like gravity and time that defy anthropomorphizing even as they are cast as villainous antagonists. Nevertheless, all confront human protagonists in ways that accord with expanded understandings of the face-to-face encounter, per Levinas's ethics, as a site wherein the demands of ethical responsibility are brought to bear. Per Hollywood convention, disaster movies centre on heroic figures and thus a major focus for my analysis in this chapter is the prominence of disaster movie heroes as subjects, how they are shown to be called into encounter with alterity that threatens to decentre them and destabilize humanity, and what their responses signal with regard to human subjectivity, history and the non-human environment. I have highlighted an overriding interest in what ethical responsibility in the face of disaster looks like, but we shall discover here how the narrative and aesthetic formulas that govern Hollywood disaster movies are more interested in advancing a type of irresponsibility, and more likely to look away from the historical disasters that they index or represent, from the post-war period to the contemporary context of the Anthropocene and climate change.

Disaster as encounter in genre films from the 1950s to the 1970s

Prior to industrial conceptualization of a disaster genre, Susan Sontag describes a set of science-fiction films emerging mainly from Hollywood during the late 1950s and early 1960s as being not about science but, rather, 'about disaster' (213). These films share 'a form as predictable as a Western' (209) and constitute an 'independent subgenre' (212). They belong to a lineage of films about mass destruction that includes monster movies like *King Kong* (1933), in which cities are destroyed by rampaging beasts, and share themes and motifs with superhero comic books (214) but are distinguished from prior large-scale spectacles of destruction by their 'decided grimness,' which is 'bolstered by their much greater degree of visual credibility' (215). This credibility is bound up in perceived verisimilitude, as these films present shocking, seemingly unreal events and phenomena like alien invasion and bodily mutation with unprecedented lifelikeness, making use of emergent cinematic technologies to render the unreal real.

These films' interlacing of fantastic unreality and visual authenticity bears similarity to the way that death is seen to erupt and pervade across the world in the Anthropocene. Their science-fictional scenarios frequently hinge on disastrous events wherein, as Timothy Morton notes of our contemporary moment, 'beings no longer coincide with their phenomena' and 'things become misty, shifty, nebulous, uncanny' (*Dark Ecology* 74). Although their style is absolutely contra to conventional realism, they feature precisely the type of post-mortem protagonist identified by Thomas Elsaesser in world cinema, for whom 'it is not clear to either themselves or the audience whether they are still alive or dead' ('World Cinema' 10). The uncertainty and ambiguity that these films invoke, however, is purely antagonistic, signalling the threat of death. Many depict situations wherein, Sontag writes, 'the person is really dead, but he doesn't know it. He is "undead", he has become an "unperson"' (221). Ambiguous presences in films like *It Came from Outer Space* (1953), *This Island Earth* (1955), *Invasion of the Body Snatchers* (1956), *Attack of the Puppet People* (1958) and *The Brain Eaters* (1958) are seen by Sontag as evidence of wider themes of depersonalization: extraterrestrial invaders, mutants, animalistic monsters and experimental technologies are forces of alterity that threaten to usurp or radically destabilize humanity.

Objects, especially machines, attain significant meaning in many of these films as they 'stand in for different values' (216), their mysterious capacities promising obliteration. In *The Fly* (1958), a film analysed by Sontag, a teleportation device evidences evolving technology's power to bring about death in previously unimaginable ways. The inventor of the experimental 'disintegrator–integrator' machine tests it on himself while, unbeknownst to him, a housefly has invaded the equipment in his basement laboratory and he is thusly transformed into a part-human, part-insect monster. A sudden reveal when his wife pulls a black cloth away from him shows viewers that his head has been replaced with that of the fly, and in this moment of literal face-to-face encounter, viewers, confronted with the fly's bulging eyes and quivering labella, share the wife's experience of revulsion. Perspective shots show that reconciling via this face-to-face encounter is impossible as the mutated scientist advances, zombie-like, and his wife flees. The machine's atomic reorganization of the world violently disturbs ontological and moral categories, bringing horror into the domestic environment. Ultimately, the destruction of the machine as well as the mutants it created, and a cover-up facilitated by a detective, soothes the anxieties of other characters in the film and of viewers. Only this complete banishment and denial of the deathly unperson-ness the machine brought about can enact a repairing of ruptured conditions, keeping wider catastrophe at bay.

The Fly is exemplary of the way these films depict non-human forces – aliens, animals, technology – as threatening to human sovereignty, and enact the neutralization of anything that might cause human death. Sontag highlights several model scenarios, each one concluding with heroes prevailing 'against the invaders' (211). This signals a formulaic generic approach wherein narratives are repeatedly deployed that reify a binary view of the self and the other that is constituent throughout modernity, informing understandings of alterity and difference as irreconcilable. Writing on H. G. Wells' novel *The War of the Worlds*, which inspired the 1953 film of the same name, Eva Horn elucidates a 'model of total enmity' that characterizes political rhetoric following the First World War: the idea of an enemy that, without any specific reason to be hostile, is so simply by virtue of being 'essentially different' (103–4). This model channels notions of self and other that Rosi Braidotti observes entrenched in European history wherein the self is a Eurocentric, masculinist vision of humanity: 'Subjectivity is equated with consciousness, universal rationality, and self-regulating ethical behaviour, whereas Otherness is defined as its negative and specular counterpart' (*The Posthuman* 15). In these sci-fi films, disaster is imbued in objects and entities that take the form of a totalizing negative: an irrational, unreasonable, irredeemable mirror for human characters who, when confronted, act in a regulatory capacity. Showcasing the triumph of humans over various hostile forces, this subgenre of films envisions humanity in a superior position over all kinds of alterity, its repeated defeat functioning to allay anxieties about the vulnerability of modern humanity.

These anxieties are specifically bound up in the advent of the nuclear bomb, and Sontag positions this sci-fi disaster imaginary as a response to the post-war context (224). *The Fly*'s teleportation device, with its atomic capabilities, stands in for nuclear weaponry. Horn argues that depictions of catastrophe somewhat paradoxically 'reveal something *that already exists*' because, in them, 'something that we previously just feared, suspected, imagined, possibly misunderstood will become an event and take on a tangible – horrific – form' (11, italics in the original). The teleportation device and the mutated fly can thus be seen as forms that embody and give face to the calamitous potentials of nuclear technology. However, in these depictions of disaster, an even broader array of already-existing fears becomes both underscored and allayed. Just as *The Fly* seemingly attests to humanity's courage to overcome atomic threats. it also, in a more literal way, reifies the abject alterity of flies and other insects. In this way, the depersonalizing sci-fi disasters observed by Sontag extend beyond their post-war specificities to corroborate other entrenched modern divisions between humans, who are sovereign, courageous and heroic, and non-human others that, cast as bearers of disaster, become ever more horrifying and dangerous.

Nuclear detonations mark a disastrous epochal shift not just in their dispersal of isotopes, but also because they necessitate a new understanding of death at a global level. This awareness is felt as a shock: a change in widespread awareness of human agencies, and of a particular shared predicament. As Sontag elaborates the sci-fi disaster subgenre, she describes this shock at the level of lived experience, noting

> the trauma suffered by everyone in the middle of the 20th century when it became clear that, from now on to the end of human history, every person would spend his individual life under the threat not only of individual death, which is certain, but of something almost insupportable psychologically – collective incineration and extinction which could come at any time, virtually without warning. (224)

This realization, brought about by the incineration of Hiroshima and Nagasaki, is proximal to the post-war conditions of overwhelming trauma noted in Bazin's post-war writing. However, while Bazin focuses critical attention on filmmakers who respond to mass death by searching for ways to honestly convey the realities instituted by the war, Sontag concludes that 'the imagery of disaster in science fiction is above all the emblem of an *inadequate response*' (224, italics in the original). The films she describes attest to a culture of inability or unwillingness to confront the 'unassimilable terrors' (224) of nuclear Armageddon. These films thus embody a refusal to meet historical disaster. Like the wife of the scientist who turns to flee from her mutated husband in *The Fly*, they constitute a looking away in the face of catastrophe. Rather than confronting trauma and seeking to understand the ramifications of the potential for atomic annihilation, these sci-fi disaster films function on a social level to exorcise anxiety by presenting the defeat of all threats as inevitable. They imagine disaster as deathly alterity that places humans in positions of extreme ontological vulnerability, but only temporarily; just long enough for them to act quickly and recover. By doing so, they elide the type of ethics this book is interested in, foreclosing any possibility for an altered or renewed consciousness of the human self to emerge via encounter, working instead to continuously re-inscribe extant human dominance.

A decade later, another distinct group of films emerges from Hollywood that also stages disaster as encounter between humans and powerful forces of alterity. Critically regarded as the first cycle of disaster movies, they figure forces of nature as they deal with widespread anxieties about new technologies and the broad course of modernity. Nick Roddick explains that while 'fear of the bomb was very much a folk nightmare of the fifties and early sixties', 1970s disaster movies reflect concerns about 'tampering with The Ecology' (248), and their threats 'arise without exception from earth … air … fire … or water' (253–4). Indeed, elemental threats are invoked in the names of the most prominent of these films: *Airport* (1970), *The Poseidon Adventure* (1972), *Earthquake* (1974) and *The Towering Inferno* (1974). Roddick offers a working definition of this genre: 'a film in which the central pivot or impulse of the narrative was provided by a natural or man-made disaster occurring, either without warning or after unheeded warnings, in a setting or environment close enough to the audience's experience for identification to be possible' (246–7).

Roddick stipulates that disaster scenarios should be 'factually possible' (246), excluding extraterrestrial invasion. This categorical insistence on a kind of relatability to the ordinary lives of viewers intimates how, although the disaster scenarios of these films are high-stakes and spectacular, they remain plausible rather than fantastical.

These films continue in the tradition of extravagant grimness outlined by Sontag. Disaster is rendered in spectacular ways that make use of tricks and effects like shaking of the camera and distortion of the frame such that objects, like *Earthquake*'s high-rise buildings, seem to wobble, distort and lose cohesion. Forces of nature often impact human protagonists from outside the frame, emphasizing their large scale and emphatic otherness. When a gigantic wave hits the titular cruise ship in *The Poseidon Adventure*, for example, viewers see the wave approach from a withdrawn, aerial perspective but witness the moment of impact mostly from the inside of the capsizing luxury liner, seeing passengers in the ballroom panic as their environment is literally turned upside down. Similarly, in *Earthquake*, debris from crumbling buildings falls from above the frame onto street scenes. The disasters of these films bring threat of death into the cinematic frame from the outside, transforming modernity's everyday spaces into spaces of death.

This cycle of films can be situated in relation to prior trends via an exploration of the way they thematize technology. Their narrative strategies are, as Roddick notes, essentially identical to older monster movies in which 'man's scientific arrogance or commercial greed are the more or less direct causes of the disaster' (247). Like the sci-fi of the 1950s and early 1960s, these films hinge on figuring machinations that precipitate disaster by disturbing ontological categories but, rather than detailing futuristic, speculative inventions, they simply feature things regularly used by contemporary viewers. Planes, ocean liners, skyscrapers, cars and sprawling cities, as the componentry of industrialized modernity, had by the early 1970s disrupted understandings of space and time in anxiety-provoking, traumatic and death-inducing ways. As Paul Virilio notes, 'When you invent the ship, you also invent the shipwreck; when you invent the plane, you invent the plane crash' (89). In these films, Roddick observes accordingly, 'technological and economic marvels of the capitalist world' figure as emblematic of a luxuriant humanity: 'sybaritic, self-centred beings totally reliant on a technology which they utilize without understanding and which proves incapable of resisting the basic elemental forces' (252). Yacowar even posits that disaster, in these narratives, might be understood as a kind of divine punishment for humanity's utilization of technology to usurp their position in the world by, for example, 'hubristically presuming to fly' in *Airport* (315), which depicts an airport crippled by a snowstorm. The machinations of greedy, naïve humans are thus shown to invite disaster by occasioning new kinds of vulnerabilities that highlight modern humanity's inadequacy.

Disaster scenarios therefore function as platforms for staging humanity's recovery from this fallen state. This recovery is enabled via the installation, in protagonists, of a particular heroic subjectivity. Roddick describes a narrative formula in which encounter between humans and elemental forces occasions extreme vulnerability: 'as a result of a catastrophe which kills most of the people around them, a random selection of people find themselves cut off from the outside world and threatened with death' (250). Among these survivors 'a natural "leader" emerges' who is male, 'invariably white' and embodies institutional power: a priest played by Gene Hackman in *The Poseidon Adventure*, or a fire chief played by Steve McQueen in *The Towering Inferno*, for example. He 'averts the disaster or leads its victims to safety', demonstrating that he can reliably handle whatever technology has been thrown into doubt (Roddick 256). The traits of this leader are shown to be the qualities necessary to overcome disaster, and the heroes of disaster movies thus model an idealized modern humanity. Uniformed male heroes stand for 'brave, morally upright and technologically brilliant' leadership (Roddick 261), functioning to conjoin 'traditional individualism' with 'new corporatism' (Ryan and Kellner 56) and bringing old-fashioned values into the technological era. Disaster movie heroes are comparable to the heroes of Westerns, sharing their 'muscles, good looks, sexual aggressiveness' (Roddick 257). Just as those heroes on horseback master the frontier, 'the hero of the disaster movie must know the technological environment in which he and his flock find themselves adrift', becoming 'a hero for the technological age: Charlton Heston with a degree in electrical engineering' (Roddick 257).

Heston crucially embodies this heroic figure, appearing in numerous science-fiction and disaster movies around this time. Disaster movies of the 1970s devote little screen time to character development, depending instead on the familiarity of their stars from previous films (Yacowar 321) and on their celebrity personalities more generally (Roddick 252). Heston's renown as a macho, gun-toting US conservative thus conditions the heroic characters he plays. As disaster movies service a return to prior genre conventions, their heroes also, as Michael Ryan and Douglas Kellner observe, enact 'ritualized legitimation of strong male leadership' (52). Similarly, J. Hoberman posits that they celebrate 'the inherent virtue of decent, everyday Middle Americans' by linking survival to 'traditional social roles and conventional moral values' (198). Heston's public image matches these traits remarkably: 1972, this cycle's starting point, is noted by biographer Emilie Raymond as the beginning of a stage of Heston's public activism marked by a 'newly partisan and combative style' (6), his persona hinging on an 'image of hardened masculinity' (7). In his recurring role as the face of a macho, uniformed, white, old-fashioned morality, Heston plays a US Army Colonel in *The Omega Man* (1971), an airline captain in *Skyjacked* (1972) and *Airport 1975* (1974), an NYPD detective in *Soylent Green* (1973) and a grizzled Navy submarine captain in *Gray Lady Down* (1978). In *Earthquake*, his former football player character is first shown vigorously exercising and arguing with his wife. Across these films, his image consolidates as the emblem of a particular brand of authority that is aggressively masculinist, distinctly American, physical, practical and common-sensical.

Heroic characters such as these played by Heston stand out in ensemble casts, being elevated over other identities and social strata by their capacity to overcome disaster. As much as conflict exists between heroes and the elements, it also features between heroic response to disaster and other potential responses. Yacowar even suggests that a disaster movie 'dramatizes class conflict', offering a cast that reflects a cross-section of society (321). Roddick furthers this suggestion, asserting that all disaster movie characters are 'archetypes who react to the given situation in function of their sex, class or profession' (252). Race, too, is a feature of these redemptive, heroic dynamics. Though Heston famously supported the 1964 Civil Rights Act, the rhetoric of his later outspoken conservatism found favour with white supremacists and, belittling the histories and status of Indigenous peoples of the Americas, he proudly categorized himself as a 'Native American' (Hornblower). Apocalyptic narratives, a storytelling mode adjacent to disaster, April Anson writes, are 'associated with a Judeo-Christian tradition that narrates revelation and judgement day, the promise of the end of the world and a new beginning for a *particular* people' (61). Anson describes how 'fictional appeals to the apocalypse that rely on a state of emergency are wedded to the exceptionalism of the white settler state' and 'entrench Western political structures' (62). Reiterating the Western's themes of conquest and centring of cowboys and gunslingers as masters of nature, disaster movies narrate the proper inauguration of a perfected technological modernity delineated by the prowess of their mostly white heroes. By invoking seemingly random gatherings of people who stand in for different social groups, bringing them into collective encounter with death and then foregrounding a masterful white, male protagonist whose inherent capacities enable him to overcome disaster, the formulaic narratives of 1970s disaster movies lend renewed legitimacy to extant social hierarchies, upholding power structures dictated by gender roles, white supremacy and institutional or corporate authority.

Just like the sci-fi movies categorized by Sontag, 1970s disaster movies thusly reify the powers of the regulatory, normative, masculinist human self-critiqued by theorists like Braidotti, contextualizing it firmly within the United States. Their heroes more clearly aim at an apotheosis of the unitary subject position that Braidotti names 'Him:' an 'ideal of bodily perfection' initially represented in Leonardo da Vinci's *Vitruvian Man* that doubles into 'a set of mental, discursive and spiritual values' to assert, throughout modern history, 'the almost boundless capacity of humans to pursue their individual and collective perfectibility' (*The Posthuman* 13). As disaster movie heroes become emblems for the unflinching progression of rational humanity, scenarios of risk and vulnerability, wherein humans are overwhelmed by forces of nature that might prompt a new, differentiated awareness of modern humanity's position in (and effect on) the world, instead catalyse the reification of age-old masculinist approaches. Hollywood's disaster genre thus ultimately illustrates the upgrading of humanity such that it is capable of managing the traumatic conditions of modernity without having to accommodate any kind of earthly alterity. Male protagonists are figureheads for the response to the crises of modernity that the genre articulates: a claim that when the sovereign power of humanity is properly channelled, it can easily master the modern milieu. As stories of human triumph over elemental forces, their narrative patterns set in motion a predominant social attitude reflected in media and scientific discourse that, as noted by Joanna Zylinska, 'salvation from the Anthropocene's alleged finalism' will come from 'an actual upgrade of humans to the status of *Homo deus*' (*The End of Man* 12). These films both project and attest to humanity's durability, lending an aura of permanence to a pervasive imaginary of humanity as a species that, overcoming adversity, advances rationally and progressively, indifferent to forces that might confront it. The encounters staged in these films imply an ongoing faith in humanity's capacities to regulate itself and manage all other forces, known and unknown, unnatural and natural, that are constituent in the world.

From the 1990s into the Anthropocene

By the late 1990s, when another distinct group of disaster movies cycled into popularity, faith in humanity's technological and managerial capacities was being tested due to growing awareness of global warming and climate change, and impending uncertainty surrounding Y2K. This second cycle permutes elements of both 1970s disaster movies and earlier science-fiction films, complicating their narrative formulas, updating the heroism that they invoke and visualizing disaster in newly spectacular ways. While some of these films like *Twister* (1996) and *Volcano* (1997) feature natural disasters and recover the conventions of the 1970s, others are more complex. *Independence Day* (1996), perhaps Hollywood's most successful disaster movie both popularly and critically, is described by Stephen Keane as an intermeshing of both *The War of the Worlds* and *Earthquake* (85). As it recycles and updates prior conventions, *Independence Day* exemplifies an evolved 1990s disaster movie, and it also establishes Roland Emmerich as a prominent disaster movie director for the 1990s and beyond. Like other films of this cycle, as its depiction of disaster foregrounds the interaction of technology and ecology, it provokes a feeling of the finitude of humanity's powers.

The disasters of this 1990s cycle are bigger than those of the 1970s, as human protagonists often encounter forces that threaten the entire planet or multiple locations across the globe. In *Independence Day*, alien spaceships arrive above thirty-six cities, while in *Deep Impact* (1998) and *Armageddon* (1998), Earth is imperilled by comets and meteorites. These larger-scale disasters can be seen to stand in for more pervasive, urgent and perhaps more deeply entrenched social anxieties than those present in the 1950s or 1970s. Critical discussion of these films tends to frame them, much as Sontag and Roddick frame prior

Hollywood disaster films, as a response to social anxieties attendant to the far-reaching, complex problem of climate change. Invoking a sense of ethical encounter and responsibility, Keane posits that the task of these films is 'to face up to … the end of the world' (73). While he notes the significance of ecology, arguing that weather films like *Twister* and *Waterworld* (1995) are read with a message regarding humanity's 'poisoning the planet' in mind (78), he delineates a broader, all-encompassing context: 'Pertinent concerns such as global warming quickly bled into rather more hysterical millennial concerns about Satan, aliens and asteroids. Hence disaster became an all-round bandwagon: natural disasters here, aliens there, lava bombs and meteor fragments everywhere' (78).

Even 1990s disaster movies seemingly not concerned with nature frequently thematize ecology, incorporating elemental forces and animalistic presences into their spectacular rendering of disaster. Water, air and fire are a major aspect of how this cycle advances Hollywood's tradition of mass destruction utilizing the 'new sheen' of computer-generated imagery (Keane 74) to show cataclysmic events in ways previously impossible. The impact of *Deep Impact*'s comet, for example, is shown from space as it affects Earth's atmosphere, displacing clouds before smashing into the sea. From a ground-level perspective, viewers then see the sky turn flame red before an immense wave sweeps across the screen. In the Emmerich-directed 1998 *Godzilla* remake, the titular monster, a lizard mutated after exposure to nuclear radiation, is linked with water as it generates a huge wave when it travels undersea, and also when it rampages through New York City under sheeting rain. *Independence Day* incorporates the elements as it stages global disaster by showing encounters between human cities and alien vessels. When aliens arrive above New York, their menacing spaceship emerges through a fiery cloud formation, appearing like a sudden, terrifying change in the weather. Later, the ship's weapons create firestorms in Manhattan streets as they explode landmark buildings. The aliens themselves are a chimerical melange: insectoid, reptilian and cephalopod all at once; absolutely non-human, irredeemably other and purely antagonistic. Concerns about non-human nature thus remain key to the ways that these films visualize disaster.

Disaster movies of the 1990s feature a broader range of characters collaborating in heroic roles. *Independence Day* is especially indicative of this trend, as the ensemble cast demonstrates shared capacity to overcome the alien threat. As Keane observes, Emmerich's film leaves Earth's fate 'in the hands of a strategic group of people' (87). The importance of diversity to its distinctly American group is explained by Despina Kakoudaki ('Representing

Politics in Disaster Films' 350) who, viewing the film through the lens of racial melodrama, explains that alongside spectacles of destruction, it also offers minor 'spectacles of reconciliation, multicultural understanding and collaboration' (352). Collaboration across classes and identities is key to defeating the aliens. A scientist, David Levinson, hatches a plan to upload a computer virus to the alien technology and needs the help of an Air Force pilot, Steven Hiller, to deliver it to the mothership. In the final act, Levinson, who is Jewish, and Hiller, who is Black, confront an alien face to face, laughing together as they blow it up with a missile. Meanwhile, the President of the United States recruits a washed-up, alcoholic crop duster and other volunteers to attack and destroy an alien craft at Area 51. These scenes exemplify how 1990s disaster movies, as Kakoudaki posits, provide resolutions 'preoccupied with how to coordinate massive military and police mobilization, how to reorganize the chain of command, and how to make the human group more effective by resolving racial tension' (141). As collaborative efforts are required to overcome scaled-up global catastrophe and humans come together to defeat threatening aliens or survive natural disasters, the possibilities of heroism seem to be opened up to more kinds of people.

However, as militarism, technological expertise and physical strength continue to be foregrounded, the qualities that connote heroism remain largely unchanged. The componentry of the rational, modern, masculinist heroic subject remains at work, continuing to assert humanistic sovereignty in the face of alterity. Despite their race and class differences, the active heroes of *Independence Day* are all male. Levinson and Hiller celebrate their gloating triumph over the aliens by lighting cigars, a clear symbol of masculine potency. A subplot involving Hiller's fiancée, an exotic dancer, rescuing the First Lady indicates that a redemptive but less impactful type of heroism is available to women. Even if they are not literally uniformed, the film's male heroes are all linked to militaristic authority: the President and the crop duster are both military veterans and Hiller is an active marine. Similarly, *Volcano*, in which a volcano forms underneath Los Angeles, offers a diverse set of heroes who nonetheless subscribe to the same values and reify a masculinist, militaristic vision for humanity that overcomes all antagonism. Echoing the ideological critique deployed in prior theorization of Hollywood disaster genres wherein forces of disaster are seen as proxies for social concerns, Kakoudaki posits that the underground volcano stands in for racial tension and immanent 'eruption of racial violence' in Los Angeles (137). The heroes of this film are all professionals: 'each at their workplace, doing what they are paid to do' (137) and, intimating a less optimistic social outcome,

Kakoudaki notes that the film's 'coordination of professionals' resembles the mobilization of law enforcement agencies during the 1992 Los Angeles riots (138). 1990s disaster movies' location in a lineage of macho heroism is most explicit in *Armageddon*, as Charlton Heston narrates an opening prologue that shows the extinction of dinosaurs and presages a similar fate for humanity.

Across this 1990s disaster cycle, masculine strength and coordinated militarism are continually shown as the appropriate response to the demands of disaster. While these films gesture towards diversity, their heroes remain overwhelmingly white, male and linked to institutional and professional authority. Faced with larger, more complex threats than their 1970s antecedents, in which elemental nature and science-fictional entities become intermeshed, these characters model strategic management and controlled violence rather than virtuoso mastery of their environments as a means to ensure the continuation of human sovereignty. Collectively, these films articulate a response to social anxieties about global ecological crises by steadfastly maintaining the outlook of earlier generic responses to radically new threats of disaster. They continue to elide both moral complexity and ethical responsibility in the face of disaster like 1950s and 1960s sci-fi, and to reify dominant social hierarchies like 1970s disaster movies. Continued foregrounding of a masculinist heroic subjectivity that masters both nature and technology to overcome death further embellishes the generic response to disaster apparent in prior Hollywood cycles, refusing to reckon with historical disaster even as its consequence grows, and complex death threatens to erupt on a planetary scale.

With their rich combination of prior generic elements, the 1990s cycle marks a turning point in the evolution of Hollywood's disaster genre. Rick Altman argues that cycles become genres 'through industry-wide imitation and adoption of their basic characteristics' (82), and this period in the late 1990s marks the consolidation of a disaster genre to such an extent that its visuality, themes and narrative formulas become adopted across Hollywood films of various genre orientations. For example, the prevalence of survival as a theme in films from the year 2000 is observed by Keane (120): *The Perfect Storm* and *Cast Away* are indicative of a survival subgenre focused on isolated post-disaster scenarios with male protagonists pitted against the elements, and by the end of the 2010s, another distinct group of films focused on post-apocalyptic survival emerges: *I Am Legend* (2007), *The Book of Eli* (2010). Amidst this shift, it must be acknowledged that in 2001, a world-changing historical event occurred that shifted popular understandings of disaster and re-oriented prospects for the cinematic representation of disaster in the United States especially. Following the September 11 terrorist attacks on the World Trade Center in New York City, Karen Randell observes the advent of a particular iconography of 'urban wreckage' that becomes prevalent as it 'repeats and infects different film contexts and genres, but particularly the superhero film and the disaster film' (139). Sites of sudden urban destruction are settings for many blockbusters of the 2000s and 2010s, including the Bay Area of *San Andreas*. Contributing to this iconography, Roland Emmerich continues to refine the narrative and visual style he established in the 1990s, most notably in *The Day After Tomorrow* which is mostly set in New York, but also in *2012* (2009) and *Independence Day: Resurgence* (2016). Similarly, following *Armageddon*, Michael Bay continues to direct war, action and science-fiction films that deploy disaster movie conventions including the *Transformers* franchise (2007–17), which showcases cutting-edge CGI (computer-generated imagery) as it enacts techno-masculine triumph (Wilson 353). Alongside *Transformers*, other prolific franchises conjoin key disaster movie conventions with comic book superheroes like Superman (referenced decades earlier in Sontag's initial theorization of a disaster subgenre), who is the hero of *Man of Steel* (2013) and the DC Extended Universe franchise. The most expansive superhero film franchise is the Marvel Cinematic Universe – inclusive of the *Iron Man* trilogy (2008–13), the *Captain America* trilogy (2011–16), four *Avengers* films and many more. The nomenclature of these films intimates the degree to which they continue to reify, via their protagonists, a modern regulatory subjectivity that is Americanist, masculinist and inevitably overcomes forces of threatening alterity. The grim visuality observed by Sontag is also further advanced in these films, which become ever more spectacular as newer special effects and camera technologies render disasters that continually expand to include new, increasingly complex dimensions.

As this widespread expansion, imitation and adoption of disaster characteristics continue, in the mid-2010s, a notable interest in disaster movie thematics becomes apparent in the work of film writers and theorists. Compounding concerns about ecology and global warming articulated previously, this work begins to feature and even centre on the concept of the Anthropocene, notably including human complicity with disaster and highlighting issues of scale. Hollywood blockbusters feature heavily in Anil Narine's theorization, in 2014, of eco-trauma cinema – a cinema based around encounters between human protagonists and ecological forces or presences that play out largely along the lines of the narrative formulas I have highlighted. For example, when 'urbanites leave the city for an experience in a challenging natural landscape' in *Antichrist* (2009) and *The Thing* (2011) or when an 'external threat infiltrates an idealised community, destabilizing the social order and testing the values of each resident' in *The Host* (2006) and *Teeth* (2007). Narine also highlights 'stories that depict the aftermath of ecological catastrophes' (9), and films like *I Am Legend*, *The Road* (2009) and *Mad Max: Fury Road* (2015) that feature male heroes wandering through despoiled, corrupted environments can be understood as descendent from post-disaster films associated with prior cycles like *Soylent Green* and *Waterworld*.

Also in 2014, McKenzie Wark theorizes that contemporary blockbusters 'belong to the genre of the Anthropocene' as they offer 'narratives about a civilization confronting limits of its own making' ('Anthropo{mise-en-s}cene'). The films she analyses 'opt for apocalypse' and, in doing so, centre disaster movie conventions. *Edge of Tomorrow* (2014), for example, is set some time after hostile aliens have invaded Earth and stars Tom Cruise, known for playing macho action heroes. Cruise's character is killed but, via a sci-fi plot device, is allowed to repeatedly restart his battle against the aliens and the film is, for Wark, 'about video game time' wherein death signals 'a beginning, a do-over.' *Edge of Tomorrow* indicates how disaster continues to expand in more recent Hollywood movies, erupting in new ways, becoming a force that pervades temporal dimensions until it is ultimately overcome. The time-loop structure of this narrative can also be understood to allay social anxieties about extinction, wherein the finality of death is incontrovertible. Wark's analysis ties the film to prior disaster movies, as she notes that 'weird weather' features in many Anthropocene movies and in this film the final encounter between the hero and the 'boss alien' occurs underwater. Once more, then, alien alterity is allied to elemental nature to augur death in an unprecedented way.

Gravity (2013), also discussed by Wark, showcases a type of disaster movie earlier suggested by Yacowar: 'The Ship of Fools', a travel disaster category about 'the dangers of an isolated journey', most commonly involving flying (315). Where *Airport* deals with the hubris of aviation in 1972, in 2013, *Gravity* deals with some disastrous consequences of space flight as the destruction of a satellite catalyses a cloud of debris that destroys a shuttle and leaves an astronaut stranded alone. *Gravity* is discussed at greater length by Selmin Kara, who more thoroughly formulates 'Anthropocenema: Cinema in the Age of Mass Extinctions'. 'Anthropocenema' is a grouping of films about extinction and the limits of humanity, many of which are Hollywood blockbusters and/or partake in the disaster movie tradition, including *Beasts of the Southern Wild* (2013) and *Snowpiercer* (2015). Kara posits:

> The proliferation of films with ecological disaster and extinction narratives in recent years suggests that the Anthropocene might also signal a new epoch in the ecology and temporality of cinema. Through the aid of new technologies and CGI, films increasingly stretch the boundaries of cinematic time and space across deep pasts, vast futures, and previously unmappable topographies in order to project visions of humanity under constant threat by factors of its own making. (3–4)

Accordingly, Kara's analysis of *Gravity* focuses on the film's representation of waste as a type of villain. This usefully highlights the complicity of industrial humanity with ecological disaster and extinction. However, as much as space debris is a villainous, disastrous presence in *Gravity*, so too are Earth's gravity and the vacuum of outer space, and these forces, promising immediate death, present a clearer semblance of threatening alterity. Like *Cast Away*, this film posits an isolated scenario in which a sole survivor faces death, but its spectacular scenes of orbital destruction also offer ample opportunity for visualizing Earth from space in a manner reminiscent of *Armageddon* and *Independence Day*, invoking a global scale in its dynamics of extreme endangerment. Orbital scenes are rendered entirely with CGI and showcase dizzying camera perspectives, attesting to the continued advancement of cinematic technology in the service of spectacularly visualizing catastrophe.

Updating Sontag's appraisal of post-war science fiction's capacities for reflecting post-war anxieties around nuclear threat in a 2019 article titled 'Different Death Stars and Devastated Earths: Contemporary SF Cinema's Imagination of Disaster in the Anthropocene', Toby Neilson posits a 'need to assess whether contemporary sf cinema can operate as a similar staging post for presenting the sense of crisis and disaster tied to the very different shape and form of the Anthropocene's eco-apocalypse narrative' (243). Neilson's analysis focuses on how recent *Star Wars* films and *After Earth* (2013), operating within the bounds of science fiction, resituate and renegotiate social anxieties around planetary destruction to evidence 'the genre's shifting imaginations of disaster' (249). Issues of scale are crucial to his appraisal of the way that these films figure human complicity in temporally stretched, ecologically attuned narratives of global destabilization. Representation of the planet-destroying Death Star in recent *Star Wars* films *The Force Awakens* (2015) and *Rogue One*

(2016) updates the franchise's disaster imagery to involve visuality of ecological catastrophe alongside the sudden planetary immolation of its 1970s forebears, as in *Rogue One* when a destructive blast that initially appears to reproduce nuclear imagery 'mutates into an Anthropocene-inflected behemoth' in a drawn-out sequence of heaving mountains and volcano-like ash and dust (249). *After Earth*, meanwhile, set far in our planet's future, depicts future humans' return to an Earth despoiled and made hostile by their irresponsible forebears and are 'forced into an encounter with their ancestors' relentless ecological entanglement' (253). Both films, for Neilson, signal larger shifts in which 'deep time, human history and unruly environments' function as touchstones for contemporary imaginations of disaster (257), wherein death looms in ever-larger and more complex ways.

These reflections and groupings of 2000s and 2010s blockbusters offered by Narine, Wark, Kara and Neilson echo prior theorization of disaster genres as they delineate concerns around alterity, ecology, destruction, despoliation and extinction. The numerous films they draw attention to can thus be categorized as the most recent articulation of Hollywood's generic tradition of mass destruction, and from the 1950s to the present moment, we can trace the consistent acceleration of Hollywood disaster as a multifaceted cinematic force, pervading across blockbuster genres, taking forms that are ever more spectacular and rendered with ever more sophisticated technologies. Having accounted for this historical formation of Hollywood's disaster genre, this chapter now shifts to offer more in-depth analysis of *Gravity* and *Avengers: Age of Ultron*, returning also to *San Andreas*. Exploring these films makes it possible to more completely contextualize the present shape of Hollywood disaster, as each one deploys formal tendencies evolved from the history detailed here in different ways, staging encounter with disaster in which possibilities for ethics are at stake in the manner that human response is enacted.

Gravity

Directed by Alfonso Cuarón and popularly categorized as a sci-fi thriller or space survival film, *Gravity* was co-produced across Hollywood and the UK and so has a partial industrial relationship with Hollywood. However, the presence of American stars Sandra Bullock and George Clooney as the only actors appearing in the film gives credence to the notion that it can best be understood as a Hollywood disaster movie. By further exploring how *Gravity* works within disaster movie conventions and their formulaic reification of the sovereign, masculinist self, a better understanding of how it functions in relation to the Anthropocene issues foregrounded by Kara can be established.

While *Gravity*'s narrative trajectory and visualization of disaster largely conform to disaster movie convention, it also potentially constitutes a significant break. Kara notes that directors like Cuarón, who has directed blockbusters as well as films better categorized as world cinema, occasionally comment on moving away from "macho heroism" (17) by centring female protagonists. *Gravity*'s protagonist is Bullock's Dr Ryan Stone, a specialist on her first space mission. Dr Stone embodies a 'hysteric vulnerability' framed by Kara, in the context of the Anthropocene, as 'a refreshing disavowal of an aggressive environmental politics that responds to ecological threats with destructive technofixes (often associated with masculinity and colonial attitudes)' (17). Kara notes, though, that the character remains somewhat problematic in its reproduction of stereotyped 'damsels in existential distress' (17).

As I have noted, star power is important in disaster movies because it creates expectations for viewers and facilitates the reification of archetypal characters. Dr Stone can be better understood via comparison with an earlier starring role of Bullock's from the 1994 blockbuster *Speed* which, as Keane notes, combines disaster movie conventions with action movie 'narrative drive' (71). Both films are concerned with acceleration, velocity and out-of-control vehicles. In *Speed*, Bullock stars with Keanu Reeves as their characters are isolated together on a doomed bus. Reeves plays a typical disaster movie hero, a calm LAPD officer who supports Bullock's more visibly traumatized character, a civilian unprepared for disaster. Remarkably similarly, in *Gravity*, Bullock stars with Clooney who plays the veteran mission commander Matt Kowalski. Kowalski's death is assured early in the film when he sets himself adrift to save Stone, but Kowalski continues to calmly comfort her via radio as he drifts away, his calm disposition in the face of impending death a counterpoint to her distress. His death is a sacrificial gesture that confirms his heroic qualities, but Kowalski also returns much later in the film to motivate Stone again when, alone in a Soyuz capsule, she gives up trying to return to Earth. Cheerily sipping vodka, he instructs her to use the capsule's landing jets to manoeuvre it towards a Chinese space station, his mastery of the technology is made clear when he asks her, 'Didn't you learn about that in training?' This post-mortem return is revealed as a hallucination, but even after Kowalski's death, the film persists with the image of his heroic mastery. So, while *Gravity* certainly does centre on the vulnerability of its female protagonist, tropes of masculinist heroism are not disavowed but endure, remaining essential to how the film represents humanity's capacity to overcome disaster.

As an exemplar of an Anthropocene genre, *Gravity* is best seen not as an altogether new form, but as an evolution or extension of Hollywood's disaster genre. Continuing from the 1990s cycle, it accounts for anxieties about global extinction and also gestures towards humanity's role in eco-catastrophe. It attempts, with partial success, to move away from modelling masculinist heroism as the best response to disaster. Corollaries between *Gravity* and the state of humanity in the Anthropocene are succinctly articulated by Stephanie Wakefield: 'the infrastructures that were supposed to have been mastered and perfected the world not only cannot, but moreover it is increasingly from within these networked infrastructures themselves that disasters emerge, disasters producing more disasters producing more cascading disasters, which Man can only watch helplessly' ('Man in the Anthropocene').

A pointedly gendered contemporary humanity is critically positioned as a viewer: In the Anthropocene, the masculinist modern subject watches disasters of his own making continually multiply. At the same time, disaster movies and the irresponsible ethics of encounter that they posit, wherein human sovereignty continually wins out against threatening alterity, are reiterated across 2010s blockbusters. Hollywood's disaster genre and its formulaic methods of folding together themes of human–nature relationships, emergent technology and masculine subjectivity clearly bear incredible relevance to broader Anthropocene discourse.

Two other recent blockbusters, however, while hewing less closely to genre formulas, more productively centre female protagonists as they recoup disaster movie elements and more clearly stage encounters wherein a more hopeful ethics might lie. In *Arrival* (2016) and *Annihilation* (2018), aliens land on Earth to inaugurate prolonged confrontations. The arrival of *Arrival*'s aliens, Mark Bould writes, 'condenses climate change into a single ruptural, if ambiguous, event' (113). Arriving at multiple global locations, as in *Independence Day*, they are 'envoys of the weird' come 'from the future to infect us with their language so that we begin to perceive time differently' (113). The protagonist is a linguist, played by Amy Adams, who contends with over-aggressive, impatient military leaders as she works to understand the aliens, rather than overcome them. In *Annihilation*, an alien force establishes a zone named the 'shimmer,' separated from the world by an oil-like barrier in which biological life goes haywire. An army veteran and biology professor, played by Natalie Portman, is the final survivor of an expedition group that witnesses and falls prey to mutated flora and fauna.

Both films offer conclusions based not on domination or heroism but on connection and reciprocity, whether through empathy and communication, as in *Arrival*, or cellular exchange and biomimicry, as in *Annihilation*. As with *Edge of Tomorrow*, *Arrival*'s thematizing of non-linear time may be understood as a response to the historical possibility of extinction, and for Bould, this is about impasse: 'there is no way out' (117) from humanity's contemporary crisis. However, focusing on encounter yields another interpretation. The linguist communicates with the aliens in a safe room where species are separated by a screen. Her process towards understanding coincides with incrementally becoming closer to the aliens. The alien 'heptapods' don't have faces, but a capacity for reciprocity and perhaps ethical responsibility is signalled at various moments of breakthrough, for example, a human hand and a heptapod appendage touching the screen from either side. As global violence threatens near the film's end, the linguist becomes immersed in the alien's smoky atmosphere and comprehends their language, transcending human experience of time, attaining a new awareness of the world and forestalling disaster. *Annihilation*'s conclusion is darker and more spectacular. The protagonist, at the shimmer's core, confronts an alien entity – a pulsating fractal form – that absorbs a drop of her blood and mutates to mimic a human body. Choosing violence, the protagonist hands it a grenade and it mutates again into her doppelganger. The shimmer burns, but an ambiguous final scene reveals that something alien lives on when the version of the protagonist who escapes reconciles with her husband and, as they both look towards the future, their eyes shimmer. The film presents this not as a victory or a defeat over alterity but simply a biological alteration.

Both *Annihilation* and *Arrival* remain party to some gender tropes, in particular, figuring their female protagonists, who, like *Gravity*'s Dr Stone, are expert scientists, as mothers. But they also refuse and frustrate the masculinist heroism of disaster movies as their scenarios become platforms for staging something like ethical responsibility. Where *Gravity* produces a partial variation of disaster movie conventions but cleaves to dominant notions about human subjectivity, these two films usurp convention more completely. Contextualizing their narratives within the thematic territory of extraterrestrial invasion, global endangerment and militaristic deployment, they resonate with anxieties, pronounced in discussion of the Anthropocene, around both planetary and human finitude. But they offer, in their female protagonists, visions of a human subjectivity not bent on continuing dominion over non-human alterity and maintaining sovereignty at all costs but, rather, responsible to alien others and, as death threatens their 'ontological right to exist' (Cohen, *Face to Face with Levinas* 24), open to compromise and coercion in their commingling with disaster. In an ethical sense, these encounters demonstrate how accommodation of the other might leave the self irrevocably altered, 'marked by a change in the status of "me"' (Blanchot, *The Writing of the Disaster* 25). In the context of the Anthropocene, these films signal the intertwining of the human subject and the non-human in ways that carry potential for mutual flourishing into the future. At the level of film form, as they begin departing from genre convention and incorporate these less-antagonistic encounters, their narratives necessarily become ambiguous rather than formulaic, a tendency that will be discussed in much greater detail in Chapter 2.

Avengers: Age of Ultron and disaster franchises

Avengers: Age of Ultron is a superhero and sci-fi action movie about a group of heroes who combat a rogue artificial intelligence (AI) that seeks to destroy humanity by triggering an extinction-level event. It clearly takes part in the disaster genre, involving a heroic ensemble and featuring a spectacular disaster scenario at its core. It is exemplary of how disaster blockbusters of the 2010s update the planetary disasters of the 1990s cycle by invoking even more complex, world-bending scenarios of extinction like interdimensional conflict, the upending of gravity and the harvesting of Earth's resources by aliens. It also exemplifies, again, how human complicity is frequently foregrounded in such scenarios.

Age of Ultron's heroes are a true ensemble, each one played by a star actor and clearly standing in for a socio-political value or moral perspective. Tony Stark, alias 'Iron Man', is a playboy inventor and former weapons manufacturer – an embodiment of entrepreneurial neoliberalism. Steve Rogers, alias 'Captain America', is a wholesome, all-American supersoldier. Bruce Banner, alias 'Hulk', is a biochemist and nuclear physicist who unwittingly transforms into a bestial green monster, echoing the protagonist of *The Fly* – his implied riskiness a counterpoint to the self-assuredness of Iron Man's neoliberal approach and Captain America's patriotic militarism. Alongside several other mostly male and white characters, these heroes stand for varied responses to disaster that are somewhat distinct but aligned in their outlook. They work together to overcome disaster much like the cast of *Independence Day*, wielding their shared power and commanding a military organization named 'S.H.I.E.L.D.'. At various turns, they display the requisite qualities of disaster movie heroes: not only strength, resourcefulness and blue-collar grit, but also corporate professionalism, mastery of new technologies and willingness to sacrifice themselves.

Stark's and Banner's technological inventions make them complicit in the disaster that arises in *Age of Ultron*. Ultron is an artificial intelligence, designed by Stark as a defence against inter-dimensional or extraterrestrial threats, that malfunctions and attempts to eradicate humanity which it perceives (somewhat sympathetically) as the ultimate threat to Earth's survival. Ultron commands a swarm of humanoid robots with chrome surfaces that emulate pronounced male musculature, visually reminiscent of *The Terminator* (1984). The AI inhabits a main body: it is larger, emits a red glow and speaks in the first person – at one point threatening 'There is no Man in charge', intimating simultaneously the feeling of out-of-control planetary catastrophe and the futility of a masculinist approach to resolving it. This AI technology is fantastical like that of early sci-fi, but also mundane like that of 1970s disaster movies, resembling virtual assistants like Siri and Alexa that came into use in the 2010s as much as militaristic surveillance and drone technologies. To trigger an extinction event, Ultron rends skyward a large chunk of Earth on which the capital city of the fictional Eastern European nation Sokovia is built, threatening to drop it suddenly in emulation of a meteor strike. This disaster is teased at several points in the film when viewers are shown premonitions experienced by psychic superheroes: a large object impacts Earth and fiery shock waves engulf the planet, the same type of imagery that characterizes the disasters of *Deep Impact* and *Armageddon*, but as with 1970s disaster movies, the origin of the large-scale threat, appearing as a force of alterity, actually lies within the hubris of rational humanity's attempts to assert technological mastery.

Scenes depicting the raising of Sokovia mesh the visuality of natural disaster and advanced warfare, recombining tropes from earlier disaster cycles. The first images show a crack forming in a cobbled street and citizens fleeing as rubble falls from crumbling buildings. A bridge collapses as the city begins to rise. The cleaving ground reveals massive engines emitting screams of blue energy, an apparatus built into the mobile chunk of Earth beneath an ancient-looking church – perhaps a suggestion that technology usurps religion, and certainly a signal of the heroes' hubris. Ultron proselytizes the disaster to its victims – 'you are my meteor' – as drones jet through the sky harrying fleeing citizens.

As this sequence builds from a localized disaster scenario into a global apocalyptic situation, it maintains a convincingly realistic aesthetic, evincing and advancing the 'visual credibility' (Sontag 215) apparent throughout Hollywood's disaster tradition via the evolved lustre of CGI. Writing of recently advanced special effects technologies in 2008, Dan North describes a 'perceptual realism' that is distinct from 'conventional discussions of filmic realism' and emphasizes a sense of tactility as it centres on evoking textures like 'dinosaur skins, metallic sheens, fur, moisture, ice' (21). The timeliness of this evolved technology is apparent in Randell's observations of a post-9/11 blockbuster aesthetic, as she posits that since the early 2000s, such effects 'echo and replicate the images of 9/11 in extraordinary detail in a way that is not seen in more realist cinema' (138). Randell observes a kind of 9/11-obsessed imagery in *Age of Ultron*: 'the vertically falling building, enveloping ash clouds, people running toward news cameras, paper raining, and the mangled metal wreckage' (141). This disaster sequence is notable for the way that the solid chrome of the robot bodies and the glow of their eyes contrast the aged, granular bricks and tiles of the city, and there is a potent irony in the way that the film advances technologically enabled, perceptually realistic imagery in service of its cautionary tale about technological advancement. A relentlessly fast, indestructible and anti-human technological polish visually supplants both impermanent nature and friable European buildings, objects of interest for traditionally realist post-war cinema, which here stand in for an outmoded, doomed humanity.

Extinction events of this sort recur with similarly convincing textural visual verisimilitude in dozens of 2010s blockbuster franchises, lending yet another type of visual sheen to formulaic figurations of non-human alterity as purely antagonistic fodder for conquering heroes, threatening death as planetary disasters that erupt and pervade in new ways. In 2016, *Slate* magazine compiles a 'succession of new clichés' enabled by advanced CGI including implosions where objects or planets 'crumple inward', emphasizing disaster sequences in which cities or massive objects are lifted skyward and dropped down again (Wickman). In these scenarios, the disruption of gravity is a key feature of the meshes of elemental nature and advanced alien technology that threaten humanity. *Independence Day: Resurgence* shows aliens returning to harvest Earth with a spaceship so large that, as one character observes, 'It has its own gravity', uplifting parts of Asia and the Middle East and depositing their ruins over Europe and the UK: the Burj Khalifa crashes downward onto London. Later in the film, another character, aboard the alien vessel, remarks that 'it has its own ecology', and thus the film posits the appearance of an entire alien nature that upends humanity's Earth. Similarly, in *Man of Steel*, an alien spaceship that looks like a giant insect uses a gravity weapon to terraform Earth, and in *Transformers: Age of Extinction*, robotic aliens use a giant magnet to carry metal objects – buses, ships, buildings, the objects of earlier disaster movies – before dropping them over Hong Kong. Another disaster-related trope of the 2010s is human overpopulation, described as the cinematic 'crisis du jour' in a 2018 *Guardian* article (Hilton) and thematically apparent in *Avengers: Infinity War* (2018), a sequel to *Age of Ultron* in which the superhero team must defeat a genocidal, alien supervillain named Thanos, after Thanatos, the mythological personification of death. All of these franchise films reflect massive, epochal disasters that exceed the global threats of the 1990s cycle. Even in their collective nomenclature, they inaugurate a new age defined by pervasive death as they seek new ways of spectacularly staging disaster as something for macho heroes to overcome.

The forces of disaster in these blockbusters might usefully be considered as hyperobjects, correlating in several ways including being necessarily more-than-human. Threat of global death permeates Morton's elaboration of hyperobjects as 'things that are massively distributed in time and space relative to humans' (*Hyperobjects* 1): global warming is the hyperobject par excellence, and while hyperobjects thus seem comparable to disasters, Morton argues that they are 'more deeply challenging' (16) because of how thoroughly they displace the human. Along these lines, blockbuster disasters of the 2010s are more challenging than their generic forebears in many ways: in their sheer scale; in the complexity of their merging of elemental nature, aliens, fictional technology and human complicity; and in their visual textural verisimilitude which so convincingly resembles reality, displacing human features from the mise-en-scène. A characterizing feature of hyperobjects is that their 'primordial reality' remains withdrawn from humans (15): it is impossible for us to perceive them in their entirety. This is also a feature of many immense, multiform 2010s blockbuster disasters. *Independence Day: Resurgence* signals the impossibility of apprehending the aliens by repeatedly showing the sheer size of their vessel, the entirety of which is never pictured in the frame. The aliens themselves are hidden, concealed, within organic exoskeletons. Ultron, too, is withdrawn from humans as his essence operates in virtual realms where he continually eludes the heroes even as his material presence multiplies when his army amasses.

Age of Ultron is unique among 2010s disaster blockbusters because of how explicitly it foregrounds human complicity. In the heroes' militaristic and technological aspirations, they create Ultron as a force of death that far exceeds them in both scale and perceptual capacity. While Ultron most directly echoes nuclear technology, it could also stand in for global warming or climate change or the Anthropocene or even all of modernity. As such, even the super-powered humans cannot directly destroy Ultron at the conclusion of the film. The familiar face of masculinist heroism is nonetheless present, though, as it is overcome by another artificial intelligence named Vision, also created by Stark and Banner but placed within a body that is softer, organically textured and bearing a more human-like face. Vision's physical strength is apparent, but his reflexivity, rationality and empathy are his defining characteristics. If Ultron is understood as standing in for any kind of extinction threat, then Vision stands in for the fantasy of the techno-fix, the notion that a friendlier version of the same technology that precipitated disaster, or better human mastery of it, can avert catastrophe. With this dynamic at its core, *Age of Ultron* functions to allay anxieties about the cataclysmic impact of human civilizations on Earth just as scientists are proposing that the Anthropocene be formally inaugurated into the geological timescale. Recombining and further upgrading Hollywood disaster tropes, it continues to assert humanity's ability to triumph over death.

San Andreas

Amidst the box office dominance of blockbuster franchises, *San Andreas* represents another distinct strategy for Hollywood disaster in the 2010s. While those films present increasingly complex scenarios, *San Andreas* adheres to the formulas outlined in Roddick's categorization of 1970s disaster movies as 'an essentially earthbound form' (246), directly recovering the natural disaster scenarios and narrative schema of that cycle. In *Age of Ultron* and other films that rework sci-fi tropes, the disaster scenario is typically the centrepiece of a third act, a component of a final showdown between human heroes and evil alterity. In *San Andreas* though, as in the 1970s cycle, disaster strikes early to isolate characters, setting the stage for the hero's fight to reunite his family. Disaster in *San Andreas* subsequently encompasses many kinds of elemental threat as the earthquakes catalyse a series of events that spectacularly threaten death on the ground, in the air, in skyscrapers and in water. These cascading narrative events allow the film to spectacularly visualize threatening nature by repeatedly smashing the built human environment and its technologies to pieces.

Throughout the film, the technologies of Californian civilization are completely overwhelmed by the tectonic force of the earthquakes, and key sequences show the destruction of the Hoover Dam as well as downtown San Francisco and the Golden Gate Bridge. The dam fails in the first fifteen minutes of the film and scenes showing its destruction echo prior Pacific Coast disaster movies including *Earthquake* and *Dante's Peak* (1997). People are thrown to the ground as the camera shakes and computer-generated dust spits from cracking concrete. This dust hangs in the air for much of the film, a ghost-like elemental presence invading urbanized spaces. A later sequence shows a much larger quake striking San Francisco, where much of the action takes place inside doomed high-rises. One character is trapped in an underground carpark amidst falling concrete. Another is trapped at the top of a crumbling tower attempting to escape from a luxuriant restaurant. Exterior shots show reflective glass sheeting away from skyscrapers, falling building fragments evidencing a continuation of post-9/11 wreckage iconography. Thus, as with *Age of Ultron*, the CGI textures of these disasters recall past films and American historical moments. Natural disasters familiar from the 1970s cycle become recombined and enlarged, as *Earthquake*'s tremors combine with the wave of *The Poseidon Adventure* and the skyscraper peril of *The Towering Inferno*.

The characters of *San Andreas*, similarly, recover facets of the 1970s cycle, especially hypermasculinity. Ray Gaines, the hero, is a Fire Department air rescue helicopter pilot and veteran of the US War in Afghanistan. He is briskly introduced as a strong, professional hero in the film's opening sequence when he tells a journalist 'just doin' my job, ma'am' before manoeuvring a helicopter into a crevasse and single-handedly ripping a door from a wrecked car to save a woman's life. Throughout the film his mastery of technology and nature becomes apparent: Ray pilots his helicopter through a maze of falling skyscrapers, steers a small boat over the crest of a tsunami, performs a skydive and drives at least two pickup trucks. During most of the film, Ray is accompanied by Emma, his estranged wife, as they search for their daughter Blake, and his redemption as a husband and father is a major component of the film's narrative. Besides the force of the earthquakes, the film's main villain is Emma's new partner Daniel, who is emblematic of humanity's sybaritic, selfish and hubristic tendencies. He is an exploitative arch-capitalist: a property developer building San Francisco's tallest skyscraper (which is ultimately wrecked by the quakes). Posing differing responses to disaster in Ray and Daniel, *San Andreas* dramatizes class conflict. Daniel reacts with cowardice, abandoning Blake and fleeing his own damaged building. This unheroic behaviour assures he will not be redeemed and, indeed, he is unceremoniously crushed by a shipping container. Ray, Emma and Blake, meanwhile, model resilience and courage, and thus their survival is assured. Daniel's slickness is contrasted with Ray's courage, grit and resourcefulness. By the end of the film, these qualities have helped Ray's family reunite and, as helicopters fly into the city and an American flag unfurls on the remains of the Golden Gate Bridge, he proclaims, 'Now we rebuild'. This is in keeping with how disaster movie conclusions posit 'a new world whose inhabitants have learned from the mistakes of the old' (Roddick 258–9). Heroic masculinity is recapitulated on a larger scale as *San Andreas* gestures towards the post-disaster resurrection of the city led by the military and rescue workers like Ray rather than unscrupulous tycoons like Daniel.

Just as the scale of threat is greatly increased in this 2010s natural disaster movie, so too is the hero's musculature. The type of star power that 1970s disaster movies relied on is in full effect here, as Ray is played by Dwayne Johnson, the actor and professional wrestler also known as The Rock. Johnson stars in many other 2010s disaster blockbusters including the monster movie *Rampage* (2018) and *Skyscraper* (2018), which has many similarities to *The Towering Inferno* and *Die Hard*. A 2018 *Rolling Stone* feature identifies a sympathetic character type that he returns to: 'highly skilled bad-asses who are also sensitive and vulnerable, flawed yet decent men with big biceps and bigger hearts' (Eells). Johnson's celebrity persona also mirrors these qualities, as a 2017 *GQ* article frequently references his charm, calmness and commitment while also noting his 'industrial-strength patriotism' and dedication to the armed forces (Weaver). If Charlton Heston with an engineering degree is the 'new hero' for the 1970s (Ryan and Kellner 252), then the updated hero for the 2010s is an ex-military, gym-junkie Dwayne Johnson.

Heroic realism

Gravity, *Age of Ultron* and *San Andreas* exemplify the status and significance of Hollywood's disaster genre at the dawn of widespread awareness of the Anthropocene. *San Andreas* amplifies the characteristics of 1970s disaster, offering more muscular American heroism. *Age of Ultron* incorporates science-fictional elements and features a super-powered hero squad resembling the diverse but distinctly American and militaristic groups of 1990s disaster movies. *Gravity* probes the genre's gender dynamics without overhauling them as it focuses on endangerment in a survival scenario. All three utilize advanced CGI to convincingly render disaster, which takes the form of elemental nature, extraterrestrial objects and technology gone awry. David Martin-Jones pays special attention to scholarly discussion of *Gravity*, highlighting it alongside *Interstellar* (2014), *The Road* and *Mad Max: Fury Road* as the type of eco-catastrophist, disaster-adjacent film 'typically used to illustrate discussions of the Anthropocene' (55). Critical of this fact, he details that 'how scholars attempt to understand this ecological idea by selecting certain specific representative films is very revealing of the structuring presence of Eurocentric views of world history', particularly in their focus on technology (55). Echoing Martin-Jones, I posit that these films resonate in this way because they represent a cinematic capacity, perfected in Hollywood since at least the 1950s, for sustained thematic engagement with socio-historical dilemmas and simultaneous evasion of the ethical ramifications of those dilemmas. In these films, as in previous disaster movie cycles, humanity may be presented as complicit in the emergence of disaster due to hubris or folly, but heroic protagonists are always capable of mastering both the situation and the technologies at hand, averting death by subjugating all threats and, in doing so, asserting the pre-eminence of a Eurocentric, masculinist vision of humanity over whichever other forces are vanquished. Just as Ryan and Kellner suggest that 1970s disaster movies update patriarchal figures for a modern context (*Camera Politica*), so too do these films refresh masculinist dominance of the world for the exigencies of the Anthropocene. They thus represent a well-honed strategy for maintaining and asserting the primacy of a particular vision for humanity – a strategy that, as Sontag observes (*Against Interpretation*), has always been inadequate because of its refusal to entertain or accommodate the threat of death that arises in encounter with disastrous alterity.

From the inception of a Hollywood disaster genre in the 1950s, through two cycles in the 1970s and the 1990s, to these more recent iterations, the way this simultaneous engagement and evasion is continually effected via the essential componentry of Hollywood disaster becomes apparent. Disaster is always represented spectacularly using the latest cinematic technologies. As the genre evolves, the disasters it depicts become bigger, growing from isolated earthbound incidents to situations of planetary endangerment and beyond. Heroes are continually foregrounded, and they are almost universally characterized by physical strength, assertiveness, rationality, whiteness and technological prowess; they embody institutional hegemony, often being military service people. Encountering disaster, they remorselessly assert their dominance over alterity and especially the dominance of humanity over the non-human and elemental nature, the sorts of presences Rosi Braidotti names ' "earth" others' (*The Posthuman* 27). These formal and narrative tendencies combine to constitute a form of realism, a response to historical exigency particular to this genre.

Initially, visual verisimilitude may be perceived as crucial to any potential realism in Hollywood's disasters. The convincing appearance of Hollywood disaster is seen as a major factor in their appeal, apparent in Sontag's references to the credibility of science-fiction movies' 'sensual elaboration' of destruction (212) and Keane's observations of CGI's 'sheen' (74). But this type of lifelikeness, the 'perceptual realism' (North 21) enabled by special effects and digital technology, diverges sharply from conventional understandings of realism that are contingent on a relationship with the world involving indexicality. Indeed, the spectacular and violent visual style of these films – large-scale effects, computer-generated mise-en-scène, rapid cutting, extreme cinematographic dynamics – works in clear contradistinction not just to traditional atmospheric realist sensibilities, but more significantly to notions of responsiveness, being necessarily closed off from the flux of the world via their virtuality: their absence of indexicality. The technical apparatuses that enable the verisimilitude of these films are constitutive of what Ian Aitken terms 'intentional constructs' that impose an inauthentic 'synthetic structure' ('The European Realist Tradition' 181–2). The simulated visual verisimilitude of Hollywood disasters therefore does not correspond with the notions of responsive realism that this book investigates.

As this genre does operate in clear response to social anxieties, though, it engages notions of realism in another major way that helps explicate this lack of correspondence: through its melodramatic narrative tendencies. This genre conforms to popular understandings of melodrama, and Linda Williams' framing of melodrama as a category of films 'that move us to pathos for protagonists beset by forces more powerful than they' ('Melodrama Revised' 42) relates powerfully to the films considered here. Williams goes on to detail how melodrama constitutes a narrative vernacular that 'generates sympathy for a hero who is also a victim and that leads to a climax that permits the audience … to recognize that character's moral value' (58). If Hollywood disaster movies are understood as melodrama, they can be aligned with notions of realism and verisimilitude that involve narrative motivation, causal linearity and psychological plausibility (Bordwell 19). Such an alignment may seem to place the genre at odds with notions of realism as a materially and historically responsive tendency; however, Williams pushes for a situated and complex understanding of melodrama, posing it as 'in tension with and transformed by realism and the more realistic techniques of cinema, yet best understood *as melodrama*, not failed tragedy or inadequate realism' (50, italics in the original). Pursuing this further, she explicitly contextualizes melodrama as a persistent formal response to history and the pressures of modernity when she writes that 'faced with the familiar dilemmas of modernity – the decentred self, the failure of language to say what is meant – melodrama responded with a heightened personalization and expression of the self' (78). The realism of disaster movies, as the realism of melodrama, is bound up in the way that narrative structures invariably foreground the psychological disposition and moral values embodied in beleaguered but triumphant protagonists, who are recentred at all costs.

The inadequacy of Hollywood disaster movies as a response to our present historical moment revolves not around their capacity to generate *a* realism, but more precisely around the renunciation of ethics apparent in the realism of pathos and triumphant spectacle that they formulaically generate as they repeatedly assert their vision for human selfhood. Evoking disaster-consciousness, Haytham El-Wardany calls for 'a completely new language' to address disaster, but these films unequivocally restate the dynamics that have defined human presence on Earth for centuries. Engaging the melodramatic mode, disaster movies embody what Williams calls a 'realism of action' apparent across Hollywood's 'infinite varieties of rescues, accidents, chases, and fights' – the '"masculine" action-centered multiple climaxes' of blockbusters ('Melodrama Revised' 57). In this macho form of melodrama, protagonists are positioned in situations of vulnerability that, via psychological association, elicit sympathy from viewers before moments of violent spectacle – destruction, escape, battle – reveal the protagonist's moral strength. Fine-tuning the assertion of this moral strength, the response to history offered by disaster movies amounts to precisely the reification and justification of the rational, masculinist, Eurocentric self – the subjective disposition of the 'Man' critiqued by Braidotti who throughout history has subjected all others to pejoration (*The Posthuman* 27). Just as 1970s disaster movies update traditional patriarchal figures for a modern context, so too do the disaster blockbusters of the 2010s refresh masculinist dominance over Earth for the present historical moment, where global extinction looms.

In the context of the Anthropocene, the increasingly large-scale, real-time catastrophes it enfolds, and the ethical questions they raise, rehashing this triumphal disavowal of alterity has far-reaching consequences. In disaster movies, the Earth exists solely as an antagonizing mirror for a moralizing, triumphal human subject, rather than something that may be imperilled itself, or that could occasion more broadly inclusive understandings of shared vulnerability. Spectacularly restating the dynamics that have defined so much human presence on Earth for centuries, these films refuse that threat of extinction might provoke an adjustment in human self-awareness, might give us pause to reconsider ways of knowing and encountering our world. Instead they distil the way that, as Haraway posits, our historical moment is characterized by 'refusing to know and cultivate the capacity of response-ability' (*Staying with the Trouble* 35). Upholding the sovereignty of a particular kind of humanity over the world as well as its mastery over its own dangerous technologies, they iconize the abrogation of ethical responsibility, preferring the status quo wherein the masculinist, corporate, scientific humans of modernity encounter the world not as replete with all kinds of life but as an object they have already mastered.

2

Strange disaster in American independent cinema

Pivoting away from Hollywood, this chapter explores how American independent cinema unsettles the imagination of disaster offered in blockbuster disaster movies, addressing a subgenre of films produced mostly during the 1990s and early 2000s, roughly coinciding with Hollywood's 1990s disaster cycle. It begins with an exploration of how Robert Altman's *Short Cuts* (1993) and Paul Thomas Anderson's *Magnolia* (1999) configure an understanding of disastrous non-human alterity, crucially differentiated from Hollywood's monstrous and elemental antagonists, that calls human characters into encounter. Following this, it offers more detailed analysis of how similar encounters are staged and demands are placed on protagonists in Todd Haynes' *Safe* (1995) and two films directed by Richard Kelly: *Donnie Darko* and *Southland Tales* (2006). These films all employ formal strategies divergent from those discussed in the previous chapter, being characterized primarily by overwhelming ambiguity, including alienated characters who do not overcome disaster but, rather, are overcome by it. Contra Hollywood disaster's spectacularity, the disasters of these films are not foregrounded visually, nor does threat of death necessarily appear as a main narrative hinge. Rather, disaster is something that lurks, a background presence or ambient force that contours existence nonetheless.

American independent cinema is often framed by its opposition to Hollywood, sometimes in rather confrontational terms, but the films discussed in this chapter have complex relationships with Hollywood both formally and institutionally. Yannis Tzoumakis explains that while 'mainstream Hollywood' films are 'bound by many conventions', independent films 'can depart from the dominant and the established in a large number of ways' (7). More bluntly, in 'Against Hollywood', Sherry Ortner articulates a view that independent films can be 'the antithesis of a Hollywood studio film' (2). The films analysed here are contrary to Hollywood in many ways, employing crucially divergent formal strategies, especially narratives that muddle linear expectations. At the same time, though, they are 'against' Hollywood not only in an oppositional sense, remaining adjacent to it and frequently leaning on this adjacency both commercially and formally. This is especially apparent in the case of *Donnie Darko* which, as Geoff King notes, was produced 'on the back of traditional Hollywood star power' (8) with assistance from Drew Barrymore's production company, and benefitted from her appearance in the film. Similarly to their reliance on Hollywood celebrity and finance, as my analysis below explores, the films discussed here also draw meaning from Hollywood's disaster tropes even as they advance a distinct imaginary for ethical encounter with forces of disaster in the shadow of 1990s disaster blockbusters.

Independent cinema in the United States shadows Hollywood in this almost literal sense, falling always alongside it. But the notion of the shadow resonates here in another way, at these points of dissonance and connection between Hollywood and independent cinema, and during this book's search for cinematic imaginaries adequate to reality's exigencies. Levinas invokes it in his early essay on aesthetics 'Reality and Its Shadow', and this essay is the locus for much subsequent diagnosis and debate concerning Levinas's attitude towards art and art's possibilities for ethics (see introduction by Seán Hand, in Levinas, *The Levinas Reader*). On the one hand, scholars, including Hand introducing Levinas's essay in *The Levinas Reader*, have posited that for Levinas art's images are a 'closed world' that is interesting 'without being useful', and that art's disengagement from the world makes it an 'evasion of responsibility' that 'offers consolation rather than a challenge' (129). This line of thought corresponds with the way I elaborated, in the previous chapter, Hollywood disaster movies' evasion of responsibility and reification of extant hierarchical relationships, particularly in the context of the Anthropocene and its attendant non-human forces. Meanwhile, others hone in on an articulation of art's power for something slightly more revelatory: Tanja Staehler posits that Levinas also 'realizes that art alienates us and interrupts the usual course of things' and that by focusing on shadows, art 'brings to the fore what is already present in reality itself' (128). As the films discussed here probe the strangeness that inheres in the designation of the Anthropocene, they oscillate towards these latter possibilities while remaining indebted to the former, bringing forward an awareness that something odd is afoot in late modernity. As Levinas himself writes of reality, 'it is what it is and it is a stranger to itself, and there is a relationship between these two moments' (*The Levinas Reader* 135). As this chapter works to understand strangeness and disaster, Levinas also arises as faces, shown in close-up and during moments of recognition in several of these films, become 'hyper-signaletic' (Ivakhiv 64) and key in to a desire for ethical revelation.

Strange disaster as encounter in *Short Cuts* and *Magnolia*

Short Cuts and *Magnolia* are both set in Los Angeles and concerned with California, particularly insofar as California can signify more expansive, vaguely American themes: the nuclear family, suburbia, show business, technology and progress. Both films also end with disaster: *Short Cuts* concludes immediately after a major earthquake; and *Magnolia* finishes, as Adrian Ivakhiv writes, with a 'biblically proportioned rain of frogs pounding on windshields, splattering onto wet roads, and plopping into spotlit San Fernando Valley swimming pools' (*Ecologies of the Moving Image* 269). Ivakhiv positions these films as a pair not only due to their apparently incidental disasters, but also due to their decentred network or 'patchwork' narratives, their 'juxtaposition of interpersonal and emotional predicaments' and their punctuation with references to weather (269). Alongside *The Ice Storm* (1997), *The Sweet Hereafter* (1997) and *American Beauty* (1999), they constitute a group of independent 1990s films he designates '"indirect disaster" films': 'films about social relations that include portents of ecological disaster in their backgrounds' (268). As these furtive, portentous disasters appear before human characters, they present heavy demands, but also intimate far-reaching possibilities for ethical dynamics with respect to the non-human and emergent eco-catastrophe.

Ivakhiv's designation suggests an inversion of Hollywood's spectacular disaster movies that accords with oppositional understandings of American independent films: indirect or background disaster being opposed to the spectacular disasters of Hollywood. Intimating the type of unspectacular but weird, pervasive and creepily traumatic catastrophe these films include, Ivakhiv posits their disasters take the form of 'strange weather' (266). This term is borrowed from Andrew Ross's 1991 book *Strange Weather: Culture, Science, and Technology in the Age of Limits* that explores relationships between technocratic systems and ecological thinking by chronicling encounters with then-emerging trends and phenomena like New Age, cyberpunk, futurology and global warming (13). Ross explains that in the late 1980s, 'the spectre of climate change' had 'come to haunt the political soul of popular consciousness' (197), and Ivakhiv's analysis excavates this consciousness, conceptualizing indirect disaster as 'unconscious eruptions, storms, quakes, and freezes' (276) that are background properties of films more overtly concerned with social drama, particularly the collapsing of normative, affluent suburban communities and their subjects. These disasters operate as an unbidden return of the repressed wherein the repressed 'other' is 'recognition of our complicity with the ecological crisis' of climate change, which is 'the collective trauma of postmodernity' (274). Spookily destabilizing, strange disasters are conducive of extreme uncertainty and ambiguity rather than reification, and accordingly these films are not lent to the tidy narrative resolution and centring of heroic subjectivity conventional in Hollywood. Prompting an awareness of vulnerability that cannot be overcome, they signify rupture with no hope of repair.

Short Cuts and *Magnolia* also begin with allusions to disaster that presage their conclusions and engage non-human alterity. The opening of *Short Cuts* stitches several seemingly discrete scenarios together by intercutting shots of helicopters flying at night, spraying pesticides over Los Angeles. The whirring of their blades accompanies a television pundit's declaration: 'The time has come to go to war again. Not with Iraq, international terrorists, or what was once Yugoslavia, but with the medfly; a potentially devastating insect. ... The war's objective is clear: to destroy the medfly before it has a chance to destroy us.' Meanwhile: a limousine driver speeds along a highway discreetly sipping booze; a cellist plays while her audience gossips; a phone sex worker changes a baby's diaper while talking to a client; a jazz singer overtones, 'If you're lookin' for a rainbow, you know there's gonna be some rain'. The disaster at hand is the medfly invasion, hovering over everything, unspectacularly echoing the alien invasions of Hollywood sci-fi. But the disaster is also an effort to overcome this invasion: the film's strange weather is the pesticide, a deadly technological rain deployed as disaster management. Rachel Carson describes insecticides as 'the most modern and terrible weapons' and suggests that by deploying them against insects, humans have also 'turned them against the earth' (297). A husband and wife argue over whether the pesticide will give their dog cancer, the husband roaring, 'Don't you get environmental on me, Sharon!' Every networked narrative thread subsequently proceeds under and in relation to the apparatus of a military operation: a repelling of invasion, holding at bay a strange, unseen force. But this operation has guaranteed friendly fire casualties. The quake that concludes the film is not clearly foreshadowed, but occurs just after an eruption of another kind of violence when a violent murder is committed by the phone sex worker's husband, an expression of repressed jealous rage. Considered in relation to these opening scenes, it can be understood as a sudden, shocking assertion of non-human nature: the strange, unseen force can no longer be repelled or managed.

Magnolia begins with a series of deaths described in rapid sequence by a narrator. First, vagrants murder a pharmacist. Second, a scuba diver is lifted accidentally from a lake by a firefighting airplane and the guilt-ridden pilot kills himself. Finally, another man attempting suicide is hit by a bullet shot from a window of the building he jumps from, impacting his chest as he falls. Speaking with the serious tone of a public service announcement, the narrator remarks on extreme coincidences pertaining to each event: 'this was not just a matter of chance; these strange things happen all the time.' These deaths are not connected to any of what follows in the film, except in that they are marked by uncannily bad timing, as if each apparently coincidental event were occasioned by an unknown order. Following this, similarly to Altman's film, a musical montage introduces the film's network of characters. A final introductory shot before the narrative properly begins shows a cloudy sky and the text of a weather forecast appears centre-screen: 'Partly Cloudy, 82% Chance of Rain.' Forecasts like this repeat as intertitles throughout the film foreshadowing the concluding rain of frogs, which fall onto wet night-time streets lit by fluorescent lights, their nocturnal appearance resembling the medflies of *Short Cuts*: a random, unwelcome incursion of non-human nature. They become evidence that disaster can strike, weirdly, like a change in the weather. One falls first onto a car windscreen, then gradually more, as viewers see the characters react and the narrator's voice adds the events of the film to the chronicle of strange deaths at its beginning.

These strange weather disasters, wherein non-human nature returns like a revenant, are encounters with alterity in which an ethics of encounter is at stake in the manner described, following Levinas, by theorists of post-anthropocentric thought, and demands are placed on humanity. A sense of encounter inheres in the designation of these events as strange, as strangeness connotes a certain understanding of alterity: a hostile presence or disruptive force that hides in the corners of the world we strive to make habitable, within our homes or even ourselves. Mark Fisher allies the strange with 'a fascination for the outside, for that which lies beyond standard perception, cognition and experience' (*The Weird and the Eerie* 1). In these films, strange disasters fall into ostensibly comfortable suburban worlds, collapsing them and blurring distinctions between outside and inside, other and self. In his brief exploration of indirect disaster films, Ivakhiv describes this type of disaster as an oblique encounter with an alternative order: 'Appearances of disorderly, uncanny nature ... invoke an alternative, unhuman order, one whose very incommensurability sets up a jarring moral counter-oscillation to the social realities portrayed ... . Like the threat of global warming they hover, with a kind of reptilian stare, on the horizon of collective unconsciousness' (271).

This order is slippery and shapeshifting, not aesthetically fixed: in *American Beauty*, it is 'the barest cypher of nature', the wind that animates an empty plastic bag, trash whooshing in the air. It corresponds to Timothy Morton's description of 'spectral beings whose ontological status is uncertain' precisely because we cannot encounter them directly even as they appear at the juncture of the Anthropocene proposal (*Dark Ecology* 126). But it does take a specific shape in the beginning of *Short Cuts* and the ending of *Magnolia* when, in the animal forms of medflies and frogs, it infiltrates and plops into the cinematic frame: it is insectoid and amphibian, wet and nocturnal, airborne, and meteorologically bound. Its bookend presence means that the remainder of each film, their narrative bulk, is framed by apparently random encounters with mostly hidden forces of disaster that are distinctly non-human and enmeshed within large-scale networks that exceed any individual character, but in which a type of human subject – American, suburban – is hailed as it is imperilled. In these encounters, alterity is barely glimpsed but its presence is irrevocably confirmed, and its uncertain ontological status – its connection to climate change, and human complicity with its ascendance – makes it impossible to overcome, necessitating a different response.

Ivakhiv's ecocritical analysis of these disasters resonates with the phenomenological approach that undergirds Levinasian approaches to ethics. His identification of a repressed other, latent in the mise-en-scène, is made possible by attention to the background environmental features of these films and heightened awareness of the cinematic presence of ambient textures. Writing on *Magnolia*, for example, Ivakhiv evokes the 'splattering', 'plopping' materiality of rain (269), and his description of the helicopters in *Short Cuts* involves a simile that muddles distinction between human and non-human as it draws attention to the film's background: 'looking like giant bugs against the night skies' (268). In Levinas's ethics, phenomenology is 'a way of becoming aware of where we are in the world' (Cohen, *Face to Face with Levinas* 15), and the weather in these films – the literal weather, the strange weather of helicopter-borne pesticides and the apocalyptic weather of frog-fall – functions to locate viewers within an experiential frame demarcated by large-scale ecological collapse, suggesting that wherever we may be in the world, disaster and imminent disorientation is not far away. Levinas observes that 'human experience ... is always intending or tending toward something in the world that preoccupies it', and a phenomenological approach to philosophical ethics 'permits consciousness to understand its own preoccupations' (14). The background disasters of these films, threatening to encroach, evince a preoccupation with disastrous, traumatic events that deny resolution. As each film concludes with the recursion of disaster, denouement is made impossible. *Short Cuts* and *Magnolia* stage encounters in which disaster cannot be overcome but, rather, is incessantly present, provoking indirect confrontation regardless of attempts to look elsewhere.

Safe: Face to face with strange materiality

Safe makes possible an exploration of what might happen to the human subject in a more sustained face-to-face confrontation with disastrous strange weather. Intimate attention to the film's protagonist Carol allows for analysis of what an attempted response to the deathly demands of strange disaster might look like, as she struggles to accommodate the way disaster manifests in the matter of her suburban lifestyle, dislodging her sense of security and her selfhood. As Carol, a housewife, succumbs to an ambiguous sickness, her face appears to slowly decay, evident in multiple scenes where Carol confronts her reflection in mirrors. In one pivotal scene, she examines herself in the bathroom mirror at a friend's lavish San Fernando Valley house before returning to a baby shower in the living room where, nestled amid indoor plants, party balloons and glaring 1980s décor, she has a seizure. Unable to breathe, she shrieks inhalations as her friends surround her. Carol's face contorts, the edges of her mouth peeling back and her brow creasing. The disastrous Los Angeles atmosphere of *Short Cuts* and *Magnolia* is here too, but rather than literal weather phenomena like rain, it is evident in widespread material toxicity and ambient pollution. By the end of the film, Carol's face is blotched red, her eyes dark and sunken. She sits alone in her room at Wrenwood, a retreat for sufferers of Environmental Illness. As the camera slowly zooms towards her, she turns, as if to look at viewers, and stands. A reverse angle shot reveals Carol is actually looking into a mirror again. She sees herself, bruised by encounter with disaster, and says 'I love you. I really love you. I love you' before a fade to black.

Safe furthers understandings of the kind of strange, uncanny disaster presented in *Short Cuts* and *Magnolia*. The film furthers Ivakhiv's theorizing of 'indirect disaster' independent films (268) by staging an explication of relationships between foreground and background, inside and outside, and subject and environment (or object, or entity). Its closing scene is visually reminiscent of Edward Hopper's 1952 painting *Morning Sun* which depicts a woman alone on a bed facing a window, assaulted by light pouring through it. The painting is referenced in Rob White's discussion of *Safe*, and White cites Haynes' own description of it: 'There's darks in it, but there's nothing as black as her eyes, and her eyes aren't detailed. It's almost like a bullet hole, it's a void. There's nothing in her gaze' (40). Framing Haynes' comments, White intimates far-reaching contexts of post-war catastrophe and apocalyptic disaster when he suggests that 'it is as if an atomic bomb were exploding outside that had somehow already incinerated her eyes' (40). Elsewhere, Haynes notes that in Hopper's later paintings, such as *Sun in an Empty Room* (1963) where sunlight also pours through a window, painted light takes on a material quality, a thickness (qtd in Dyer, 'Double Indemnity'). It is in these ways that disaster pervades Carol's material environment: strange weather suffuses the houses and other spaces she inhabits, permeates her body and radiates through her eyes.

Carol's illness is frequently interpreted as allegoric of AIDS, and Haynes' filmmaking connected to the independent movement of New Queer Cinema emergent in the early 1990s. Haynes' affiliation with the movement, and the movement's definition in relation to the AIDS crisis are relevant here, as this book begins charting formal tendencies beyond Hollywood. Explicating New Queer Cinema's relationship to AIDS, Monica B. Pearl configures the movement as 'a form and expression that emerges from the cataclysm of AIDS in the Western World' because HIV disrupts conventional narratives around science, the body and identity (24–5). New Queer Cinema thus 'provides another way of making sense … that does not placate and does not provide easy answers – that reflects rather than corrects the experience of fragmentation, disruption' (33). Nicole Seymour refers specifically to Haynes' 'queer techniques' (73), positing that aspects of *Safe* – particularly its narrative arc which 'feels rather limp' – may be recognized as 'politicized shiftings of narrative standards, rather than simple failures to meet them' (78). Departing from conventional, generic narrative formulas in favour of narrative ambiguity or obliqueness is commonly associated with independent filmmaking (and apparent in the network narratives of *Short Cuts* and *Magnolia*), and with New Queer Cinema, such departures are a means of enabling a more honest, accurate representation of traumatic events than Hollywood might allow. In this sense, it works towards a kind of realism in the same way that Bazin suggests when he intimates Hollywood's inadequacy in the wake of the Second World War. *Safe*, like *Magnolia* and *Short Cuts*, does not attempt to narrate the overcoming of disaster. Instead, it intimately details the traumatic disruption and fragmentation of the self that disaster occasions as Carol faces up to it.

Carol's illness can also be productively understood as more literally environmental and linked with global ecological catastrophe, which is ciphered through the film in multiple ways. Carol's face, marked by her encounters with various environments – the backgrounds of the film, where alterity lurks – reflects the notion that the social structures of the modern world are, as Suzi Gablik posits, 'profoundly anti-ecological, unhealthy, and destructive' (5). For Carol, the upper-class Californian environment is experienced as a world of relentless, traumatic disaster. As she traverses domestic spaces, health clubs, cafés and freeways, often accompanied by radio or television signals, she is impinged upon by a harmful miasma of fumes and chemicals that cause her apparent decay. Looking in another mirror to appreciate her appearance after getting a perm, for example, Carol is shocked by a sudden nosebleed. This is preceded by a close-up of her hair treatment, chemical lotion dripping onto her scalp. Another seizure is triggered by pesticides sprayed at her drycleaner, which turn on Carol in the manner Carson suggests: like a weapon, leaving her convulsing on the ground, her face bloodied.

Los Angeles becomes thick with threats of death that thwart and impede Carol, rendering her post-mortem: out of place, wounded, traumatized, inarticulate. Repeatedly disrupted by damaging chemical encounters, Carol is unable to locate herself in the world. Sitting in her own bedroom, where one wall is covered in mirrors, she exclaims 'Oh God, what is this? Where am I right now?' Characters across Haynes' films, according to James Morrison, 'describe a spectrum of "dead subjects" duly coordinated with appropriate theoretical cognates', of which Carol is emblematic: 'pathetic nonentities unwittingly enduring the benumbed death-in-life of late capitalism' (134). Carol is certainly a subject of late capitalism, but it is difficult to pinpoint where her silencing deathliness comes from. White describes her distress and alienation as a state of 'strange internal exile' from her surroundings, positing 'she is present but somehow not resident' (41). But it is precisely the fullness of her presence in encounter with her surroundings that occasions the blooming of disaster into her life. Carol's illness is symptomatic of a kind of anti-ecological accommodation, an overload of toxic interrelatedness. As Morton writes, 'we are scarred with the traces of object cathexes' (*Dark Ecology* 135). Carol cathects with chemicals, fumes, radiation and a myriad of apparently mundane household objects: furniture, appliances, adornments that, as Mary Ann Doane suggests, 'exert constant pressure' on her (7). Her intertwining with the materials and objects of her life leaves her brutalized because they are profoundly anti-ecological, they come to be associated with global ecological catastrophe and they are shot through with death.

Susan Potter corroborates Doane's suggestion, further positing that as the film's cinematography, sound and mise-en-scène combine 'the material presence of objects, rooms, and buildings is always emphasized and threatens to overwhelm the people within or near them' (132). Carol blends in (or, perhaps, is permeated) such that 'she almost vanishes into the materiality of her surroundings' (139). Much writing on the film is attentive to how it mostly eschews close-ups, placing emphasis on environments and creating an impression of distance typical of independent cinema that, as Roddey Reid argues, seeks to 'work against Hollywood's manipulation of the process of viewers' desires to identify with characters' (32). *Safe* becomes as much about environments, backgrounds and ambience – the chemical tangle of Los Angeles – as it is about Carol. Reid explains how the film's long shots confront viewers 'with the very "thereness" of things and social relations', describing 'the thicket of their materiality' (35). As Carol's muteness and inability to plot her way out of her situation make it difficult for viewers to identify with her in a pathos-driven psychological way, we instead simply see her amidst a disastrous diorama of everyday objects. In one scene, she is confronted by a black sofa that sinisterly appears in her living room after she had ordered a teal one. Reid even ascribes agency in this encounter to the sofa, suggesting it 'stares back at her' (35). This further underscores the potential for face-to-face encounters with forces of strange, indirect disaster, echoing Ivakhiv's evocations of an 'unhuman order' and a reptilian stare (271). Carol's urban environment, having become anti-ecological and disastrous, calls on her to respond in ethical terms.

Carol faces up to these strange forces with confusion and distress. Like Haynes' description of the woman in Hopper's *Morning Sun*, having glimpsed disaster, she becomes void. The lurid 'pastel perfection' (Reid 35) of suburbia that Carol moves through (and that moves through her) figures Morton's position that in the Anthropocene humans coexist with 'ghosts, strangers, and specters' (*Hyperobjects* 195). Morton evokes how reality is 'becoming more vivid and "unreal"' as 'nonhumans crowd into human spaces, leering like faces in a James Ensor painting' (*Hyperobjects* 194) and indeed, the scene where Carol is gripped by a seizure at the baby shower resembles Ensor's *Masks Confronting Death*. In Ensor's painting, extravagant masked figures surround and leer towards an adorned skull in the centre of the canvas that looks outward, mutely appealing. Carol's eyes, desperately glancing about, are darkened like the black holes of Ensor's death-skull. Her brightly dressed friends move from the corners of the decorated room, trying to give comfort but becoming intimidating as they confront her. Posthuman anthropologist Eduardo Kohn suggests poetically that 'how other kinds of beings see us matters' (1), and the objects and entities in Carol's milieu regard her with menace. In *Safe*, the hovering, disastrous presence described by Ivakhiv is given the form of a mask of domesticity, as if the threatening medflies of *Short Cuts* have disguised themselves as a sofa or dressed up in human costume.

Strange disaster crowds in on Carol in other ways too, as *Safe* positions her amidst media static and carbon-dependent transportation infrastructure – the substance of Ross's *Strange Weather*. These networks are global, as the inclusion of mediated whole-Earth imagery in the film suggests, and Carol's intensely subjective experiences become situated within larger contexts of global ecological catastrophe. Sounds of planes, helicopters and cars factor significantly in the film's networked suburban Los Angeles ambiance, linking it to *Short Cuts* and *Magnolia* (and perhaps also transport disaster movies like *Airport* and *Speed*). In a sequence of transport danger that conveys the city's deathly atmosphere, Carol drives while listening to a radio interview that foreshadows apocalypse, and as we hear a snippet – 'if I told you that the end of the world was coming...' – a truck suddenly changes lanes in front of her. Exhaust fumes cause a coughing fit, and death intrudes sonically as the voices on the radio are overtaken by the grumbling truck engine, then Carol's uncontrollable hacking. The film cuts to a point of view shot from a car, presumably Carol's as she drives home, freeway traffic flowing under a purplish sky (in *Safe*'s Los Angeles, the sky is unnaturally dark, suggestive not only of encroaching night but also of radiation). Next, the film cuts to a whole-Earth image, represented on a television screen. The image on the screen cuts to a waterfall as a male voice speaks – 'A movement to save the trees? Some say it goes deeper than that ...' – and we see in quick succession billowing clouds, windswept grasses and rolling waves. Carol is at home, watching an advertisement about deep ecology, a 'new paradigm' of interconnectedness. The vision of nature presented here fits seamlessly among the film's luxurious domestic interiors and health clubs because it is positioned as a fetishized, advertised object. As this sequence shows the ambience of industrial late modernity affecting Carol, it introduces continuity and resonance between illness and ecology as modes of bodily encounter with the world. It also foreshadows the introduction of Wrenwood, the desert retreat run by a quack guru that Carol stays at when she eventually flees Los Angeles.

Despite Carol's vulnerability, the most optimistic moments in *Safe* hint at the emergence of a hopeful subjectivity. A scene midway through the film details Carol's growing awareness of the disaster inherent in the world around her, and the beginnings of her attempts to confront it. It occurs just after Carol attends a meeting for sufferers of Environmental Illness but, crucially, before she decides to go to Wrenwood. Viewers see Carol outside of her usual material environments, away from her friends and her husband. She sits outside with a group of women as they discuss their experience of illness. The setting is minimal rather than lavish, the women dress in duller colours than Carol's friends, their hair moves in the breeze and in the background sunlight falls on a bush. Carol sits apart, listening, as the women laugh and joke about the bottled water and oxygen masks their illness necessitates. The scene plays in a different, lighter register to the remainder of the film. Haynes locates 'a sort of radical hope' that 'Carol might actually learn something and make a change in her life for the better – and revolt' (qtd in White 146), and it is at this point in Carol's encounter with strange disaster that she demonstrates a desire, if not a capacity, to look disaster in the eye and apprehend its power without fleeing or trying to manage it. Haynes explains further: 'everything is completely falling apart, and in a way she doesn't even know who she is anymore. But maybe that's the beginning of something potentially great' (147). White agrees, suggesting the possibility that Carol might 'let herself be unmade by this world she can't deal with' (147), alluding to the potential for a transformative outcome: that in encounter with disaster, Carol might become reconstituted as a subject and embrace a new kind of consciousness against the grain of her garish, anti-ecological milieu.

The women Carol listens to embody a differentiated subjective response to strange disaster. Where Morrison reads Haynes' films through the 'theoretical cognates' of Marx and Adorno to describe Carol as a 'dead subject' (134), some alternative cognates in ecofeminist theory can help us to see how Carol might also stand in for a different subjective disposition that is more ecological and more ethically open. Stacy Alaimo elaborates trans-corporeality as a means of understanding interrelations between humans and material forces, describing a recent historical 'shift in subjectivity': 'As the material self cannot be disentangled from the networks that are simultaneously economic, political, cultural, scientific, and substantial, what was once the ostensibly bounded human subject finds herself in a swirling landscape of uncertainty where practices and actions that were once not even remotely ethical or political matters suddenly become the very stuff of the crises at hand' (*Bodily Natures* 20).

This describes Carol's predicament precisely, as she struggles to orient herself amidst enmeshments she experiences as harmful and destabilizing. In such situations, Alaimo posits, 'the sense of self is transformed by the recognition that the very substance of the self is interconnected with vast biological, economic, and industrial systems that can never be entirely mapped or understood' (23). In this wider context, Alaimo frames Environmental Illness outside of medical discourses, identifying value in the way it 'demonstrates how attention to the flows and interchanges between body and environment catalyze new modes of thinking about and being within the emergent material world' (114). The women Carol listens to seem to come to terms with the ways their interconnection with the emergent material world of late modernity endangers them, embracing the precarity that disaster thrusts upon them and forging solidarity with each other.

Alaimo cites Lorraine Code, who formulates the ecological subject in distinction from the abstracted, autonomous 'individual of liberal moral-political theory':

> He/she is self-critically cognizant of being part of and specifically located within a social-physical world that constrains and enables human practices, where knowing and acting always generate consequences. For this subject, internal interdependence within communities and their external dependence on one another are given – neither to be repudiated in illusory gestures of self-sufficiency nor elaborated in a nostalgic immersion of self in nature or in Others. (*Ecological Thinking* 5)

Approaching something like this ecological subjectivity, these women are open and vulnerable: they articulate their coping mechanisms (laughter, perhaps, is one) and signal supportive dependency and honest communication with each other. In contrast to Carol's presence in encounter with disaster – alone and brutalized – theirs is both communal and contingent. They evince awareness of how the city's toxic materiality has decentred them, but from this position they do not try to reinstate their own mastery. Instead, they collectively explore the new reality inaugurated by the disaster that has befallen them, situating themselves on this new terrain. Alaimo posits that when faced with trans-corporeal toxicity, 'a nearly unrecognizable sort of ethics emerges – one that demands that we enquire about all of the substances that surround us, those for which we may be somewhat responsible, those that may harm us' (*Bodily Natures* 18). Carol's apprehension intimates that she might join these women, aligning with their ethical response to the strange eruption of death, which would call on her to be enquiring, honest, vulnerable and patient, seeking not to overcome or master the forces and presences at hand but to accommodate alterity. In Levinasian terms, such a response equates to a respect for the presence of the other, inclusive of attendant strangeness, its 'irreducibility to the I, to my thoughts and my possessions' (*Totality and Infinity* 43).

Unfortunately for Carol, however, the path she chooses involves both illusory gestures towards self-sufficiency and nostalgic immersion of herself in nature. As Seymour writes, 'Carol frustrates narrative conventions by never fully triumphing over her health-related adversities, never reaching enlightenment, and never achieving self-knowledge' (78). Per Code's description of ecological subjectivity, Carol's response to anti-ecological disaster can be seen as anti-ecological itself. Going to Wrenwood, Carol pursues wellness in an individualized, corporatized lodge in the desert wilderness that is as socially and politically toxic as the fumes and chemicals of suburban Los Angeles. In the final scene of *Safe*, as viewers are confronted by Carol's bombed-out eyes, we see an acknowledgement of her failure to face up to disaster in ethical terms. As we look into the mirror with her, we share in her demise, witnessing the futility of her efforts to overcome disaster and perceiving her failure to reckon with strange forces in ethical terms.

Strange apocalypse in *Donnie Darko*

Early in *Donnie Darko*, the type of aviation disaster threatened in Hollywood's *Airport* or, more recently, *Sully* (2016) occurs. A jet engine, shorn from the wing of a plane, falls through a stormy night sky. Rather than showing panicking passengers or pilots plotting an emergency landing, however, *Donnie Darko* positions viewers inside a middle-class family home where, as the father snoozes in front of television static, the engine smashes through the roof. According with notions of independent cinema's oppositional relationship with Hollywood, this inverse view shifts the focus away from potential heroics, reorienting viewers in an apparently mundane suburban milieu. The pesticide rain of *Short Cuts* and

Magnolia's rain of frogs are precursors for this nocturnal disaster in which a technological object, falling from the sky, transforms the domestic space of the nuclear family into a territory delineated by the sudden eruption of death.

The engine falls directly onto a bedroom belonging to Donnie, the family's troubled teenage son, but the scene immediately prior has demonstrated Donnie is not home because he wanders in his sleep. The film begins with a sound like thunder cracking, invoking stormy weather, but as the first shot fades in, we see clear morning sky and Donnie waking up on a road in the hills next to his bicycle, which he rides home. The exact location of Donnie's town Middlesex is not specified, but the film was shot in California, and its suburban world is similar to that of *Short Cuts*, *Magnolia* and *Safe*. As Donnie pedals through town, a song plays, echoing the opening scenes of Altman's and Anderson's films. It is 'The Killing Moon' by Echo and the Bunnymen, which presages disaster lyrically and also foreshadows Donnie's encounters with Frank, a ghostly figure in a stylized bunny suit whose sheer alterity prompts a transformation in Donnie's consciousness. Donnie's own nocturnal encounter with disaster occurs soon after when Frank lures him from his bedroom to a golf course to tell him: 'Twenty-eight days, six hours, forty-two minutes, twelve seconds. That is when the world will end.' The film then chronicles these twenty-eight strange days.

Donnie finds himself inhabiting a suddenly unfamiliar world of disastrous forces that, unbeknownst to others, call him to encounter. Disaster in this film is not overtly natural or (anti-)ecological: it is apocalyptic. Just as Hollywood pivots in the late 1990s from films about isolated disaster (*Twister*, *Titanic*) to larger-scale films (*Independence Day*, *Armageddon*) and then more obviously apocalyptic films (*End of Days* (1999), *28 Days Later* (2002)), in a parallel extension of strange weather disaster, *Donnie Darko* and *Southland Tales* can be understood as strange apocalypse films. In Ivakhiv's theorization of an indirect disaster subgenre, ecological disaster functions as a 'framing signifier' (270) for narratives foremostly concerned with interpersonal or familial tension. *Donnie Darko* is primarily concerned with its teenage protagonist, and the immanent end of the world frames and conditions his interactions with peers and adults throughout the film as Donnie alone is aware of the unfolding disaster, and adult characters especially are irritatingly oblivious to the impending apocalypse. Richard Kelly's post-2000 films, like late-1990s disaster movies, reintroduce elements of science fiction observed by Susan Sontag in post-war Hollywood. But they do so in accord with independent cinema's preference for ongoing ambiguity and uncertainty over straightforward, moralizing resolution. Donnie therefore has far more in common with Carol than with Hollywood's male heroes as he faces up to the end of the world alone, alienated, disturbed and decentred from his suburban idyll.

More than the other films discussed in this chapter, *Donnie Darko* is interrelated with Hollywood's 1990s disaster movies. It is located at the commercial end of the independent spectrum, as noted by Geoff King, including the appearance of Hollywood actress Drew Barrymore as Donnie's English teacher Karen Pomeroy, one of the film's few sympathetic adults. King observes that the film 'conforms in general to classical narrative conventions' with the crucial exception that 'key sources of information have been left out' (69), making the narrative enigmatic, provoking unease for viewers. King positions *Donnie Darko* in relation to many genres – 'science fiction, horror, teen or high school drama' (43) – and analyses its incorporation of science fictional elements at length. The 1990s disaster movie cycle that preceded *Donnie Darko* is not substantively noted in analysis of Kelly's film, but it can nevertheless be clearly read against them in both oppositional and proximal ways. Mirroring *Armageddon* and *Independence Day*, *Donnie Darko* premises a countdown to calamity and tasks its protagonist with saving the world. Unlike those films, however, there is no explicit threat that Donnie must overcome. Instead, there is Frank, a mysterious force of disaster calling out to Donnie, compelling a more complex face-to-face encounter.

Donnie is cited by Thomas Elsaesser as an exemplary post-mortem protagonist whose status as living or dead is uncertain ('World Cinema' 10), and this ontological uncertainty is engendered via encounter with Frank. Their initial meeting marks Donnie's entry into an alternate temporality referred to as a 'tangent universe', and the film insinuates that temporality is malleable by featuring what King describes as 'accelerated motion imagery' that 'seems to manifest something beyond the fabric of the everyday' (16). This imagery takes the form of sped-up sequences that allude to an alternate, transcendent perceptual framework, intimating how Donnie has brushed up against presences and forces that wholly exceed him. More mundanely, however, Donnie's attunement to something beyond the everyday is associated with mental illness: his therapist diagnoses him as a paranoid schizophrenic experiencing daylight hallucinations. This is Donnie's 'restriction' in Elsaesser's formulation of posthumous presence: an apparent limitation on his mental faculties that is actually enabling, only 'in some other register' (9). Only Donnie can see Frank, and Frank's appearance is not just linked to Donnie's subjective disposition, but also his mental consciousness. Donnie sees Frank's face when he looks in the bathroom mirror while taking his medication (an echo of

Safe's Carol looking at her own degrading semblance). During these encounters, Donnie touches the mirror – the boundary separating the self and the other – which then ripples as the material world, too, becomes malleable. Frank's alterity literally disturbs the fabric of Donnie's suburban life. Claire Perkins suggests that Donnie's illness might work as an interpretive framework, and reading the film thusly means it 'doesn't diverge from realism' as it engages the 'contemporary therapeutic imagination' (152). Perkins also notes the significance of the 'ordinary emotional confusion of being a teenager' (154) and indeed, Frank may initially be perceived as a hallucinatory mirror-manifestation of Donnie's pronounced teen angst. As a force of strange disaster, however, Frank exceeds this personal scale and his presence is more complex, as he ultimately becomes a helpful haunting who leads Donnie to save the world.

Rather than presenting Donnie's fracturing subjectivity as a splitting personality, which might be more conventionally be symbolized with a cracked mirror, the film reflects Donnie's unsettling encounters with disaster as mirror-glass made liquid. This suggests a state of becoming or transformation, a reflexive awareness of growing understanding and morphing consciousness. Indeed, Jake Gyllenhaal, who plays Donnie, remarks that the film 'beautifully captured the experience of moving into adulthood: the world that felt so solid becoming moveable and liquid' ('How We Made *Donnie Darko*'). During one bathroom meeting with Frank, Donnie stabs at the mirror with a knife. The point of the blade connects with Frank's right eye and a rupture is implied: a transcendent breaking through, a violent caress of the other. Contrasting with Carol's bombed-out eyes that evince aloneness and failure, between Donnie and Frank there is an irrevocable wounding but also a profound, productive connection.

Disaster inheres in this connection. In addition to foretelling apocalypse, Frank compels Donnie to become an agent of the type of elemental event that features in Hollywood disaster movies by flooding his high school and burning down a house. The flooding is presaged by a spectacular dream of Donnie's in which parts of a school hallway appear flooded. The ceiling is replaced with blue sky and an expanse of water, stretching to the horizon, surrounds lockers that tower like skyscrapers. This surrealistic image echoes more literal scenes from Hollywood's *Waterworld* in which eco-catastrophe causes global flooding, but it signals serene resolve rather than foreboding futurity. Strange alterity inheres in this image that suggests a non-human order with the ability to remake the world lurks beneath the surface of suburban existence. Indeed, King observes a sort of lurking, undefined, incommensurable alterity when he notes that *Donnie Darko* is 'characterized by evocations of the otherworldly, the precise nature of which are not easy to pin down' (80), and as Donnie cooperates with Frank, he becomes increasingly attuned to this otherworldliness. Within the film's narrative, the destructive tendencies that Frank impels in Donnie turn out to have positive functions. For example, the house that Donnie burns down belongs to Jim Cunningham, a corporate motivational speaker who has been concealing a child pornography operation in his basement, which is revealed when the house is destroyed. Because of the school flood, Donnie walks home with Gretchen, who becomes his love interest. At Frank's urging, forces of disaster thus come to operate generatively. For Donnie, embracing their attendant strangeness is conducive of clarity and heightened awareness.

Though it engages trauma and extreme disaffection, with its tendencies towards the transcendent, *Donnie Darko* demonstrates a hopeful awareness of disaster. Perkins positions Kelly's film alongside other independent films about suburbia and trauma – *Happiness* (1998), *The Safety of Objects* (2001), *The Chumscrubber* (2005) – that she suggests 'feed upon disaster and *yearn* for apocalypse' (148). Perkins argues the scenarios of these films, which eschew regeneration and are anti-utopian, can be 'described in terms of satire, hyperbole, ambiguity or emptiness' (terms not dissimilar to those of *Short Cuts*, *Magnolia* and *Safe*), but *Donnie Darko* offers a challenge by being utopian (151–4). Frank is framed by Perkins, via a deployment of Deleuze's and Guattari's concept of becoming-democratic, as 'the intensity that disrupts the film' (152), and she argues that he 'transpires as Donnie's act of becoming-animal – he is an active alternative, a refusal' that allows Donnie to escape from binary limitations (153). Donnie transforms in his encounter with Frank: he is moved by Frank's alterity to transcend the normative, adult world that is most concisely articulated in hypocritical characters like Jim Cunningham and Kitty Farmer, Donnie's condescending physical education teacher. Perkins elaborates:

> Donnie's transformation amounts to an awareness of himself not as a unique origin for a perceived world (as the adults see themselves) but as one more form itself becoming-different. For Donnie, this is not a positive recognition that fleshes out an existing system of understanding but it is the subtraction of everything that he does 'know' … . Donnie's 'insights' amount to a virtual awareness of the immanence of life that may or may not destroy him. (154)

Having gained true awareness of the world around him and his decentred position within it, Donnie refuses that world. He revolts in precisely the way that

Carol might, but ultimately does not. Frank, as the disaster, augurs this revolt by invoking another, strange order. But Frank also becomes disaster in a more straightforward way, as the eruption of death into life: at the film's conclusion, we learn he is actually a time-travelling dead man killed by Donnie who shoots a bullet through his eye, their final encounter making the wounding of their cathexis undeniably material.

In his openness to being coerced and commanded by Frank, and the insight he thus gains, Donnie evinces an awareness outside of conventional knowledge. In this sense, his encounter with Frank can be framed as ethical in an explicitly Levinasian sense. For Levinas, Richard Cohen explains, 'the other's alterity is experienced as a command… . The other disturbs, pierces, ruptures, disrupts the immanence into which the subject falls when free of unassimilable alterity' (*Face to Face with Levinas* 7). Frank's alterity pierces Donnie's suburban world from outside and compels Donnie to exceed it himself. Donnie's association with Frank leads him to satirize the moral simplification and hypocrisy of the adults who surround him, asserting contingent complexity over universalizing morality. For example, when Donnie is asked by Kitty to participate in a 'lifeline exercise' predicated on the binary categorization of human behaviour according to either love or fear, he refuses, remonstrating 'life isn't that simple … you can't just lump everything into these two categories and then just deny everything else'. The moralizing performed by Kitty is not dissimilar to the simplified morality of Hollywood's disaster genre, and as viewers see it from Donnie's perspective, it appears sanctimonious, self-serving, ironically childish and ill-equipped for complex situations. Donnie acts ethically to dispute this vision of reality, disrupting it by burning it down, flooding it, telling it where to shove its lifeline exercise, becoming a force of disaster himself. His response to disaster is to work with it rather than attempt to overcome it.

The apocalypse that *Donnie Darko* yearns for is expressed via this transformation in its protagonist's consciousness, and this becomes evident in the film's repeated allusions to eyes, suggesting new ways of seeing and perceiving the world. *Donnie Darko* draws attention to eyes and the act of looking at several significant moments, including Donnie and Frank's bathroom mirror confrontations. Before Donnie burns down Jim Cunningham's house, he and Gretchen are alone at the cinema when Gretchen falls asleep and Frank appears in the next seat. Donnie's gaze turns from the screen as he looks Frank in the eye, then they both look at the screen and Donnie asks, 'Why are you wearing the stupid Bunny suit?' Frank turns to face Donnie and viewers see his suit's creepily insectoid eyes in close-up as he retorts, 'Why are you wearing that stupid *man* suit?' Donnie tells him to take it off and when Frank reveals his human face, we see his mutilated eye, blood trickling down his cheek. In this moment of strange encounter, Frank instructs Donnie, saying to watch the movie screen as a hole appears in the middle of it, through which bright sky is visible, and Frank asks, 'Have you ever seen a portal?' The screen tears open and sunlight pours from it, like in Edward Hopper's paintings. In this encounter, Frank, with his bloodied eye socket, shows Donnie how to see the world differently. Donnie sees through things, material surfaces become permeable, new kinds of interrelation are made possible. Amid its time-loop strangeness, *Donnie Darko* thusly conceptualizes ethics in a way remarkably resonant with Levinas: through his face-to-face meetings with Frank, Donnie is forced into contact with death. This contact compels in him the emergence of a new subjectivity, marked by the subjection of his will to Frank, and increased awareness of and responsibility for the world around him.

Here and throughout the entire film, viewers see the world from Donnie's perspective. While *Safe* employs techniques of distanciation that discourage viewers from identifying with Carol in a conventional psychological way typical of Hollywood, Kelly's film positions viewers nearer to its protagonist. Indeed, that the film encourages this kind of identification to occur can be understood as component of its proximity to Hollywood. The inclusion of a conventional romantic subplot between Donnie and Gretchen amidst all the film's strangeness, for example, makes Donnie more like a Hollywood hero (for Carol, even in her relationship with her husband, there is no romance). Most interestingly, however, the identification of viewers with Donnie means that the enigmatic nature of the film's narrative, with its time travel, tangent universe and portals, unfolds for us as it does for him. This means that for much of the film, viewers are unsure what, precisely, is transpiring, and must become content with the omission of narrative information and a lack of sense-making. Viewers become post-mortem, in a sense, sharing in Donnie's subjective experiences of disorientation and revelation.

This sense of disorientation grows as the film moves towards a paradoxical resolution of sorts. Donnie comes to understand that for the timeline to be restored and the apocalypse prevented, he must return to his bed to be crushed by the jet engine. Time collapses and rewinds and, in the penultimate scene, Donnie is where he should have been at the beginning: in his room on the night the jet engine smashes into it. During this second version of the scene, disaster movie elements are more evident, and powers of strange coincidence are also at work. Viewers learn that the engine falls from a plane Donnie's mother and sister are on, and travels through a portal – a passage through time and space that appears as a streak of dark cloud in a clear sky – leading to the Darko home. This cloud gathers, circling like a tornado, over the suburban house. As Donnie lies on his bed waiting to die, the camera lingers on a drawing of an eye stuck to the wall. Inside the dark pupil is a skull, as if to suggest a reflection and a face-to-face encounter with death. This hints at a more ultimate alterity than that posed by Frank alone, the kind of alterity described by Maurice Blanchot in his evocation of ethical responsibility: 'the Other is death already, and weights upon me like an obsession with death' (*The Writing of the Disaster* 19). As the camera moves back to allow a fuller view of Donnie, he laughs and, in voiceover, says 'I hope that when the world comes to an end I can breathe a sigh of relief, because there will be so much to look forward to', his last words echoing the obliqueness and seeming contradiction of Blanchot's writing. Rather than being bombed out black holes, as Carol's eyes are in the final moments of *Safe*, the deathly eyes that repeatedly appear in *Donnie Darko* become portals, conduits for a transcendent power located in recognition and vulnerability, conducive of new ways of perceiving.

The way the world has ended: *Southland Tales*

Richard Kelly's subsequent film *Southland Tales* recoups the network narratives of *Short Cuts* and *Magnolia*, similarly stitching together a cast of characters spread across Los Angeles. But strangeness here is writ larger, the notions of anti-ecology and splintered subjectivity apparent in *Safe* and *Donnie Darko* being interwoven with some spectacular tendencies of Hollywood disaster movies. *Southland Tales* emerges from American independent cinema at roughly the same time as two major US movies about disaster, *The Day After Tomorrow* and *An Inconvenient Truth*, which are discussed in the next chapter, and its instantiation of a disaster imaginary both spectacular and strange remains uniquely provocative. It can initially be understood along the lines of the 1950s and 1960s sci-fi movies discussed by Susan Sontag in which new technologies are ontologically disturbing harbingers of death. The fictional technology at the film's centre is also its strange weather, its disastrous background: 'fluid karma' is both a psychedelic drug and a method for harnessing energy from Earth's oceans, an 'alternative fuel', the production of which is causing the planet's rotation to slow. This deceleration precipitates anti-ecological catastrophe, creating what one character calls 'environmental anomalies' including a rift in the fabric of time and space located in Nevada. These resemblances to Hollywood's disaster genre are significant. David Ingram notes that the film's 'narrative of technological hubris follows generic expectations' (54), characterizing it in part as a 'science fiction moral fable' (55), and like older science fiction films, much of the technology in *Southland Tales* is scientifically unsound or outright ridiculous. Except, that is, for the various media and surveillance technologies, central to the film's particular imagination of disaster, that constantly record and reflect characters, catching them in procedures of splitting and doubling, creating amnesiac feedback loops that take the place of conventional narrative progression.

The film is blown apart at the outset, beginning with a recorded disaster. Viewers first see an Independence Day street party in Texas through a video camera wielded by two young boys: tables laden with food, water pistol fights, a bouncy castle. The screen flashes white and, as the camera weaves through a gathering crowd and dust fills the frame, a mushroom cloud rises in the distance. A nuclear bomb has exploded. This home video perspective does not return in the film, but a multitude of other audio-visual modes are immediately deployed as it cuts to the 'Doomsday Scenario Interface', a multifaceted infographic display that synthesizes a range of visualizations. This display conveys story details covering the subsequent three years, leading up to the beginning of the film's narrative: the Third World War, the invention of fluid karma and the appearance of the Nevadan rift. When disaster intrudes into domestic space here, it coincides with an abrupt break in film style: from a first-person camcorder aesthetic to a view-from-above, live-update modality that surveils and compiles images of different kinds. During the remainder of the film, conventional cinematic presentation is blended with newsfeeds, advertisements, music videos, HUDs (head-up display), aerial visualizations and other kinds of imagery. *Southland Tales* also contains a variety of image sources – recordings, broadcasts, replays: one character carries a camera, obsessively recording events; another is an adult film star creating a reality TV show; another controls a nationwide surveillance operation. At the end of this two-part opening sequence, the narrator Pilot Abilene, a scarred military veteran suffering from post-traumatic stress disorder (PTSD), tells viewers, 'This is the way the world ends, this is the way the world ends, this is the way the world ends. Not with a whimper but with a bang'. His reversal of the famous final line of T. S. Eliot's 'The Hollow Men' augurs an amplified recursion of disaster, an apocalypse that is continually deferred until the film's end.

Disaster operates, once again, as a framing signifier. These scenes function as an affective epigraph, signalling the ways that world-ending disaster and a whorl of media regimes chaotically intermesh throughout *Southland Tales*. Beginning with the detonation of a nuclear bomb and featuring an anomalous rift near post-war nuclear test sites in Nevada, the film clearly echoes the nuclear fear and technological anxiety of post-war sci-fi films. Simultaneously, it locates itself within the dispersive, fragmented affective modes more recently provoked by digital media technologies. Steven Shaviro, one of few theorists to engage substantively with *Southland Tales*, devotes a chapter of *Post Cinematic Affect* to exploring ways the film signals how 'digital technologies, together with neoliberal economic relations, have given birth to radically new ways of manufacturing and articulating lived experience' (2). He observes that on a formal level the film works contrary to Hollywood convention as it is 'not edited according to any traditional cinematic logic' (73). Rather, Shaviro explains, it is 'filled with inserts, it overlays, juxtaposes, and restlessly moves between multiple images and sound sources' without providing hierarchical organization (71). In this way, the film is even more radically decentred than *Short Cuts* and *Magnolia*. Rather than weaving distinct threads together to compose a network or 'patchwork' (Ivakhiv 269), it allows some threads to unravel and disappear into a cascade of images, picking up other threads and making unexpected, unpredictable narrative divergences including military manoeuvres, political machinations, entrepreneurial ventures, abductions and impersonations.

Where *Donnie Darko* has the shape of a conventional classical narrative with crucial parts occluded (King 69), *Southland Tales* creates the impression that a cohesive, continuous narrative probably exists, but offers viewers diffracted glimpses of it rather than a straightforward through-line. In Shaviro's initial impressions of the film, published online, he describes its compositional logic as 'paratactic and additive', writing that 'in defiance of linear or narrative logic; everything in the film is a matter, neither of causality, nor of action grounded in character, nor even of dialectical contrast; but rather of juxtaposition, "free" association, and the proliferation of multiple levels of self-referential feedback loops' ('Southland Tales'). *Southland Tales* is polyphonic to an extreme degree, and in this sense, its generation of affect is consonant with the lived experience of disaster, with the splitting of the world such that it can only be reckoned with partially or obliquely. (As Haytham El-Wardany writes, 'It is impossible to present a complete picture of disaster or to apprehend it in its entirety.... . More fitting to make partial appraisals, to reckon it in fragments' ('Notes on Disaster').) Fragmentation and obliqueness thus become the crucial formal elements of *Southland Tales*. The bomb blast that is silently ciphered through Carol's eyes in the final moments of *Safe* is unleashed on viewers at the outset of this film. It figuratively incinerates viewers' eyes, and the destabilization of visual modality that it prompts calls on them to look differently at what follows.

With this catastrophic formal logic, *Southland Tales* configures a sense of realism that is responsive to specific contemporary cultural conditions in the sense of Bazin's suggestion that 'each period looks for its own' realism (*Bazin at Work* 6). The rapidity of the film's cuts and its proliferative progression are firmly against the slower, atmospheric tendencies of conventional realist form, but they also proceed far beyond Hollywood convention. Destabilizing Hollywood aesthetics in an accelerative way, the film's style enables a critical reflexivity and establishes precisely the type of 'immediate, concrete, intuitive understanding of reality' that Ian Aitken posits is sought by realism ('The European Realist Tradition' 178). *Southland Tales* authentically renders the traumatic collapse of temporality that Shaviro suggests is inaugurated by the conjunction of neoliberalism and digital media. To articulate this contemporary reality, Shaviro cites Mark Fisher's *Capitalist Realism*, in which Fisher echoes Žižek and Jameson to suggest 'it is easier to imagine the end of the world than it is to imagine the end of capitalism' (2). Elsewhere, Fisher writes of 'the slow cancellation of the future' (*Ghosts of My Life* 6). In this reality, Shaviro asserts, 'the world can end, but it cannot change' as 'duration implodes; it shrinks down to a dimensionless, infinitesimal point' (*Post Cinematic Affect* 58). Kelly's film becomes 'as radical as reality itself'; a 'demented fabulation' that 'reflects upon our actual situation, while at the same time inserting itself within that situation' (92).

Southland Tales presents our actual situation as one of traumatic disaster and rampant death. As the film's spasmodic addition of variegated imagery and scattershot narrative fragments proceeds, it details the relentless proliferation of disaster rather than any kind of progression towards apprehending or overcoming it. Beyond the formulaic narrative trajectories of Hollywood disaster movies, and even the decentred narratives of the indirect disaster films discussed by Ivakhiv, *Southland Tales* not only diegetically represents, but also formally simulates the type of 'breach in the mind's experience of time, self, and the world' that Cathy Caruth describes when defining trauma (3). The film posits traumatic rupture as a constant force rather than a singular, interrupting event, and this precludes progression or temporal advancement. From the moment of detonation in its opening scene, *Southland Tales* asserts a world punctuated by instances and returns of disaster (both lived and mediated) so frequently that the punctuations become like striations on a plane, a terrain constituted by recursive rupture. It posits that as subjects of neoliberalism and digital media, our temporal experience of disastrous modernity cannot be delimited by categories of pre- or post-, but, rather, as Blanchot writes, 'we are on the edge of disaster without being able to situate it in the future: it is rather always already past, and yet we are on the edge or under the threat' (*The Writing of the Disaster* 1).

Another touchstone for the mediated perspective on disaster posited by *Southland Tales* is apparent in the work of filmmaker and writer Hito Steyerl, who describes a particular visual subjectivity engendered by digital media. Steyerl argues that with the recent advent of new visualization technologies – '3-D nosedives, Google Maps, and surveillance panoramas' – the heretofore conventional visual paradigm of linear perspective is usurped by a 'free-fall' vertical visuality rooted in 'surveillance technology and screen-based distraction' (24). In this de-linearized, abyssal world, 'time is out of joint and we no longer know whether we are objects or subjects' (26). For Steyerl, the advent of digital imagery and its meshing with extant cinematic modes occasions a kind of representational freedom: 'As it merges with graphic-design practices, drawing, and collage, cinema has gained independence from the prescribed focal dimensions that have normalized and limited the realm of its vision' and consequently, 'the viewer is no longer unified' but instead becomes 'dissociated and overwhelmed, drafted into the production of content' (27). Incorporating a multiplicity of visual modes outside of cinema (surveillance recordings, advertisements, schematics, news tickers, etc.), *Southland Tales* renders the schema of visual and subjective experience articulated by Steyerl. The film's realism – its capacity for authentically representing a world in which temporality becomes uncertain – is made possible precisely by the inclusion of these images at a point of formal tension between conventions of Hollywood disaster spectacle and the oppositional ambiguities and occlusions of independent cinema.

Viewers encounter the characters of *Southland Tales* as emissaries of these atemporal, free-fall dynamics. They extend the dissociative and death-driven tendencies of Donnie, Kelly's previous protagonist, being supremely post-mortem in multiple ways. They are amnesiac, experience post-traumatic stress, use mind-altering drugs, are clones of themselves and travel through time. They watch themselves and each other reflected and projected onto screens, echoing the ways that Donnie and *Safe*'s Carol repeatedly look into mirrors as they are confronted by disaster. They are actors thrust into roles they are unprepared for. The entire cast of *Southland Tales* is evidential of Hollywood star power and operates similarly to the ensemble casts of Hollywood disaster movies, each character offering a differentiated response to disaster. Though the film spoils Hollywood narrative conventions, it is, like *Short Cuts*, *Magnolia* and *Safe*, concerned with Los Angeles, and especially with celebrity. Its primary characters are played by star actors and celebrities who are cast (and thus must act) in opposition to their popular identities. Shaviro notes that 'their acting cuts sharply against their familiar personas' (*Post Cinematic Affect* 89), a clear inversion of the way Hollywood disaster blockbusters rely on and bolster the celebrity personalities of their stars. The disfigured, drug-addicted narrator Pilot Abilene is played by the boyishly good-looking Justin Timberlake. Sarah Michelle Gellar, known for her titular role in *Buffy the Vampire Slayer*, plays Krysta Now, a porn star turned reality television star turned energy drink entrepreneur. Dwayne Johnson, the former professional wrestler who I have framed as the archetypal masculinist hero for 2010s Hollywood disaster movies, in this film (produced a decade earlier) plays Boxer Santaros, a timid, anxious actor whose memory has been wiped. Seann William Scott plays Roland Taverner, another war veteran and a Southland police officer, as well as his duplicate Ronald – ostensibly a twin brother but actually a clone created during a passage through the time–space rift. This cast concentrates the affective and subjective experiential modes outlined by Shaviro and Steyerl. Temporally displaced, hallucinatory, out of joint, caught in representational feedback loops, the mediated edge of disaster makes them subjects of endless liminality.

Furthering *Donnie Darko*'s impulse towards eschatology, *Southland Tales* imbues a sense of transcendence in its male protagonists, who ultimately all become martyr-like figures. Santaros's muscled arms and torso are tattooed with a panoply of religious iconography, including a portrait of Jesus Christ that bleeds through his white shirt near the end of the film when he raises his arms, mimicking crucifixion, as the burn of an incoming missile haloes around him. Abilene recites passages from the Book of Revelation as he sits atop a gun emplacement on Venice Beach and his fluid karma trips enable him to speak to God and to 'angels who can see through time'. Taverner is designated 'the new messiah' by Abilene at the conclusion of the film, when he encounters himself face to face in a scene that stages, most explicitly, the kind of subjectivity that the film posits in response to strange forces of disaster. In this scene, which plays out in parallel with other events at the end of the world (including Santaros's death), the two Taverners are in an ice cream truck that has somehow levitated into the sky. One of Ronald's eyes has been shot out, just like Frank's in *Donnie Darko*, leaving a pulpy mess of blood. An eye, opening a new way of seeing and a new, heightened consciousness, becomes a motif for Kelly. A tunnel of light swirls outside. Briefly intercut images show rapidly moving clouds above buildings and a gaseous emission billowing purple across the frame. Substances of strange weather are shown morphing state – solid, liquid and gas. The wounded Taverner holds a pistol, threatening to shoot the other, then himself, apparently due to guilt over a friendly fire incident during the war that caused Abilene's wounding. Roland tells him, 'It wasn't our fault' and they speak in antiphony the words 'friendly fire' and 'I forgive you' as their faces are shown in close-up. Ronald drops the gun and Roland repeats, 'I forgive you, I forgive you, I forgive you', his tripling of the line recalling Abilene's earlier repetition of Eliot's poem. Finally, Abilene interrupts, speaking in voiceover: 'Revelation twenty-one. And God wiped away the tears from his eyes so that the new messiah could see out to the New Jerusalem. His name was Officer Roland Taverner of Hermosa Beach, California. My best friend.' A brief intercut shows him partying as the world ends.

The ending of *Southland Tales* is far more ambiguous than that of any other film discussed in this chapter, but it includes some productive points of comparison with *Safe* and *Donnie Darko*. Viewers last see both Carol and Donnie alone in the dark, private spaces of their bedrooms, confronted with their personal dooms: Carol with her failure to conceive of a way to live with disaster, and Donnie with his sacrifice that allows the world to go on for his family and for Gretchen. The final image of *Southland Tales* is Roland's face engulfed in light. A cataclysmic sear is reflected in his eyes as he remains facing his double. Above all else, this encounter between the Taverners, who face the end of the world together and/or face each other at the end of the world, is one of acceptance and forgiveness. Mixing the words repeated by Abilene at the beginning of the film with the words repeated by Taverner at its conclusion creates a poetic summation of the film's oddly ameliorating imagination of apocalyptic disaster: Friendly fire / the world ends // This is the way / I forgive you.

Deborah Bird Rose writes that the 'question of our time', a time of mass extinction, death and disaster, is 'to ask to whom, or to what, does one come face to face' (*Wild Dog Dreaming* 13). Throughout *Southland Tales*, characters, faced with disaster and apocalypse, look at images of themselves and each other, ciphering a sense of complicity with ecological degradation and the possibility of the end of the world. But in this final moment, face-to-face confrontation is made overwhelmingly literal: there is no recording or playback, no mirror and no drawing on the wall. Taverner looks into a living double of his own eyes. He appears like a Hollywood hero, another ex-military, uniformed white man, but is addled in a world constituted by trauma-inducing technologies and mediatic procedures of doubling. Lacking the power to overcome disaster and poised between transcendent levitation and free-fall to death, he can only offer forgiveness to himself for the damaging role he has played as a soldier.

Kelly states a desire for the film's ending to be hopeful, but his comments reveal a lingering ambivalence: 'all that's left is this floating ice-cream truck and this gateway, maybe to heaven or maybe to some other place' (qtd in Ingram, 'The Aesthetics and Ethics of Eco-Film Criticism' 56–7). *Southland Tales* meets Haytham El-Wardany's imperative to look disaster in the eye, positing that looking disaster in the eye involves looking ourselves in the eye. Like *Short Cuts* and *Magnolia*, *Southland Tales* is bookended by disastrous events: the bomb in Abilene and the apocalypse reflected in Taverner's eyes. Between them, it configures a haunted consciousness of disaster not unlike that observed by Andrew Ross in the changing, post-industrial world of the early 1990s that is haunted by the encroaching spectre of climate change, and also not unlike that post-war consciousness observed by Sontag in which sudden nuclear annihilation looms. The other films discussed in this chapter channel strange disaster through non-human presences: *Short Cuts* with its medflies and the pesticide that combats them; *Magnolia* with its anuran apocalypse; *Donnie Darko* with the animal-esque figure of Frank and *Safe* with its allusions to ecology and anti-ecological objects. This film, however, presents a collective human consciousness preoccupied with itself, framed by the mediatic proliferation of human images. *Southland Tales* shows viewers a world of human-technological doubles; recordings, images, clones, spectres, versions of self, splintered into strange alterity to become forces of disaster themselves.

Strange weather and capitalist realism

In Don DeLillo's novel *White Noise*, a character opines, 'Californians invented the concept of lifestyle. This alone warrants their doom' (65). Above all else, the strange disaster films catalogued in this chapter create an impression of a paranoid, insecure, particularly Californian subject unsure of its place in a rapidly dissolving world it assumed to be stable. The deadly havoc that its fossil-fuelled lifestyles have wrought on the world is catching up to it and, though there may be some recognition of complicity, it is mostly clueless about how to fix things. These are films about middle-class, mostly white Americans who seem oblivious to relationships between their vain extravagance and encroaching crisis. The doom they have earned inheres in their poisoned surroundings and lurks behind their own mediatic representations and late-night bathroom mirror reflections.

Though all these films can be categorized as American independent cinema, there is great variation in their styles. Distinguishing themselves from Hollywood, they opt for different disruptive techniques. *Safe* is in some ways aligned with realist aesthetics because of its long shots and the spectatorial distance it creates, while *Southland Tales* channels digital media and doomscrolling with its distracted, fast cutting visuality. Strange disaster is difficult, if not impossible to master, and narrative strategies in particular are a way that these films frustrate Hollywood's straightforward trajectories towards heroism. *Magnolia* and *Short Cuts* are unfocused and sprawling, and *Southland Tales* exacerbates their decentred logic in its splintering of story. *Safe* focuses tightly on its protagonist, but its narrative progression is stifled, and while *Donnie Darko* resembles a Hollywood film, it omits critical narrative information. In different ways, these films call on viewers to be open to ambiguity and omission, to bear with collapse and fragmentation of familiar cinematic form.

As these approaches to narrative occasion gaps in form and presence that ultimately leave human characters faced with disaster looking not at spectacular alterity but at their own disrupted appearance, they come to resemble and effectively convey something similar to Fisher's conception of capitalist realism. Capitalist realism is a paradigm for social life that speaks to aspects of Jameson's descriptions of postmodernism that have become 'aggravated and chronic' since the 1980s (*Capitalist Realism* 7). It is 'the widespread sense that not only is capitalism the only viable political and economic system, but also that it is now impossible to even *imagine* a coherent alternative to it' (2). This impossibility brings 'a deeper, far more pervasive, sense of exhaustion, of cultural and political sterility' than that diagnosed by Jameson (7) and Fisher describes a sort of attendant subject position: 'all that's left is the consumer-spectator, trudging through the relics' (4). Disaster and climate catastrophe hold a special position as componentry of capitalist realism because they help characterize it but also, potentially, signal a way out or a world beyond. Fisher's theorization of capitalist realism begins with a brief analysis of Alfonso Cuarón's 2006 post-disaster dystopia *Children of Men*, in which he observes catastrophe 'is neither waiting down the road, nor has it already happened. Rather, it is being lived through. There is no punctual moment of disaster' (2). Environmental catastrophe, in capitalist realism, is subsumed, 'incorporated into advertising and marketing' to support a fantasy of Earth's infinite resources and capital's capacity to renew life (18). But Fisher also returns to 'environmental disaster' in his concluding remarks, positing that it augurs a disruption of 'capitalism's constituent imperative towards growth' because it will occasion a need for rationing (80), attesting to undeniable finitude.

Encounter with strange disaster in these independent films provokes a particular form of consciousness, a new awareness of the way the world is structured, like a dawning realization one is being haunted. *Safe*, *Donnie Darko* and *Southland Tales* are about processes of recognition for their post-mortem protagonists who come to understand that as they trudge through the mire of their ordinary suburban existence they are beset by deathly disaster. What Carol, Donnie and the ensemble of *Southland Tales* do with this realization can be understood in ethical terms. Carol's response highlights the futility of attempting to manage disaster with extant fantasies as she attempts openness but falls back on toxic strategies. Donnie holds himself available to astonishment as he responds to Frank's demands, embracing the responsibilities that disastrous alterity commands. The characters of *Southland Tales* seek transcendence even as their recognition of disaster comes too late for them to be saved. Vacillating between responsibility and abrogation, and working through frustration, obstinacy, disaffection and despondence, these films offer oblique glimpses and futile hints of alternatives to capitalist realism, alternatives to a disastrous life, as they seek to face up to it.

Part II

Two Documentary Views of Disaster

3

The view from above

Environmental documentary is a cinematic category encompassing many formal tendencies but frequently characterized by its highlighting of human impacts on the Earth. Doing so, it offers explicit response to the various disasters bound up in the Anthropocene and climate change, exhaustively detailing aspects of species extinction and exploitation, waste, despoliation, displacement and the like. This chapter and the next, each focusing primarily on two documentary films, outline two possibilities for the imagination of disaster in documentary: the view from above and the view from a body, each of which carries an ethical sensibility and distinct possibilities for realism. The view from above is traced from *An Inconvenient Truth* (2006), the paradigmatic, hugely influential climate change documentary directed by Davis Guggenheim and based on former vice president of the United States Al Gore's international mission to educate and advocate about global warming. *Before the Flood* (2016), released a decade later and directed by Fisher Stevens, emulates Guggenheim's film in crucial ways, positing a similar viewpoint as it shows actor and celebrity climate activist Leonardo DiCaprio on a global journey exploring impacts of climate change. The subsequent chapter turns to two lesser-known films from Oceania and Aotearoa New Zealand to explore the view from a body. *There Once Was an Island* (2010), directed by Briar March, was shot during two visits to the Takuu atoll in Papua New Guinea where the disastrous effects of sea level rise are taking hold. *On an Unknown Beach* (2016), co-directed by Adam Luxton and Summer Agnew, documents three separate traumas that intermesh in its poetic style: hypnotherapeutic exploration of past addiction, a city wrecked by earthquakes and ecological devastation caused by industrial fishing.

The view from above and the view from a body connote two ways of seeing, thus suggesting distinct approaches to intersubjective encounter and distinct ethical dispositions. To name and elaborate these ways of seeing and describe them as possibilities for the documentary representation of disaster, I draw on Donna Haraway's landmark essay 'Situated Knowledges: The Science

Question in Feminism and the Privilege of Partial Perspective', first published in 1988. Haraway invokes two opposing perspectives on knowledge and claims to objectivity, framing both in visual terms as ways of looking or viewing positions, writing 'I am arguing for the view from a body, always a complex, contradictory, structuring and structured body, versus the view from above, from nowhere, from simplicity' (589). She intimates an ethics of encounter, even echoing Levinas's expression that 'ethics is an optics' (*Totality and Infinity* 23), when she writes that 'an optics is a politics of positioning' (586). The view from above entails, for Haraway, an understanding of objectivity bound up in masculinism and false omniscience that she names 'the god trick', an 'ideology of direct, devouring, generative, and unrestricted vision' (582). She argues against 'pictures of the world' that are 'allegories of infinite mobility' and for pictures of 'elaborate specificity and difference' (583). Where the view from above suggests an abstracted, totalizing visuality and an all-seeing, dominant subject, the view from a body suggests corporeal encounter with the material of the world and intimate appraisal of its constituent forces.

'Situated Knowledges' looms instructively in post-anthropocentric thought, particularly over issues of visual representation. Stacy Alaimo makes repeated recourse to Haraway in *Exposed* as she resists the 'grand mapping' of the Anthropocene, favouring rather 'embedded modes of epistemological, ethical, and political engagement' (1). Joanna Zylinska, in *Nonhuman Photography*, challenges 'traditional tenets of the self-focussed, capital- and fossil-fuelled masculinist I' (8), instead elaborating modes of perception and subjectivity that are ecological: 'embodied, immersive, and entangled' and therefore, she argues, constitutive of 'a better ethics and a more responsible politics' (17). For both theorists, in contemporary contexts of eco-catastrophe, the view from above intimates continued sovereignty of the historically dominant masculinist subject and a disinclination to fully engage with or take stock of catastrophic contexts face-on, while the view from a body suggests a capacity for response-ability of the sort more recently called for by Haraway: attentiveness to the specificities of complex enmeshments of human and non-human presences.

Haraway herself warns against binaristic theorization, however. Despite posing a series of binaries – 'world system' versus 'local knowledges', 'master theory' versus 'webbed accounts' – she suggests that a more adequate way of framing these issues of epistemological positioning would be 'a map of tensions and resonances between the fixed ends of a charged dichotomy' (588). I have already observed a charged dichotomy of this sort in the ways realist style has historically been counterposed to Hollywood style: In Hollywood disaster movies, the sovereignty of Eurocentric, masculinist humanity over the world is confirmed, while notions of realism potentially offer avenues for the articulation of other responses to disaster. Turning to analyse documentary films here, I am interested in mapping their resonances with both Hollywood and realist style. *An Inconvenient Truth* and *Before the Flood* are far from simplistic in their outlook, as my initial framing of them might imply. They open up many possibilities for important activist praxis and awareness of contemporary environmental crises, particularly given their immense global reach. However, their immediately apparent resonances and links with Hollywood do suggest grounds for criticism, both being produced in the United States and foregrounding powerful male protagonists as they invoke global scenarios of disaster. Somewhat conversely, *There Once Was an Island* and *On an Unknown Beach*, both produced in the South Pacific, resonate with the style described by realist theorists. Composed of longer takes that emphasize the specificities of the material environments they depict and featuring sequences that make use of impressionistic camera techniques, both films foreground multiple subjects whose diverse experiences of disaster are connected to their material and geographical situation.

To account for how documentary can structure ways of seeing the historical world embroiled in disaster, Part II of this book maintains an interest in how these films look towards the Pacific Ocean. Oceans are particularly advanced disaster zones in the Anthropocene which has, as Elizabeth DeLoughrey observes, 'catalyzed a new oceanic imaginary in which, due to the visibility of sea level rise, the largest space on earth is suddenly not so external and alien to human experience' ('Submarine Futures of the Anthropocene' 34). Despite this, they remain overlooked because 'dominant rhetorics (within both science and cultural theory) figure the Anthropocene as a primarily lithic phenomenon' (Neimanis 156). Alaimo offers a catalogue of anthropogenic oceanic disaster: 'Atomic testing. Dead zones. Oil "spills". Industrial fishing, overfishing, trawling, long lines, shark finning, whaling. Bycatch, bykill, ghost nets. Deep sea mining and drilling. Cruise ship sewage. BP. Fukushima. Radioactive, plastic, and microplastic pollution. Sonic pollution. Climate change. Ocean acidification. Ecosystem collapse. Extinction' (*Exposed* 111).

Many of these slow and strange disasters take hold specifically in the South Pacific, in nations and locales that were sites of colonial encounter and are still conditioned by violent power matrices of colonialism and nuclearism. This means that, as the president of Palau tells DiCaprio in *Before the Flood*, 'the small island nations who contribute the least to the process of climate change are actually going to feel the worst impacts, the worst scenarios, because of global warming'. The region is consequently visited by many documentary filmmakers, who run the risk of recapitulating colonial encounter. Indeed, the Pacific is central in a slew of environmental documentaries: *Time and Tide* (2005), *Someplace with a Mountain* (2010), *The Hungry Tide* (2011), *ThuleTuvalu* (2014), *Blue* (2016), *Anote's Ark* (2018) and more. Meanwhile, in popular imaginaries and feature filmmaking, the ocean is commonly regarded as an (often racialized) site of ultimate alterity. Despite the clear and deadly impacts of humans on oceanic life listed by Alaimo, in Hollywood disaster movies, the water of the ocean is usually figured as a vast elemental force, threatening to wipe out humanity and a site of irredeemable, unstable alterity. These understandings and perceptions are succinctly highlighted by Alice Te Punga Somerville when, metaphorically observing the transit of scholarly knowledges and '(colonial) discourses about cultural integrity,' she writes of an assumption 'that the land is always at risk of danger from the sea (erosion, flood, tsunami) rather than the other way around. This reinforces the sanctity of land … and in turn quietly affirms that the ocean is the place where danger and risk are located' (325). Both *An Inconvenient Truth* and *Before the Flood* incorporate short visits to the Pacific into global trajectories. These visits are moments of encounter in which their purview, and their ethical outlook, is made clear.

The god tricks of *An Inconvenient Truth*

Framing environmental documentary as a genre in its own right, Charles Musser designates the early 2000s as the moment of its 'full constitution' (55). The thematic and formal contours of this genre remain varied, however, and attempts to critique and categorize environmental documentaries often account for the tenor of response they pose to contemporary environmental crises. The 'green wave' of film and television newly apparent at this time, observes Gregg Mitman, acknowledges, as in the case of the documentary *Arctic Tale* (2007), that 'human actions are changing the (hi)stories of other living creatures' (215). A socio-political positioning is apparent when Belinda Smaill describes environmental documentary as 'a broader body of films tasked with critiquing corporate dominance and investigating and advocating on issues concerning the decimation of the environment and its natural resources' (*Regarding Life* 1).

This is, then, a recently emergent genre (coming to prominence in the same historical moment that, as I have discussed in Chapter 1, marks the end of Hollywood's 1990s disaster movie cycle and the proliferation of disaster movie style and themes into a range of genres) that has explicitly ethical aims, seeking to bear witness to environmental crises and reckon with the disastrous impact of humans on earth.

A kind of realism is thus at hand. As Bazin suggests, realism searches for techniques and aesthetics that 'best capture, retain, and render' reality (*Bazin at Work* 6) and, in a contemporary context, environmental documentary endeavours to realistically retain and render facets of environmental crisis. *An Inconvenient Truth* is often positioned as a figurehead of environmental documentary and, as such, emblematic of a particular documentary realism premised on scientific truth, ostensible objectivity and convincing argument. These associations become readily apparent to viewers due to the film's slideshow presentation format, which positions Gore as a bearer of scientific knowledge about the advancement and impacts of climate change. Contextualizing these associations historically, Helen Hughes links the slideshow presentation format with established documentary traditions by citing John Grierson's interest in how 'documentary film could represent an advance on the lecture' (16) and locating it as exemplary of an argumentative type of environmental documentary, which puts forth 'an explicit argument about an environmental issue' and sets about achieving activist goals and promoting political and social change (117). The potential for realism conveyed by the film is thus bound up in its assertion of scientific fact and its capacity to convince viewers of the realities of environmental crisis. Documentary has a ready association with science, courtesy of Bill Nichols' formative writing, in *Representing Reality*, of its 'kinship' with 'discourses of sobriety', chief among which is science (3). Nichols posits that 'in documentary, realism serves to make an argument about the historical world persuasive' (165), so environmental documentary can be approached as a genre that truthfully articulates the uncomfortable realities of climate change and sets about convincing viewers of the severity of associated disasters. Documentary attempts to convincingly render reality in this manner risk partaking in the totalizing tendencies of the view from above. This is particularly the case for *An Inconvenient Truth*, with its titular invocation of a singular, universalizing truth, and its masterful male protagonist.

The film swiftly establishes Gore's centrality as it introduces viewers to the global scale of environmental crisis. Its opening moments create an oscillation between a localized viewpoint belonging to its protagonist and a literal aerial view from above. Firstly, viewers see a flowing river glimpsed through trees rustling in a breeze as Gore's voice wistfully evokes the scenario: 'in the distance you hear a cow ... it's quiet, it's peaceful.' The film cuts abruptly to a laptop screen on which the Earthrise photograph is displayed. The image of Earth, taken from lunar orbit, fills the frame. This is the first image of the slideshow, and it begins his lecture presentation. Gore stands before a live audience, another enormous screen behind him and yet more dotted around the room such that Earthrise proliferates in a way resembling the 'doomsday scenario interface' of *Southland Tales*. Although vastly different in style, these two American films, released the same year, are united in their rapid cutting between dispersed locations and their collation of different media modes as throughout *An Inconvenient Truth*, Gore interprets data and different media shown on these screens, also discussing his associations with politicians and scientists. Viewers quickly understand that he is knowledgeable and well connected across the world. Thus, while the film begins with a whimsical, nostalgic overture seemingly grounded in nature, it is established properly in this hyper-connected lecture scenario.

Gore shows more images of Earth: The Blue Marble, a photograph taken from Apollo 17 in which the Sun illuminates all of Earth's face; a time-lapse image of the planet's rotation taken from the Galileo spacecraft; a globe composed of 3000 thousand satellite images stitched together such that there are no clouds blocking the view of continents and oceans. The final image morphs and squiggly lines representing solar radiation appear across it as Gore explains 'the basic science of global warming'. In this sequence, the advancing technical apparatuses of spacecraft, photography and digital technology picture the planet from above in increasingly sophisticated ways, each image revealing more of the Earth's surface than the last. Haraway writes of how modern instruments of visualization are 'without apparent limit', and this sequence is almost a literalization of 'the god trick of seeing everything from nowhere' (581). Given the film's genre-defining significance, this sequence also illustrates Alaimo's contention that abstracted aerial visioning is 'the dominant visual apparatus of the anthropocene' (*Exposed* 146). These images link science and truth with omniscience and literal visual capacity (i.e. the ability to see as much as possible). Following Gore's contemplative musings, they serve as the proper introduction to the perspective on the environment and climate change posited by *An Inconvenient Truth*. The river glimpsed by viewers in the film's opening moments is unnamed and remains nowhere. Though it presumably exists somewhere, its specificity is unimportant. Only the totalizing, abstracted image of Earth is real in the sense of documentary realism offered by Nichols: technological abstraction and aerial distance work to generate the historical world that the film persuades us to care about when Gore says of The Blue Marble, 'Isn't that beautiful?'

Analysing Gore's role throughout *An Inconvenient Truth* helps contextualize the way the film utilizes this type of aerial imagery to represent disaster. With his attire and demeanour, Gore becomes a uniformed, corporate, scientifically astute hero not unlike those of Hollywood disaster movies. Indeed, Janet Walker notes a prevailing criticism of the film: it insults viewers' 'ability to connect with a film minus a crusading hero' ('Projecting Sea Level Rise' 63). Walker's observation intimates how the foregrounding of an active, activist male hero (often a celebrity actor) has become a convention in high profile environmental documentary and indicates how Gore's heroic representation is key to both the format and the reception of *An Inconvenient Truth*. Resonance between Gore's representation and the heroic protagonist of Roland Emmerich's *The Day After Tomorrow* is particularly striking, and there are further resonances between these two films that are frequently referenced together as a 'touchstone moment in the history of environmental cinema' (Rust 192). The disaster blockbuster may even be seen as instructive for the environmental documentary, as producer and environmental activist Laurie David saw Gore present his slide show at a New York premiere party for Emmerich's film (Rust 200). Some broad formal similarities between Hollywood films and argumentative environmental documentaries are noted by Hughes, who observes that both activist documentaries and environmental features 'display a shared structure, a consistent set of characters and a recognizable iconography', being 'peopled by good and bad scientists, passionate but rational campaigners, committed journalists, farmers and agricultural workers, enlightened consumers, politicians of all kinds, die-hard and reformed entrepreneurs, and good and evil corporate managers' (8). *The Day After Tomorrow*'s hero Jack Hall is a passionate scientist who becomes a political campaigner. A paleoclimatologist, he travels from a scientific outpost in Antarctica to a UN conference in New Delhi where misguided politicians dismiss his urgent concerns about an impending global catastrophe. Returning to the United States, he braves a frozen-over New York City to save his son. Gore, in *An Inconvenient Truth*, is an enlightened American politician, a passionate campaigner who befriends good scientists and activists, facing down bad politicians and sceptics across the globe. Gore is, Stephen Rust posits, crafted into 'an image of intellectual and ethical authority on global warming' (200).

Like disaster movie protagonists, he is represented in a way that draws on an iconography of heroic masculinity, granting him the attributes of the Hollywood hero who saves the day. As he invokes technological, masterful images of Earth, he echoes the dominant frameworks of masculinism, corporate managerialism and Americanism prevalent in Hollywood disaster movies.

Whole earth imagery also compounds Gore's cosmopolitan identity; his representation as someone who first hand navigates the entire world with ease, transcending national boundaries and geographical situatedness. As Gore demonstrates and discusses a range of climate-related issues during his lecture, the film cuts to show him at various locations around the world. He discusses his travels extensively, even nonchalantly saying, 'I went up to the North Pole, I went under that ice cap in a nuclear submarine'. In his slides, viewers see remote places: Antarctica, Greenland, Alaska, Patagonia and Mount Kilimanjaro. Cutting between locations, the film takes on a circumnavigatory logic. Toggling between nations where global disaster manifests in different ways emulates *The Day After Tomorrow* which, like *Independence Day* and various other Hollywood disaster movies, cuts between multiple global locations: a hailstorm in Tokyo, tornadoes in Los Angeles and flooding in New York. Gore's representation in *An Inconvenient Truth* is cited by Ursula Heise as exemplary of a contemporary identity and subject-position she names 'the world traveller as an epic, global self' (64); 'a Western environmentalist self that at the beginning of the twenty-first century is nomadic and cosmopolitan' (67). Centring the powerful, world-travelling Gore, *An Inconvenient Truth* configures an ethics and a politics of positioning that is based on the traversal of disparate locations and the simultaneous accretion of their images.

By accumulating images thusly, the film conquers the world as it attempts to save it from disaster. For Heise, a problem with this global perspective on environmental issues is that it countermands 'older commitments to the local' that 'sought to base an environmentalist ethic on the in-depth knowledge and care for the place one inhabits' (64). Tensions between globally nomadic cosmopolitanism and localized care may be understood as manifestations of the dichotomous opposition of 'world system' to 'local knowledge' posited by Haraway (588). Attempting to redress this tension, *An Inconvenient Truth* repeatedly returns to the American South, balancing its travels with sequences described by Heise as 'autobiographical reminiscences' (64). Sepia-toned and seemingly composed of archival footage, these sequences operate in the slower, introspective register of the film's opening shot as Gore discusses his upbringing in Tennessee and espouses appreciation for the natural environment. They engage a nostalgic, romantic American frame as the basis for Gore's heroic identity, and in doing so, they anchor the subject-position he presents firmly in the United States. This emphasizes an Americanist bias, and means the global environmental issues the film details are consistently pictured from a US perspective that risks appearing domineering and self-serving. Indeed, Walker observes a general didacticism in the film (76) and notes that its autobiographical nature has been perceived as 'careerist partisan politics' (63). The extent of this domineering bias becomes most apparent when the film visualizes disaster, and particularly when it briefly turns to the Pacific.

A sequence late in the film deals with sea level rise, picturing it as a disaster that impends if global warming is not combatted adequately. Gore describes a future scenario in which 'the maps of the world will have to be redrawn' following polar ice melt, and the film cuts to a map-like aerial view of the Floridian coastline, which is rapidly inundated in a CGI-simulated flood. This visualization is repeated with aerial views of the San Francisco Bay Area, the Netherlands, Beijing, Shanghai, Kolkata and Bangladesh: all heavily populated Northern Hemisphere locations. Gore warns of a hundred million refugees displaced by floods, and the film cuts to a zoomed-in satellite view of Manhattan. This image has greater clarity than the previous ones: buildings, landmarks, even individual trees are discernible before dark water seeps through the streets, overflowing everything. Gore references the 9/11 Memorial as well as Hurricane Katrina, giving these flooding images historical resonance and lodging them in the register of 'large events' such as the Great Depression and the Second World War that Michael Renov argues are typically reflected with 'masculinist bias' in documentary (*The Subject of Documentary* xiv). The ostensibly global disaster of sea level rise is thus overlaid onto events that are firmly inscribed within and articulated by discourses of American patriotism and militarism. Use of special effects here again highlights *An Inconvenient Truth*'s proximity to Hollywood. Walker calls these sequences 'coastal inundation animations', and notes they are commissioned from 'visual effects expert' Brian Fisher whose credits also include *Avatar* (2009) and *Transformers: Dark Side of the Moon* (2011) (74), which all portray large-scale destruction. As noted in Chapter 1, formulaic and increasingly spectacular flooding sequences in which a wave careens across the frame, devastating ships, bridges, oil rigs, skyscrapers, entire cities recur in Hollywood's disaster genre since *The Poseidon Adventure*. This is often shown with aerial shots, including in *Deep Impact*, *The Day After Tomorrow*, *2012* and more recently *San Andreas*, *Geostorm* (2017) and *Moonfall* (2022). While *An Inconvenient Truth*'s inundation animations are not as sophisticated as these Hollywood shots, they share their capacity for spectacle and their rendering of the ocean as elemental mass portentous of large-scale death. As the Netherlands is submerged, Gore overtones, 'absolutely devastating'.

Simulated CGI oceans, Erika Balsom contends, 'offer all too fitting an allegory for an impossible desire prevalent in our time – namely, the total algorithmic control of reality, whereby quality becomes quantity and the complexities of life are "solved" through planning, metrics, and predictive models' (*An Oceanic Feeling* 21). Joining in Hollywood's disaster style, *An Inconvenient Truth* aspires to an indexicality that is omniscient and omnipotent, resonating with imperialist impulses towards total control. In this way, it is emblematic of a recent strain of top-down visual media located by theorists of various orientation. T. J. Demos identifies 'Anthropocene visuality' (*Against the Anthropocene* 28): schematic imagery, 'shifting data visualizations of the globe' (12) that enable visual verisimilitude and connote indexicality but do not correlate with reality as human eyes would see it. Alaimo, similarly, observes that 'prevalent depictions of the anthropocene emphasize the colossal scale of anthropogenic impact by zooming out – up and away from the planet' (*Exposed* 145). Astrida Neimanis observes that the zoomed-out CGI visuality of the website and video project *Welcome to the Anthropocene* offers 'a perspective that our living, breathing, wet bodies … could never inhabit' (162). For Sean Cubitt, *An Inconvenient Truth* typifies how 'data visualisations, embracing cartography, numbers, graphics, and simulations', which all deploy unattainable perspectives, have become 'integral to the discourse of climate change' because, he asserts, 'we are more convinced by numbers than pictures' (280). This assertion, while perhaps dismissive of the affective and political power of impressionistic images, corroborates the sober, scientific understanding of documentary's capacity for realism that *An Inconvenient Truth* trades in. The film's view from above colonizes notions of objectivity, subordinating images at ground level, de-emphasizing emotionality, subjectivity, locality and materiality beneath technological, scientific, masculinist, Americanist power. With its abstracted, aerial visioning, the film distances itself from encounter with the material forces of the disasters that it seeks to reckon with.

This becomes evident as an ethical problematic when the South Pacific locations *An Inconvenient Truth* visits are thoroughly disavowed, even as evocative images of them are deployed in service of Gore's arguments. While hypothetical sea level rise in the Northern Hemisphere is visualized with spectacular, expensive imagery, the means with which the film represents already-occurring sea level rise in the South are comparatively meagre. Gore mentions the Pacific in a single sentence, claiming that 'the people in these Pacific Islands have all had to move to New Zealand' as the film shows two still photographs. In the first, a woman wades through knee-deep water, and in the second, a wave splashes across a building on a shoreline. These images are, for Walker, an exception to how the film 'barely depicts affected individuals' (63), but this momentary depiction is not adequately contextualized, and the appearance of these photographs has been heavily criticized as misleading. David Corlett observes that viewers are not told what is happening, and there is no evidence of evacuation (24). Carol Farbotko notes that Gore does not name the island depicted, but explains the photographs are credited to Mark Lynas, whose book *High Tide* specifies that they show Funafuti, an atoll in Tuvalu (Farbotko 57). Nina Hall highlights the disjuncture between Gore's claim and the historical geopolitical context: 'Gore's claims in the documentary were mistaken. New Zealand has not, then or now, accepted anyone as a climate refugee. Although the Ministry of Foreign Affairs and Trade issued a correction, the story and image of "climate refugees" remains a powerful reference point' (151).

Functioning as visible evidence for Gore's claims and embedded closely to the CGI inundation animations, *An Inconvenient Truth*'s use of these images configures the Pacific as a place of advanced disaster and displacement, suggesting to viewers that the flooding threatening Manhattan is already underway here, in this ostensibly far-flung corner of the world. The film thus casts the Pacific as a sunken wasteland, like the dystopia of *Waterworld*. The historical and personal processes of loss and adaptation involved with rising seas in Tuvalu are obfuscated, as the film's view of the Pacific indulges wider perspectives of the region that are ignorant of both cultural history and contemporary circumstances. Just as Island nations in the Pacific have long been a locus for disaster inflicted from elsewhere – invasion, resource extraction, slavery, nuclear explosions and irradiation – they have also long been the focus for various representational tropes: fantasies of picturesque sunsets, mysterious and monstrous flora and fauna, and the like, and sea level rise and climate vulnerability can be added to both of these lists. Engaging these tropes, *An Inconvenient Truth* takes part in a larger envisioning of Pacific climate disaster: a far-reaching, widespread 'image of the "sinking islands states"' (1) and Islander vulnerability that is constituent in and 'formed around' what Charlotte Weatherill describes as 'a history of Western extinction and vulnerability narratives that are steeped in colonial logics' (2). *An Inconvenient Truth*, viewing the region from above, joins in a history of imperialist disregard for Pacific peoples and cultures as it projects an image of the region suited to its own argumentative agenda. It thus eschews ethical responsibility for its Pacific subjects, however briefly they feature.

The film concludes by instructing viewers to emulate a response to climate disaster embodied by Gore. Gore imagines a dialogue between viewers and future generations who 'ask themselves, "What were our parents thinking? Why didn't they wake up when they had a chance?"' An imperative is then delivered when he says, 'we have to hear that question from them now' and text appears onscreen: 'Are you ready to change the way you live? The climate crisis can be solved. Here's how to start.'

The film shows a list of actions that individuals can take to solve the climate crisis and avert disaster. They are mostly consumer choices: buy energy efficient lightbulbs, buy a hybrid car, switch to renewable energy sources. An upbeat song by Melissa Etheridge plays that impels action, underscoring the argumentative, persuasive tone of the film and framing its response to disaster as a renewed, feel-good vitality of consciousness. But these instructions correspond to the banal, moralistic, assignations of responsibility described by Blanchot, contra a more profound Levinasian ethical responsibility, that are associated with a particular 'bourgeoise manner' and embodied by 'a mature, lucid, conscientious man, who acts with circumspection, who takes into account all elements of a given situation, calculates and decides' (*The Writing of the Disaster* 25). *An Inconvenient Truth* posits that by behaving in accord with these instructions, viewers can join Gore's heroic crusade against climate change, becoming an informed person of action.

There is little doubt that *An Inconvenient Truth* succeeds as a call to environmentalist action. It establishes a convincing impression of the global-scale effects of anthropogenic climate change early in the twenty-first century, creates a compelling atmosphere of urgency and motivates viewers to forestall disaster. However, when considered with this book's deeper ethical concerns in mind, it remains troubling due to its disavowal of context in favour of persuasive rhetoric. The perspective of the view from above is, as Alaimo writes, problematic due to its abstracting powers: 'the viewer enjoys a comfortable position outside the systems depicted' as detached aerial images actually function to 'make risk, harm, and suffering undetectable' (146). This view from above elides ethics because it constitutes an outlook necessarily turned away from the vicissitudes of immediate, real encounter with disaster. *An Inconvenient Truth* shows Al Gore encountering and mastering disaster from afar and via technological apparatuses. Despite the film's spectacular, scientifically informed visions of flooding, it obfuscates dimensions of harm by not actually showing or giving credence to people who are already complexly affected by the global flooding disasters it poses as a future threat. Orbiting around the cosmopolitan and conventionally heroic Gore instead, the film seeks to manage disaster with masculinist, technological dominance rather than reckon with its full emergence.

Before the Flood: Complicity and bad conscience

Released ten years after *An Inconvenient Truth*, *Before the Flood* also documents a globe-trotting male subject encountering disaster across the world. However, while it emulates some key formal strategies of Guggenheim's film, it establishes a crucially differentiated subjective disposition in the way its celebrity presenter faces up to climate change and climate disaster. The film follows Leonardo DiCaprio to various locations – the United States, Greenland, China, India, Denmark, and Kiribati and Palau in the Pacific – where he interviews local experts, scientists, politicians and activists, about environmental crises and advocates for climate action. Like *An Inconvenient Truth*, it is strongly autobiographical: DiCaprio is credited as a producer, and the film is framed as a collaboration between him and director Fisher Stevens. It builds on popular recognition and media attention he received after presenting speeches at UN climate summits. It is ironic, given the prominence of sea level rise as a climate disaster, that DiCaprio's celebrity status was cemented with his lead role in *Titanic*, a disaster movie about a sinking ship. In the context of documentary, however, his renown as a performer works to distance him somewhat from the notions of scientific objectivity and empirical truth that *An Inconvenient Truth* attaches to Gore. Rather, DiCaprio's climate activism and his encounters with disaster are framed in a distinctly non-expert way that emphasizes his emotional responses. He invokes this dynamic himself in a 2014 UN speech when he pronounces, 'I stand before you not as an expert' ('Leonardo DiCaprio at the UN').

Centring DiCaprio at the outset, *Before the Flood* (like *An Inconvenient Truth*) establishes its protagonist's childhood as a narrative frame that contextualizes and balances its global purview. DiCaprio describes lying in a crib as an infant, gazing at a poster of Hieronymus Bosch's 'nightmarish' triptych *The Garden of*

Earthly Delights. The painting subsequently functions as an allegory for climate-changed Earth, each panel sequentially gesturing towards pre-disaster, trans-disaster and post-disaster phases of global eco-catastrophe. DiCaprio describes the third panel as a 'twisted, decayed, burnt landscape, a paradise that has been degraded and destroyed', engaging a mood of pessimism and contrition that persists throughout the film. As viewers see him witness degradation and destruction, DiCaprio comes to embody a more complex and emotional response to disaster than Gore. Gore echoes Hollywood's invocations, modelling a response to disaster that is relentless in its expansive, global heroism. The urgency of his quest powers his determination and optimism, with no room for doubt or reflexive questioning. DiCaprio, however, frequently reflects on his own role as a celebrity activist and expresses doubt about whether climate disaster can be averted. He even questions the value of *An Inconvenient Truth*'s climate advocacy, pessimistically saying, 'It seemed like a positive thing at the time, you know, changing your lightbulb. But it's pretty clear that we're way beyond that point now. Things have taken a massive turn for the worse'. The film's representation of DiCaprio highlights what Heise calls 'cosmopolitanism with a bad conscience' (67), an aspect of the globally nomadic environmentalist identity, the 'carbon-offset self' (64), that more clearly signals complicity with environmental degradation; 'an awareness that the necessity of mobility always seems countermanded by the imperative to be local and to avoid the damage that global nomadism inflicts' (67). DiCaprio's self-awareness and bad conscience are foregrounded especially during a long passage midway through the film when viewers see him journey from India to the Pacific via Los Angeles. At key moments, his engagements with the contexts he travels through prompt him to contemplate his own complicity with the burgeoning disasters of climate change and position himself, along with viewers in developed Western countries, as guilty of precipitating global crisis via carbon-dependent lifestyles.

As it stages a global tour, *Before the Flood* presents various local perspectives as foils to a prevailing Americanist view embodied by DiCaprio. In India, DiCaprio is shown in conversation with Sunita Narain of the Centre for Science and Environment discussing energy consumption in India and disparities between lifestyles in India and the United States. Other local experts also directly address the camera, reinforcing the notion that DiCaprio himself does not have expertise. Intercut with DiCaprio's and Narain's conversation, the Secretary of the Ministry of Environment, Forest and Climate change Ashok Lavasa informs viewers that 'about thirty percent of households in India are yet to have access to electricity' and that coal reservoirs – a non-renewable energy source, the use of which worsens climate crisis and thus hastens the eruption of disaster – can make electricity accessible and affordable. Balancing the perspectives of DiCaprio, Narain and Lavasa, this sequence establishes that it is hypocritical for wealthy American environmentalists like DiCaprio, who campaign against the use of non-renewable energy, to expect Indians to forego the advantages of the resource-dependent lifestyle they themselves have enjoyed for decades. Narain even admonishes DiCaprio, saying 'I know you're an American, and please don't take this amiss, but your consumption is really going to put a hole in the planet', and as viewers see his face in shot/reverse-shot editing, he looks uncomfortable and contrite. She shows him a chart and some graphs, clearly visible on camera, indicating that the electricity consumed by one American at home is equivalent to that consumed by thirty-four Indians. When DiCaprio attempts to respond by citing American investment in renewable energy infrastructure, arguing that financial investment can solve climate-related problems, he notices her shaking her head and pauses, allowing her admonishment to continue: 'Who will invest? Let's be *real* about this…. *We* are doing more investment in solar today, *China* is doing much more investment in solar today than the U.S. is.' When DiCaprio is shown in conversation with experts, listening as well as talking, his complicity with global ecological disaster, and that of Americans generally, is clearly established. Where *An Inconvenient Truth* makes truth the property of its masculinist, Americanist perspective, this film positions Narain, an Indian woman, as a bearer of inconvenient, uncomfortable truth delivered persuasively to its male protagonist.

Narain has the final word in their conversation, and with it she draws attention to problems of representation and global economic disparity that inhere in both climate activism and theorization of the Anthropocene. She tells DiCaprio: 'People like me, we are rich enough to withstand the first hit of climate change, but it's the poor of India, it's the poor of Africa, it's the poor of Bangladesh who are impacted today by what I believe is the first signs of climate change.'

By differentiating rich from poor as well as Indians, Bangladeshis and Africans from North Americans, Narain highlights what Neimanis refers to as the 'homogenization and levelling of human difference' (163) present in Anthropocene discourse. Narain has worked as a researcher, policy-maker and activist since at least the early 1990s to address inequalities within global environmental discourses. Writing in 1991, with words that now seem prescient of environmental documentaries like the two discussed in this chapter, she argues that 'Third World nations … cannot depend on Western institutions to present a true picture of the global situation and safeguard their interests' (Agarwal and Narain 24). Critiquing the 'mathematical jugglery' utilized in a 1990 US study of carbon emissions, she argues that its 'main intention seems to be to blame developing countries for global warming and perpetuate the current global inequality in the use of the earth's environment and its resources' (1). This inequality is, for Narain, 'an excellent example of environmental colonialism' (81), a nomenclature that augurs and resonates with more recently theorized notions of climate coloniality, a phenomenon that becomes apparent in the very forum that DiCaprio has utilized to prosecute his cosmopolitan climate action: UN Climate Change Conferences. Farhana Sultana describes the 2021 Conference held in Glasgow, COP26, as 'dismal' (1). She describes a dynamic whereby leaders and activists mostly representing the Global South and colonized nations criticize the 'failures and unkept promises' (1) of ostensible attempts at climate change mitigation by powerful Western governments, corporations and elites, identifying not just 'climate justice failures' but framing these machinations – delay, distraction, performativity, co-optation – as 'colonial and racial tactics of control and disposal of marginalised communities' (2). For example, Sultana cites Bolivian President Luis Acre who describes 'concerns about carbon offsetting and the imposition of rules from powerful countries on historically marginalized countries' as 'new carbon colonialism'' (1). Staging an interview between DiCaprio, a wealthy American climate activist, and Narain, an expert in climate politics from India, *Before the Flood* (released eight years before COP26) goes some way towards reflecting the realities of these dynamics whereas *An Inconvenient Truth*, looking over the Pacific, simply recapitulates them. DiCaprio's attempts at justification leave him appearing flustered and futile, reaching for excuses, and their exchange leaves viewers with a clear impression of Narain's frustration.

It becomes immediately supplanted, however, as *Before the Flood* refocuses intently on DiCaprio in the following sequence, staging his global travel and highlighting his emotionality as it shows him attempting to face up to his personal complicity. Emphasizing both the extremity of DiCaprio's global nomadism and the disjuncture between his American lifestyle and disaster in the Global South, the film cuts from a flooded farm in India to a travel montage with a shot of clouds, then an overhead shot of an airport terminal crowded with planes. DiCaprio walks, suitcase in hand and steps into an SUV. After another cut, he is shown driving. A road sign indicates he is in California and a wide highway is reflected in his dark glasses, which are centred in the frame in a moment that creates a sense of pensive reflexivity. This montage prompts viewers to imagine DiCaprio looking down on disaster-wracked landscapes from an aeroplane window, contemplating how his lifestyle spells disaster for others. His bad conscience is highlighted in his narration:

> My footprint is probably a lot bigger than most people's and there are times when I question: what is the right thing to do? What actions should we be taking? There are over a billion people out there without electricity and they want lights, they want heat, they want the lifestyle that we've had in the United States for the last hundred years. If we're going to solve this problem we all have a responsibility to set an example.

Showing its cosmopolitan protagonist asking questions of himself and viewers, the film conjures a sense of shared ethical responsibility, perhaps even hinting that the response to disaster it stages may be inadequate. The view from above posited by *Before the Flood* remains detached, removed from context and specificity in a similar way to *An Inconvenient Truth*. But, rather than looking at the world with ruthless heroic conviction, it turns inward to question itself. Like DiCaprio himself, it seems aware of the hypocrisy and colonialist overtures involved in dominant forms of climate action and while it compels contrition and regret, it is powerless to imagine another way of encountering or representing climate disaster.

As the travel montage continues, viewers see more aerial views: a city with skyscrapers foregrounded and urban sprawl receding in the background; an unnamed island city, mid-density structures crowding the shoreline; a mostly submerged atoll where a copse of trees stands on one island. DiCaprio has arrived in the Pacific. These rapid cuts between locations mirror *An Inconvenient Truth*'s satellite imagery and CGI simulations as urbanized human presence decreases while the water level is raised after each cut. But this film actually visits many of the locations that are only pictured in Gore's slideshow, and this indicates a greater attention to context. DiCaprio's perspective remains elevated and problematic, but not as detached as Gore's technological envisioning of sea level rise. When viewers see him witnessing disaster first-hand, through his reflexive expressions of doubt, he comes to share in some of the complexity and contradiction that Haraway seeks in a view from the body (589).

When *Before the Flood* travels to the Pacific, the pre-disaster and post-disaster tenses invoked in DiCaprio's discussion of *The Garden of Earthly Delights* become meshed in a way that validates his doubt about whether eco-catastrophe can be averted. He is shown in conversation with Anote Tong, president of Kiribati (and himself the focus of *Anote's Ark*), and Tommy Remengesau, president of Palau, and viewers also see images of buildings in disrepair, rubble-strewn clearings and waves lashing roads, in addition to idyllic beaches. Tong says, 'islands in the Pacific, we're a paradise in peril', and this reminds viewers of DiCaprio's evocation of Bosch's third panel as a 'degraded and destroyed' paradise. Rather than the burnt landscape that the film's opening prophecies, however, these images position islands in the Pacific as evidence of the storm-beaten and half-sunken world that will result from failure to manage disaster adequately. Thusly, *Before the Flood*, like *An Inconvenient Truth*, confirms that global ecological disaster is already underway for some (these Islanders can be added to Narain's list of those impacted by climate change) but remains only a looming threat for those, like DiCaprio, who chiefly perpetrate the disastrous effects of climate change such as sea level rise. Concluding the film's brief Pacific visit, the camera moves undersea to show images of vibrant, colourful marine life before cutting to stark images of bleached coral. A marine ecologist speaks about the devastation of coral reefs and his words both underscore and add another dimension to the guilt and responsibility of the industrialized Western world: 'what we've done to the rest of the world is just ... it's criminal.'

The kind of ethical response posited by *Before the Flood* is most concisely apparent in its final sequence, which reproduces an environmental documentary trope from *An Inconvenient Truth* while emphasizing key differences between DiCaprio and Gore as subjects in encounter with forces of disaster. Instructive text appears onscreen while a song plays, telling viewers how to act to mitigate the effects of climate change. The bad conscience of the 'carbon-offset self' (Heise 64) modelled by DiCaprio is pushed onto viewers as they are informed the film's carbon footprint was offset by paying a voluntary carbon tax and directed to a website where they can calculate and offset their own 'climate impact'. Where *An Inconvenient Truth* features Melissa Etheridge's upbeat music and impels an activated, bold and energized consciousness, the song that concludes *Before the Flood* is by Trent Reznor, an artist usually associated with downcast, depressive music. Sparse, lethargic piano notes circle as Reznor sings literally of a belated face-to-face encounter and a recognition of blame. This oblique, sombre song suggests a failure to face up to the disasters of the climate crisis, and another abdication of responsibility. It underscores the way that DiCaprio's vexed facial expressions as he encounters disaster throughout the film, and is shown literally face to face in conversation with Narain, hint at internalized processes of acknowledgement, responsibility and regret, before cuts whisk both him and viewers away to another location. But at the conclusion of the film, his introspection, voiced by Reznor, ultimately gives way to myopic, self-centred pessimism rather than resulting in any profoundly renewed consciousness or the emergence, via ethics, of a new subjective disposition in response to suffering. Blanchot writes that, following Levinas, the responsibility of ethical recognition 'disengages the me from me' (*The Writing of the Disaster* 24), compelling a profound overhauling of one's sense of self, but this film only consolidates the carbon-offset self as a contemporary mode of engaging with climate change's disasters more broadly where, glimpsing the harm one's lifestyle might afflict on others elsewhere, the Western, globe-trotting, high-consumption subject expresses remorse but continues apace. Thus, although *Before the Flood* stages in DiCaprio a recognition of complicity with disaster, it suggests that this recognition comes too late and is not significant enough to allay full-blown climate catastrophe and prevent the suffering of many people. Where Al Gore encounters disaster in a way that mimics the authority, certainty and action of Hollywood's disaster movie heroes, DiCaprio appears forlorn and paralysed, unable to move through his own bad conscience into any profound ethical revelation or transformation.

This chapter has drawn a set of comparisons between prominent environmental documentaries and Hollywood convention, most clearly via comparison of *An Inconvenient Truth* and the Hollywood disaster blockbuster *The Day After Tomorrow*, and analysis of how Americanist, male protagonists are shown encountering disaster. Another parallel that creates further context for understanding the significance of DiCaprio's response to climate disaster, and the way a pessimistic consciousness is imbued in *Before the Flood*, is also apparent between the documentary and Adam McKay's *Don't Look Up*. Produced five years after Stevens' and DiCaprio's documentary (and fifteen after Guggenheim's and Gore's), *Don't Look Up* meshes Hollywood's disaster genre with political satire and stars DiCaprio as Randall Mindy, a scientist attempting to warn politicians and media about a comet that threatens to wipe out life on Earth. Though *Don't Look Up* does not reference climate change or environmental crises at all, it is supported by an impact campaign focusing on climate action and, as Julie Doyle writes, 'functions as a useful reflection point for popular cultural and mainstream climate communications' (2). Blackly comedic, the film reflects darkly on celebrity and gender, and poses a conflict between scientists as bearers of truth and politicians and media figures as obstinate obstructionists, intent on inaction, invested in denying the reality of the situation and desperate for a quick, easy remedy. Doyle concisely describes how the film critiques 'existing values of late-capitalism by satirizing speculative techno-fixes, extractive capitalism and celebrity culture as interconnected social, economic and political systems preventing action' but despite this, crucially, 'fails to centre any marginalised voices, continuing to privilege global north perspectives, even as these are satirised' (6).

Though it impresses a degree of self-awareness and a depressive, forlorn disposition into its protagonist, *Before the Flood* essentially commits to the same failure, recapitulating the politics of the aerial imagery, cosmopolitan logic and ties to discourses of sobriety and scientific knowledge modelled by *An Inconvenient Truth* and eliding to work justice for those worst afflicted by climate disaster. Configuring an imagination of disaster thusly, both films indulge in aspirations towards universal rationality, common language, world system and master theory that, for Haraway, are associated with empiricism and reductionism (188). The way they work towards thorough, penetrating explanation and explication of disaster recapitulates the gaze of the historically dominant, masculinist subject who imposes a dialectics of self and other, subjugating alterity into negative presence and pejoration. As Gore and DiCaprio traverse the climate-changing world, they are shown to effectively distance themselves from its disaster – certainly materially, if not emotionally – and though DiCaprio's myopic regression represents a distinction from Gore's heroic overtures and signals a changed consciousness, an affliction of guilt, it does not necessarily come closer to ameliorating the effects of the global climate disaster it bears witness to.

4

The view from a body

There Once Was an Island and *On an Unknown Beach*, the two documentaries this chapter focuses on, are firmly anchored in their Oceanic contexts. Not as easily categorized as *An Inconvenient Truth* and *Before the Flood* nor as widely viewed, lacking global distribution and massive influence, they are nonetheless worthy of consideration because of their formal innovations, affective resonances and potential for an altogether different configuration of documentary realism that reflects their disastrous contexts and keys in to distinct ethical possibilities. This potential, emphasizing creativity, subjectivity and emotionality, centres on film's capacity to convey specific traumas and memories and honestly represent the lived experience of individuals and communities who are rooted in place and in history as they are subject to disaster.

There Once Was an Island deals with anthropogenic climate change and sea level rise and is clearly an environmental documentary, but it eschews the argumentative, persuasive approach modelled by *An Inconvenient Truth*. Rather, it is exemplary of what Helen Hughes considers a contemplative response to environmental crisis. Contemplative environmental documentaries involve viewers more deeply with the worlds they represent, 'refraining from occupying the space for thought and feeling with commentary, dialogue and music' (14). Like other films Hughes categorizes as contemplative including *Sleep Furiously* (2007), *Modern Life* (2008) and *Sweetgrass* (2009), *There Once Was an Island* is concerned with a way of life endangered in a late capitalist world, representing people whose relationship to place is forced to change because of onrushing modernity and industrialization. A specific emotional register takes hold in such films and, Hughes posits, a mournful ambivalence is connoted as they 'do not argue for the preservation of the past, but rather than presenting the future they dwell in a present that is in a kind of limbo' (15). However, *There Once Was an Island* is distinguished from the above films because of its Oceanic context and the geographical and cultural distance between its subjects and the thoroughly industrialized world whose carbon-heavy lifestyle endangers them. As filmmakers travel to the Takuu atoll in Papua New Guinea to document the lives of its Polynesian inhabitants whose home is imperilled by sea level rise, the film also resembles ethnographic films which Charles Musser argues are significant to the formation of environmental documentary as a genre, such as *The Inland Sea* (1991) and *The Saltmen of Tibet* (1997), 'focussing on peoples whose traditional lifestyles are under threat if not rapidly disappearing' (54). Situated in the Pacific, it also belongs to a sea level rise documentary subgenre, identified by Elizabeth DeLoughrey, of films that 'focus almost exclusively on village life, feature ample images of the ocean, islanders fishing, children running on the beach, sunsets, palm trees, the camera person at work on the island, images of flooded homes, and interviews with subjects who are considering migration' ('The Sea is Rising' 189).

However, while it shares many of these themes and visual tropes, my analysis explores how it offers a distinct outlook on disastrous sea level rise.

On an Unknown Beach, meanwhile, defies classificatory frameworks. It is best framed as an intermeshing of three disparate biographical threads, each of which documents the activities of a person connected to ruination or the eruption of death in and around Aotearoa New Zealand. David Hornblow is a poet and actor undergoing hypnotherapy to confront personal traumas. Bruce Russell is a musician and 'improvised sound worker' practicing and performing in Christchurch, my hometown wrecked by an earthquake. Di Tracey is a scientist surveying coral devastated by industrial fishing. The thread of the film that follows Tracey's observation of ecological extinction could be considered environmental documentary, but it is not concerned with conveying scientific knowledge or appealing to political viewpoints. Although the film incorporates dialogue-heavy sequences, including testimonial address, it is extremely poetic, mainly characterized by pronounced use of sound and music alongside fluid, impressionistic camera techniques.

Both films partake in elements of conventional realist film style, as their Oceanic aesthetics share in those aspects of reality that Kracauer calls 'physical existence' or 'material reality' (28), conveying the 'emphasis on the immediacy of experience' Ian Aitken describes as constituent of realism (35) as they represent impressions of historical, material reality. Their logics are embedded rather than circumnavigatory as they work towards deeper understandings of life (and death) in specific South Pacific locations, and the ocean itself becomes a key aesthetic component. Both films have loose narrative structures that foreground the lived experiences of vulnerable people displaced, in different ways, by disaster. The Takuu people are exemplary of a new form of displacement observed by Rob Nixon that refers not to exile or migratory movement but to 'loss of the land and resources ... that leaves communities stranded in a place stripped of the very characteristics that made it habitable' (*Slow Violence* 19). Though not post-mortem protagonists in Elsaesser's sense ('World Cinema' 9–10), they are indelibly marked by their encounter with disaster, which forces them into an unknown reality. Alongside the subjects of *On an Unknown Beach*, they are presented as exposed subjects, an understanding of positionality that Stacy Alaimo advocates: 'To counter the dominant figurations of the anthropocene, which abstract the human from the material realm and obscure differentials of responsibility and harm, I propose that we think the anthropocene subject as immersed and enmeshed in the world' (*Exposed* 157).

The people of these films are, as cinematic subjects, 'always already penetrated by substances and forces that can never be accounted for' (*Exposed* 5), as disaster constitutes the world around them and they are forced to adapt.

As these two films creatively represent traumatized, displaced peoples, they can be usefully contextualized with branches of documentary theory counterposed to the ideas of sobriety and objectivity described in Chapter 3. While Nichols notes that '"Documentary" suggests fullness and completion, knowledge and fact, explanations of the social world and its motivating mechanisms' ('Getting to Know You ...' 174), he also concedes that it 'has come to suggest incompleteness and uncertainty, recollection and impression, images of personal worlds and their subjective construction' (174), and some documentaries 'insist on ... the body itself as witness' (175). These notions of documentary are not mutually exclusive (indeed, *An Inconvenient Truth* and *Before the Flood* centre on the personal worlds of Gore and DiCaprio), but, following Haraway, they may be understood as opposing ends of a 'charged dichotomy' (588) wherein objectivity and scientific knowledge have been historically and institutionally privileged over subjective experience. However, important theoretical rejoinders highlight the value of the latter. Smaill, for example, argues that 'the emotionality inherent to sobriety should be more fully examined' (*The Documentary* 1). When Nichols theorizes the observational documentary mode, relating it to ethnographic observation rather than exposition (*Representing Reality* 41), he suggests a realism that renders 'the historical world as we, in fact, experience it, usually on a quotidian basis' (43). Accounting for personal experience and exploration of subjective identity more fully via documentary, Michael Renov posits that documentary necessarily contains '"fictive" elements' wherein 'a presumably objective experience of the world encounters the necessity of creative intervention' ('Introduction' 2).

Representing disastrous events, a documentary realism that centres on subjectivity and emotionality rather than on objectivity and scientific knowledge would foreground subjective experiences grounded in the material world, conveying emotional responses to its contingencies. It would be fluid and processual, and may involve creative intervention into perceptual verisimilitude, as with realist style more generally. As Aitken writes, 'feelings, rather than ideas, should predominate' (34). Such a documentary realism resonates with Haraway's arguments for a view from the body, for an objectivity that is 'about particular and specific embodiment' (582) and for pictures of 'elaborate specificity and difference' (583). In contemporary disastrous contexts, such a realism promises a potent counterpoint to dominating, top-down visualizations of climate crisis, and a differentiated ethical engagement that may be more responsive in the face of disaster.

The view from a body of water

There Once Was an Island expands on the erroneous supposition that the Pacific is a zone of foregone catastrophe as its title conjures an irrevocable disaster. The titular island is Nukutoa, in the Takuu atoll near Papua New Guinea. In actuality, Nukutoa is not yet sunken, but it is adversely affected by sea level rise, subject to gradual erosion and susceptible to flooding. The film is produced and directed by New Zealander Briar March, and Alexa Weik von Mossner explains that production was initiated when the Islanders became 'worried enough about the ecological changes' to request that someone visit to document their situation (178). Viewers witness the experiences of three Islanders, mainly through observational footage and direct address, as they consider the possibility of mass relocation. As von Mossner notes, March became a participant-observer during production because she 'to some degree shared the life of the people she was portraying', gaining sustained first-hand experience of climate disaster (178). The circumstances of the film's production thus position it as a potential answer to Haraway's call for pictures of 'the loving care people might take to learn how to see faithfully from another's point of view' (583), as March seeks to help viewers understand impending disaster from the complex viewpoints of the Islanders.

The opening sequence offers a visual perspective immediate and literally oppositional to the abstraction of a view from above, staging an approach to Nukutoa that begins underwater. In the first shot, the camera lingers below the surface. In the next, the camera is half submerged, bobbling uncertainly in the water, pale clouds visible above the surface line. Subsequent shots show an oar striking the ocean, a canoe and the sun low in the sky. It is dawn, a liminal time of day connoting passage from one state to another. Slow motion shots draw viewers' attention to ripples emanating across the water, disturbing reflections and creating a fragile, pensive sense of time's passage. Islands appear in the distance.

Elizabeth DeLoughrey posits that sea level rise documentaries typically 'use an aerial view to locate the island on a map' (*Allegories of the Anthropocene* 185), but this film's aesthetics constitute a distinct locative technique. Approaching Nukutoa via this sequence that renders the emersion of the camera from the ocean facilitates an understanding of the implicit risk of the island's exposure to disaster and lends specificity and complexity to the way its inhabitants are shown. Submersion in the ocean is linked with a sense of material immediacy, as geographers Philip Steinberg and Kimberly Peters suggest when they explain, 'one can hike on a mountain trail without realising that one is traversing a landform whose existence is the result of tectonic subduction. It is much more difficult to step into the surf without encountering and reflecting on both water's mobility and its depth' (258). Steinberg and Peters posit that embracing the ocean's 'three-dimensional and turbulent materiality' engages 'oceanic thinking' and 'wet ontology' (247), and that via these experiential underpinnings, 'the liquidity of the ocean complicates control' (253). Reflecting this sense of materiality, the opening sequence of *There Once Was an Island* frustrates the controlling impulses of the view from above, particularly the way it is evident in top-down 'Anthropocene visuality' (Demos 28), as the mobile line of the ocean's surface frenetically bisects the frame, a sharp contrast with the smooth cartographic demarcations of aerial visualizations. The film thus begins grounded in its Oceanic location, its perspective embedded within the very force that threatens disaster, prompting viewers to consider it not as a simplified object of alterity – vast, unknowable, threatening – but as a place of contingency, connectivity and fluid orientation. Viewers see disaster specifically from this one island, contemplating the elemental exposure of Nukutoa and the bodies of its inhabitants.

When viewers are introduced to three Islanders – Satty, Endar and Teloo – we learn each has a distinct relationship to the ocean and unique enmeshments within their endangered environment. All three address the camera, and as they speak, the film shows footage of ostensibly ordinary, everyday things in lengthy shots allowing time for complex understandings of their relationships with the ocean to emerge. Satty informs viewers that he is married with children and is a farmer and fisherman – 'That's all I do here' – and as he is shown catching a fish, it becomes apparent that the ocean allows him to provide for his family. It also grants him respite from familial obligations, bringing him calmness when he is 'fed up with the kids', and a serene feeling arises when, pictured alone on a boat, he says, 'I guess what I like best is just sitting down and waiting for the fish'. Endar, contrastingly, is associated with larger ships that visit the island irregularly. Shown caring for her father, viewers learn that she is married to a Papua New Guinean and lives in Port Moresby but has temporarily returned to see her father before he dies. It becomes obvious that she considers her life on the mainland superior to life on the island, and her preference for the Islanders to all relocate is made clear: 'I am the one who changes a lot of things. It would be worse for me to stay on this island.' Viewers also learn that Endar is Christian, unlike most on Nukutoa. As another point of contrast, Teloo is introduced via discussion of Nukutoa's unique Polynesian culture, first shown instructing children to feed fish to birds which he explains is 'the first step to teaching your sons the cultural tradition fishing'. An older man, Teloo also teaches traditional dances and is positioned as a guardian of endangered cultural practices, saying Nukutoa 'is one of those few places around Papua New Guinea who still keep their cultures and traditions', but emphasizing that these traditions are under threat: 'I have already seen signs of a bad future for my children.'

As Satty, Endar and Teloo are introduced, images of the shoreline are interspersed in the flow of the film, prompting continued contemplation of their environmental situation. Teloo's worry is emphasized as the camera lingers on water lapping at banks and tree trunks, wind-stirred waves are foregrounded and the island looks small against the sky. Endar points to a spot in the water, saying it is where her kitchen used to be. Piano music fades in as the film again shows a slowed down submerged perspective, air bubbles floating towards the surface. Time passes and Nukutoa seems to edge into the post-disaster tense insinuated by the film's title. While the ocean retains its generic role as a threatening elemental force, it is also shown in these scenes to be much more: a source of nourishment and emotional sustenance, a meditative retreat, a connection to family who have migrated, and a powerful factor in culture and tradition.

Because it features three main subjects, *There Once Was an Island* establishes the potential for a range of subjective responses to the rising sea. When Satty, Endar and Teloo face flooding, eradication of crops, scarcity and death, they respond in ways that stem from their enmeshments. Satty describes emotional loss explaining how the white, sandy beaches he played on as a child have disappeared: 'that feeling that was with me since I was a kid, it's not here anymore. I think my place is losing its beauty'. Teloo shows viewers crops of giant taro, usually used in a ceremony, that have been devastated by the incursion of salt water. Endar visits officials on Bougainville to negotiate a process for mass relocation of the Islanders, and brings scientists from Australia to Nukutoa who she says 'will help to prove that there is a serious problem'. All three are presented as 'social actors' in the sense described by Bill Nichols (*Representing Reality* 42) and, in accordance with his theorizing of the observational documentary mode, their representation functions as 'a practical testing of subjective responses as an eligible participant in as well as observer of the historical world' (43). Representing a plurality of situated responses to sea level rise, and showing how Satty, Endar and Teloo are both materially embedded and historically situated, the film is able to demonstrate the complexity and contradiction that Haraway associates with the view from a body (589).

The scientists accompanying Endar to Nukutoa become prominent figures; however, their presence does not engage expository modality or explicitly lend scientific authority to an argument. Being there to educate Islanders and advise on disaster mitigation, they are clearly constituent in climate politics and adaptation projects that, as Charlotte Weatherill notes, 'reproduce power relations ... further embedding dynamics of power and knowledge, and racialised marginalisation' (2) in the Pacific. However, their appearance in the film also has other functions as they cipher the implication of viewers, perhaps prompting awareness of complicity. A scientist addresses the Islanders at a meeting: 'At the moment the world is warming up, and it's warming up because of other people in the world. It's certainly not you; it's other people in the world who are burning things like diesel fuel in large amounts. This is putting gasses into the atmosphere which actually cause the world to warm.'

While he speaks, an aerial photograph of Nukutoa is visible on a wall, the only trace of aerial visuality in the film as the literal view from above is reduced to part of the mise-en-scène. The Islanders confer before Satty stands and replies. Scientific knowledge is here placed in a dialogic encounter with the Islanders' lived experiences, and viewers are implicitly positioned as 'other people', perpetrators of disaster like Leonardo DiCaprio, whose lifestyle precipitates the sea's slow rise.

Later in *There Once Was an Island*, disaster strikes as high tides and cyclonic weather cause dramatic flooding. The film's representation of this is notably unspectacular, engendering strange ominousness rather than shock or awe. Viewers see flooding from a ground level perspective in shots that show waves breaching the shore, washing past trees. Islanders stand amidst onrushing knee-high water and the camera lingers on their faces as they look out to sea. Endar says 'oh no, there's one great big one coming' before unhurriedly retreating. As water courses through dwellings and spreads debris, the destruction is clear, but the heightened dread it connotes remains somehow quotidian. The devastation is as slow and predictable as the tide.

An ethics of care is evident in the slow, observational style of *There Once Was an Island* which helps viewers to see disaster from the viewpoints of its three subjects, situated on their island, surrounded by the materially perilous but culturally essential force of the ocean. The film accords with Nichols' emphasis that observational documentary 'stresses the non-intervention of the filmmaker' (39), which 'gives a particular inflection to ethical considerations' (39). Notions of care that echo Haraway's evocation of the 'loving care' of working to see from another's perspective (583) abound in environmental humanities and posthumanities scholarship. Deborah Bird Rose explicitly frames care as a way of responding to disaster: 'care is an ethical response involving tenderness, generosity, and compassion ... an ongoing responsibility in the face of continuing violence and peril' ('Shimmer' 58). A similar understanding of care that more directly intimates the way that in Levinasian ethics the self is necessarily displaced by the other is explicated by Astrid Schrader, discussing the post-disaster context of Chernobyl, who posits that 'to care can mean "to trouble oneself" ... to trouble the "self" that grounds the (liberal) humanist subject' (666). The labour of March's approach to film style and her literal approach to Nukutoa suggest an attitude of generosity as, working to care for the Islanders by conveying to viewers the extent and complexity of their exposure to disaster, she absents herself from the frame rather than centring her own authorial perspective. Throughout the film, viewers may intuit March's presence behind the camera as an interlocutor but, as von Mossner writes, she 'lets her protagonists speak for themselves' (178), never employing voiceover or inserting herself into the narrative. Taking care in this way, the film avoids some problematics apparent in similarly concerned documentaries that aim to convey a situated perspective but ultimately join in the sort of disavowal evidenced by *An Inconvenient Truth*. For example, Janet Walker describes *Someplace with a Mountain* (2010) which, in effort to bring attention to rising sea levels in the Federated States of Micronesia, recapitulates colonial encounter, with 'great white men and their all-knowing technology bringing "civilization" to stunned natives', as it focuses on the filmmaker himself (62). That film, Walker explains, disregards Micronesians by positioning them as entirely isolated and 'untainted by consumerism' despite clear evidence that they are 'enmeshed within and supporting a broad geographic network' (67).

The caring ethics of March's film, by comparison, are underpinned by its focus on the physical and social environment of Nukutoa rather than moralistic argumentation, and in this sense, its observational dynamics share some impulses of realist film style. The impressions of elemental exposure and subjective response to disaster the film creates accord with Nichols' assertion that the observational mode exhibits 'three-dimensional fullness and unity' in which 'the space gives every indication of having been carved from the historical world' (39), and also with Lucia Nagib's description of a diverse realism, apparent in all kinds of film including documentary, that is 'eminently physical' and evidences 'the historical contingent and the unpredictable real' (*World Cinema and the Ethics of Realism* 8). *There Once Was an Island*'s physical realism is generated by the ocean's persistent presence in conjunction with slowness. The slow pace of editing is, for von Mossner, crucial to how the film constructs space for viewers, allowing them to 'notice the gradual collapse of distance between village and ocean' (179). Footage of the open sea, waves and the beach is intercut throughout the film, always underscoring and punctuating the testimony of human subjects. Images of the ocean pervade the film just as the ocean itself literally pervades the island, creating a slow view of disaster that has an almost tidal logic: not only protracted but also inevitable and predictable. A further link to an ethics of care is apparent in this slowness, as Swanson et al. propose and catalogue 'modes of noticing' (7) for interspecies survival in the Anthropocene, including 'slowing down to listen to the world – empirically and imaginatively at the same time' (8) – the contemplative observation of March's film could well be added to their index of careful calibrations.

The film's conclusion parallels its beginning as the camera returns to a submerged perspective, but in a way that more emphatically conveys the strange menace of sea level rise and the Islanders' vulnerability. A series of shots look out to sea at dusk, and Satty offers a reflection on scale, concluding that 'If you lose something small in the world, you lose a lot', before an emphatic piano note sounds, breaking the rhythm of the sequence and imposing a sense of finality. The next shot shows a canoe adrift in the ocean, pictured from underneath. As the credits appear, viewers see, in slow motion, the outline of a human body swimming, awash in turbulent liquid materiality. This once more attunes viewers to the bodily sensations of being underwater, slowness creating heightened awareness of the clumsiness of human limbs in water, the bubbles of expelled breath, the distinct possibility of drowning.

This perspective on bodily exposure that bookends March's film is further elaborated in an array of shorter video works by Oceanic artists that insist, in distinct ways, on questions of encounter in the context of Pacific sea level rise. Two performance videos by Sāmoan-New Zealand-Australian artist Angela Tiatia titled *Lick* (2015) and *Holding On* (2015) do even more to counter popular imaginaries of vulnerable, drowned Pacific Islands, attesting further to the endurance of Pacific peoples and cultures in the face of disaster. Shot in Tuvalu, both videos are shot from a fixed perspective showing Tiatia's body partially submerged in the ocean and are created to be seen in art gallery spaces, looping, for as long as the viewer desires. In *Lick*, the camera is positioned beneath the surface and viewers mainly see Tiatia's legs, tattooed with distinctively Samoan and culturally significant malu, as she stands in waist-deep water and uses her limbs to buffer herself against turbulence. In *Holding On*, an obverse perspective shows Tiatia from above, lying on a concrete slab that juts into the ocean at roughly surface level, and as water sloshes around her, she lifts her head and grips the sides of the slab. Jaimey Hamilton Faris poses Tiatia's work in opposition to 'the mournful gaze of environmentalist films' that frames islands and Islanders as 'on the verge of disappearance' (11). *An Inconvenient Truth* and *Before the Flood* certainly evidence this gaze, and *There Once Was an Island* is also party to it, at least in name and in the suggestions of its underwater imagery, but the encounters with the ocean and with disaster posited in *Lick* and *Holding On* constitute a refusal of it. Tiatia's movements are framed by Hamilton Faris as a 'collaboration' (7) and an embodied 'alliance' with water (8), being gestures of 'survivance' – 'a playful combination of "survival" and "resistance"', indicating the continuity of Indigenous presence and stories (8). Resistance, alongside resilience, is identified by Margaret Jolly as a way of framing stories and representation of climate change in the Pacific that can challenge fatalistic frames, which tend to be imposed by foreigners (175). Where the floating figure at the end of *There Once Was an Island* appears fragile, vulnerable and alone, Tiatia's documented oceanic encounters evidence clear connections to the ground and to culture and her repeated movements, shown in looping time, promise no resolution or conclusion of any sort but, rather, ongoing material encounter, continuing negotiation with a disastrous world.

Australian-Solomon Islander filmmaker Amie Batalibasi's virtual reality (VR) work *Aeasi* (2018), made in collaboration with her family in the Solomon Islands, promises viewers an opportunity to 'stand in the village, become a passenger in a canoe and dive down to a reef under the water' as it explores links between community, cultural history and the ocean that is 'not only the sole source of cultural and economic livelihoods but the very thing that will shift a way of life due to the affects *[sic]* of rising seas' ('"Aeasi" 360'). VR has a unique capacity for simulation wherein, as Kate Nash writes, the illusion of place 'is produced through a fore-grounding of embodied engagement' ('Virtual Reality Witness' 122). VR Simulation, Nash notes, which can include 'the illusion of physical vulnerability' (122), is linked to a 'moral force' and takes on an obviously ethical dynamic as 'imaginatively occupying the other's position, the user comes to understand that her position is only one among many and that she is immersed in the world rather than separate from it' (123). VR demonstrates a degree of continuity with cinema, including with notions of cinematic realism, and may perhaps be seen to deliver a fuller version of the objectivity promised by a wide angle long shot: a complete, concrete impression of material, if not social, reality. The word 'Aeasi' is a locative optics, referring to all that is visible above the sea, and *Aeasi* therefore seems to deliver almost literally on the possibility of seeing 'from another's point of view' (Haraway 583). But as a technology, VR also represents a totalizing desire, and Nash highlights risks involved when Western viewers virtually inhabit the worlds of others, wherein narcissistic 'experience of the self ... provides a foundation for moral response' (125), and viewers might understand themselves, caught up in the action, as a moralizing (perhaps even heroic) protagonist. These risks create conditions for understanding the ethical value of a cinematic aesthetic such as that of *There Once Was an Island*, which incorporates the rising ocean as a formal, poetic means of contextualizing an other's experience of disaster, and in doing so creates a figurative space for contemplation of their situation.

The view from the beach

On an Unknown Beach is not concerned with sea level rise, but its way of representing disaster remains inextricably tied to the ocean. The film documents two distinct disasters: the ecological devastation of coral wrought by industrial fishing on the Chatham Rise, an area of ocean floor east of New Zealand, and the earthquakes discussed briefly at the beginning of this book, which destroyed much of Christchurch city. It also documents psychological traumas related to overcoming addiction. The response to disaster articulated by the film is situated within a New Zealand context but attuned to global discourses around ecology and modernity. *On an Unknown Beach* is named for a song of the same title by Peter Jefferies that recounts a walk on the beach, and in doing so establishes an environmental setting and a situated position that connotes colonial encounter. From this inherently uncertain, exposed location of arrival, where the turbulent ocean meets land, the film establishes a way of looking at disaster by intermeshing the different scales and emotional registers of industrial, natural and personal traumas in a thickly textured poetic style. Operating as a post-traumatic record, it attests to the ways that three individuals are affected in encounter with disaster.

Like *There Once Was an Island*, this film begins at sea with a prologue sequence, composed of short shots, that situates viewers within its poetic style. First, a woman's face is pictured in close-up. The camera wavers slightly but her eyes are centred and she looks intently at something. Next, the film shows a circular porthole through which blue sky is visible and, as water comes into view, it becomes apparent this is a ship at sea. In the subsequent shot, the woman is shown moving through a corridor where untethered curtains move with the swell. The camera is fixed to the vessel such that bulkheads remain stationary in the frame and the curtains seem to be moved rhythmically by an invisible force. After another cut, viewers survey the ocean from a higher point, a wide angle shot showing the curved horizon, islands visible in the distance. The sky is purple-ish: it is dusk or dawn here, too, as this film also operates in a transitional or liminal territory. Next, the ocean is rendered on a computer display, a topographical map of the ocean floor where the words 'Gothic', 'Zombie', and 'Graveyard' denote features, suggesting the incursion of death. This cut contrasts the optical objectivity of a full wide angle shot of the sea with the objectivity connoted by the data-driven imagery of topography and surveillance. After more shipboard views are detailed, another cut shows a dog on a beach, silhouetted against the surf. Sound becomes prominent, the creaking of the ship's hull fading into the constantly sonorous crashing of waves. The dog sniffs the air, suggesting a presence beyond human perception. A distorted electric guitar shrills and wails. The final shot of this prologue shows a stormy sea. There is no land on the horizon and the camera bobs wildly. The view seems unstable.

This sequence introduces a distinct form of camera movement that inflects the cinematographic style of the entire film. *On an Unknown Beach* includes many long takes, typical of conventional realist aesthetics, offering expansive, contemplative views. But these shots are embedded alongside others that evoke the movement of the sea, the camera rocking like a ship carried by tides, swells and rolling waves. The 'turbulent materiality' of the ocean described by Steinberg and Peters (247) dictates the framing of shots, and the motion of the camera reflects what Richard Serres describes as the 'chaotic but *rhythmic* turbulence of the material world … a persistent, underlying churn' (qtd in Steinberg and Peters 248, italic in the original). These handheld shots are wonky, bobbing and weaving awash. A handheld camera, Trin T. Minh-ha writes, readily offers a worldly perspective that conveys 'urgency, immediacy, and authenticity' (99), but in *On an Unknown Beach*, this is pushed to an extreme by sloshy shots that track and pan insistently, probing across landscapes and closely following the paths and gestures of subjects. Where editing in *There Once Was an Island* is tidal – slow, patient, predictable – here it is storm-tossed: the camera seems agitated as it circles, strafes and trails angularly, often cutting abruptly. Another reference point for this camera style is shown after the film's title screen when viewers see CCTV footage of the moment an earthquake strikes, the vision blurred and destabilized by the violent shaking of the frame: grocery store shelves spill their contents onto the ground, and people on a street flee falling masonry.

More than fixed frame long takes, prolonged unstable camera movement grants *On an Unknown Beach* a realism specific to the marine and tectonic disasters it documents. This kind of mobile, erratic first-person camera movement is noted by both Bazin and Kracauer in their descriptions of realist tendencies. Bazin writes that in neorealist films, 'the camera must be equally as ready to move as to remain still. Travelling and panning shots do not have the same god-like character that the Hollywood camera crane has bestowed on them. Everything is shot from eye level or from a concrete point of view', adding that in such instances, the camera becomes 'almost a living part of the operator, instantly in tune with his awareness' (*What Is Cinema?* II.33). Kracauer describes ' "subjective" movements' wherein 'the spectator may have to identify himself with a tilting, panning, or travelling camera' (*Theory of Film* 34). The highly mobile, unstable camera of *On an Unknown Beach* pushes viewers to identify with a perspective precipitated by the elemental force of disaster. In tune with the vulnerability occasioned by disaster, the camera's movement converts exposure into a cinematic aesthetic, establishing a point of view thoroughly embedded in the material world. This is a view from a body, open to the material tumult of the world that it documents.

This view reaches an apotheosis later in the film when it seems to literally capsize, emphasizing a sense of alienation and unease within the environment. Poet David Hornblow's experiences undergoing hypnotherapy are paralleled with urban devastation and ecological extinction. He is frequently shown lying down, eyes closed, as his therapist sits above him and guides him through meditations. In one scene, he evokes a post-disaster environment: 'I'm walking through an empty city. All the shadows of who used to be in the city are still there.... It's like after a nuclear flash, but it wasn't that, it wasn't that. They're just gone clean: there's no shop signs, there's no windows. There's nothing.'

The film shows him walking through a subdivision at dusk, rows of houses receding in every direction. The camera follows him in a series of tracking shots as he begins to run, but it is unstable and wavers, eventually rolling ninety degrees as Hornblow staggers and falls. The camera leaves him behind, continuing to track in this lopsided perspective, offering a keeling view of the world where the sky fills one side of the frame and the road fills the other. Rapid cuts accelerate the sunset and show different parts of the suburban environment. Disorientation and displacement take hold as viewers are submerged into a darkening turmoil of strange, post-disaster suburbia appearing not unlike that experienced by Carol in *Safe*. Eventually the camera rights and Hornblow re-enters the frame. As he faces a row of identical houses, the film suddenly cuts to a wide panning shot of the ocean. The juxtaposed environments of the open sea and claustrophobic suburbia are conjoined by the poetics of the camera, and in their intermeshing, the film posits that human subjects in modernity are vulnerable to the encroachment of death wherever we are. Disaster is inescapable.

The unstable camera of *On an Unknown Beach* can be usefully connected to a politics of location that it partakes in as it documents disaster specific to New Zealand, a small, remote island nation and settler colonial state, colloquially referred to as the shaky isles, situated on the Pacific Rim in the South Pacific. The film engages with multiple kinds of shifting grounds at work in this context, and indeed the beach has specific resonance in New Zealand literature and cinema as a complex, contested site of encounter. Chris Prentice notes that while the idea of the 'island nation' insinuates the beach as a familiar and familial topos, a site of leisure and 'collective nostalgia', in a colonial context where it is also the site of first encounter between indigenous peoples and colonizers, it becomes 'a site and figure of liminality that destabilises the very sense of home and the local it shores up' ('"On the Beach?"' 112). Relationships to the beach and its representation are thus extremely contingent, subject to being destabilized, dislodged and remade. Prentice also writes, in another essay titled 'The Shaking of New Zealanders', of the power of the Christchurch earthquakes to destabilize foundations for culture, 'throwing into question the spatial and temporal frames that constitute "New Zealand"' (54). This unsettling power is, for Prentice, an 'ethical charge', a lens for viewing the world that 'defies totalising abstraction to insist on irreducibility and materiality' (54–5). Shifting, unstable landscapes – both literal and as methods for representation – work against desires for stable ground, frustrating the powers of the view from above. *On an Unknown Beach*, operating always in this context, does not seek to assert stability but insists on mutability and turbulence. It works with the shifting, disastrous world it documents, channelling the unstable nature of the environments it contemplates into cinematic form. In this way, the film calls on viewers to dwell in the dynamism and instability of a disastrous world, to be open to its rich materiality, its contingencies and its many claims to meaning.

There is a potent precedent for *On an Unknown Beach* in *The Quiet Earth*, a sci-fi disaster movie produced in New Zealand in 1985. In the final scene, the protagonist, a male scientist, wakes up after a cataclysmic explosion to find himself on an alien beach. He walks slowly towards the ocean as strange cloud formations and a ringed planet loom in the sky. This is a highly ambiguous ending to an otherwise relatively conventional film, providing no resolution and functioning to exacerbate the protagonist's displacement rather than reify his heroism. Scenes staging Hornblow's hypnotherapy excursions (he is credited as 'hypnotherapy explorer') take place entirely on this type of uncertain terrain of arrival, where continually shifting ground prompts ongoing displacement. Promotional material describes the film as a 'ground zero perspective of human life in the Anthropocene', and its documentation of Hornblow's post-traumatic positionality functions as one model for how humans might operate in this context. The film's destabilized camera style is used throughout the film to show him exploring, reckoning with and trying to describe the dizzying world into which he has been thrust.

Another of the film's subjects models a different post-disaster subjective disposition with ethical connotations. Bruce Russell is a musician, sound artist and writer. Known as a member of the noise rock band The Dead C and a solo artist, he has historically collaborated with Peter Jefferies, for whose song this film is named. Russell's disposition after the Christchurch earthquakes, as shown in *On an Unknown Beach*, resonates with Haraway's declaration in *Staying with the Trouble* that she is 'not interested in reconciliation or restoration' but remains 'deeply committed to the more modest possibilities of partial recuperation and getting on together' (10). Russell performs the guitar shrills heard in the opening sequence, which recur throughout the film to weave its distinct threads together. He is also shown recording the sounds of a drum and a vuvuzela amongst destroyed buildings, and re-assembling and replaying audio tapes. In his own writing, Russell frames these documented moments as performance, describing them as 'fanfares for drum and vuvuzela recorded on the site of several demolished buildings previously used as art spaces and clubs' (54). Russell's performance and recording become acts of salvage, bringing aural artefacts from the pre-disaster world into the post-disaster context, his beating and blasting like invitations to antiphony between tenses. Late in the film, Russell is shown working with a guitar, holding a glass bottle on its neck as the camera sways around his limbs and equipment. Watching him tap an amplifier to see what sort of sound comes out is like watching a science experiment. Just as the film's camera style inflects a feeling of instability, the sounds Russell creates throughout its duration channel a sense of experimental, playful retrieval and repair.

The third subject to encounter disaster in *On an Unknown Beach* is Di Tracey, a scientist surveying damaged deep-sea coral. Through her presence the film engages science thematically and conjures scientific objectivity, including aerial views and ciphers of scientific knowledge within its more embodied visuality. Viewers often see Tracey looking at navigational technologies and scientific instruments, her eyes centred in the frame. She and her team use a towed deep-sea camera to survey the seabed, and the film also shows first-person perspectives of the vessel's downward plunge, the camera approaching swathes of wrecked coral on the ocean floor. This deep-dive footage consolidates the film's mobile camera style but has an additional indexical dimension as it performs the scientific function of providing evidence that confirms ecological disaster. When paralleled with Russell's and Hornblow's more personal forays into disastrous environments, it evokes the depths of a damaged psyche as much as it plainly shows this ecological devastation. In this abyss everything usually repressed or hidden becomes visible. If, as Adrian Ivakhiv suggests and I have discussed in Chapter 2, 'recognition of complicity with the ecological crisis' is something like a 'repressed other' (*Ecologies of the Moving Image* 274), then the intermeshing of personal trauma and ecological extinction (and of science and poetics) in *On an Unknown Beach* makes the wreckage and death of the Anthropocene plain to see. As viewers see the ocean floor, we hear the voices of conferring scientists announcing what they see in plain language, repeating 'coral rubble, coral rubble, coral rubble'.

The way that Tracey is represented here de-emphasizes scientific knowledge, eschewing the proffering of expertise that characterizes films like *An Inconvenient Truth* and *Before the Flood*. Tracey doesn't directly address the camera, and viewers don't learn about the nature of her investigations until late in the film when she speaks briefly about the effects of trawl fishing on deep-sea coral. As a coral sample is pictured in her hands, Tracey says, 'it will grow about 1.3 millimetres a year, so this whole structure would take seven [hundred and] fifty to two thousand years to form. So if it was impacted by trawling it would be a long time forming these kind of structures again'. Co-director Adam Luxton contextualizes the omission of expertise in *On an Unknown Beach* as a reaction against more conventional documentary style. Explaining that an earlier edit of the film included more 'explicit information in a traditional documentary sense' involving Tracey, he emphasizes that ecological devastation is self-evident in the imagery of this film and others by paraphrasing feedback on the early edit: 'We all get that it's fucked, we all know that, we get it all the time. What we don't need is to have it told to us' (qtd in Gates and Luxton, 'Interview: Adam Luxton'). Thus, rather than didactically delivering proof of the scale of disaster or deploying scientific authority to persuade viewers to act in certain ways, *On an Unknown Beach* allows viewers to observe a scientist cataloguing death, bearing witness to disaster.

As the film progresses and the perspectives of its three subjects become increasingly interwoven, science is posited as one way among others of looking at a disastrous world, and Russell's sonic manipulations and Hornblow's hypnotherapy are shown as equally viable means for addressing disaster. Cuts between the three subjects become increasingly disorienting towards the end of the film as the mobile camera tracks incessantly, cutting between ruined seafloor ecosystems and earthquake-collapsed buildings while continuous screeching and wailing sounds overwhelm.

The final images break from this mounting cacophony to quietly centre several objects in the frame. A close shot shows a circular rock, smooth save for a single crack. It is cradled by two hands that turn it over before cleaving it in two, exposing its broken, striated centre. This motion is repeated with other rocks, and also a red brick. These whole objects broken in two stand in for disaster on the scales of the personal, of the localized earthquake devastation and of massive ecological extinction. The round rock symbolizes Earth in the Anthropocene, an object of continuity ruptured by the hand of human agency. More literally, the brick stands in for the earthquake-wrecked city. In each instance, a small earthly object, held in hand, intimates global ecology, linking the simple bodily encounter of holding to the capacity to enact disaster, to snap the world apart, but also the ability to hold it in place despite its brokenness. The hands close the two halves of the rock together again, but the crack remains. New Zealand historian Katie Pickles writes that 'the rupturing of Christchurch has shown that being open to continual change is the best way forward' (169), and *On an Unknown Beach* confirms this as it poetically attests to the irreparability of disaster's rupture and invokes a broader consciousness of disaster that, according with Haytham El-Wardany's imperatives, 'does not want to mend what it broken'. Lastly, viewers see close-up shots of several coral samples that simply stand for themselves: hundreds of years of growth laid to waste. Pictured against a black backdrop, each piece is illuminated by theatrical lighting that rises and falls. Close-up shots, Caroline Porter writes, can 'treat supposedly inanimate objects like they normally would a person's face' ('Nonhuman Subjectivity' 98), and though these pieces of coral are dead, the movement of light and shadow around them emphasizes their three-dimensional materiality. This grants the coral a kind of bruised agency, and it evidences Timothy Morton's evocations of ecological awareness wherein 'trauma is not only human' (*Dark Ecology* 135). One piece resembles a human brain, however, as if to again conjoin psychic trauma and eco-catastrophe. These final images of *On an Unknown Beach*, via these poetic close-ups, set disaster in plain sight, presenting a non-human face that bears its effects to viewers.

An oceanic ethics

The nomenclature of *There Once Was an Island* and *On an Unknown Beach*, let alone the worlds documented and the stories told in the two films, describes a specific location: an island beach exposed to the sea and wind, a meeting place for various elemental forces and cultural currents. It is from this place that these two films set forth to document encounter with anthropogenic disaster. Haytham El-Wardany, evoking disaster-consciousness, writes, 'this consciousness is like an island, borne within, and set apart from disaster' and asks, 'What message does the island have for the fertile plains?' ('Notes on Disaster'). My analysis of these two films, particularly in juxtaposition with the two films from the United States discussed in Chapter 3, illustrates how Oceanic and Southern Hemisphere contexts might carry clearly distinct ways of encountering contemporary disasters like sea level rise and ecological extinction. These films reflect materially and culturally embedded modes of knowing and as they document their contexts in the South Pacific, they invoke a positionality that aspires to immersion rather than omniscience. By featuring multiple subjects who encounter disaster in different ways, stemming from their geographical, material, cultural and emotional enmeshments, these films posit that different kinds of encounter with forces of disaster are possible, and their highly subjective approach to documenting events means that differentiated, even contradicting, responses to disaster are evidenced. The films figure these responses as variegated processes rather than as prescribed actions to be applied anyplace, in the manner of the concluding sequences of both *An Inconvenient Truth* and *Before the Flood*. These processes – of salvage for Russell, of scientific inquiry for Tracey, of therapy for Hornblow, of mourning for Satty, of reclamation for Teloo and of filial piety but also enacting change for Endar – include profound transformation of the self in encounter with the world remade by disaster, though not in a universal way. They therefore have ethical dimensions, and resonate in particular with Haraway's imperative to cultivate response-abilities, offering ways of being 'present to onrushing catastrophe' (35). Moving film cameras into and below the water that is always unstable rather than holding position high above it, these films allow the ocean to shape their cinematographic style. In this way, the two films not only figure their subjects' encounters with disastrous forces in embodied, processual ways, but convey something of that exposed experience to viewers, making us bear with the disastrous dynamism of the ocean as we work to apprehend the trouble and displacement experienced by their subjects.

Analysis of *There Once Was an Island* and *On an Unknown Beach* marks a significant turning point in the trajectory of this book. As both films are situated explicitly in the South Pacific, they propel its explorations far beyond North American contexts, and this continues in Chapter 5, which explores films from dispersed global locations and belonging to various industrial and critical categories associated with realist filmmaking. Equally importantly, however, while films discussed in prior chapters show disaster mainly as an impending threat or already-occurring event, the films discussed from this chapter onwards deal more with post-disaster scenarios. The perspectives that they offer focus the attention of viewers towards noticing the material specificities of individuals and communities who have already encountered traumatic disaster and therefore cannot act to prevent it, as so many Hollywood heroes do.

Part III

A Neorealist Legacy for Eco-Catastrophe

5

Realist auteurs after the disaster

In the first scenes of Michael Haneke's *Time of the Wolf*, which depicts a family's journey of survival after an unspecified disaster, the father dies. This grim beginning signals that the film will not track towards the reification of a patriarchal hero as Hollywood disaster blockbusters do. *Time of the Wolf* occupies the same thematic territory as many of those films but subverts their spectacular generic tropes, operating instead in the stern, slow style for which Haneke is known. It is set in an unspecified European location and conjures a sense of disaster in which the Holocaust looms as an oblique referent, dark and quiet long takes showing the subsequent travails of the surviving mother and her two children in brutal detail. Haneke's vocal defiance of Hollywood convention is one reason he is often framed as a specific type of director: a modernist whose oeuvre addresses a Western European milieu, critiquing institutions and customs but highlighting moments of unexpected humanism; a contemporary auteur in the mould of Italian neorealism.

This chapter examines three films by auteur directors linked by shared recourse to the style of post-war neorealism: *Time of the Wolf*, Abbas Kiarostami's *And Life goes On* and Lav Diaz's *Death in the Land of Encantos*. These films respond to different disastrous contexts but, embodying central elements of realist film style and according with the responsiveness that Bazin finds in post-war neorealism, present post-disaster scenarios in ways that imagine disaster as encounter attuned to an ethics of openness. Openness, in the manner described in this book's introduction with reference to Morton and particularly Rose, entails an attitude towards encounter with alterity, and especially openness to the peril of others, wherein one's sense of self may be astonished and revitalized. As Rose writes: 'To be open is to hold one's self available to others: you take risks and make yourself vulnerable', and this opening is both destabilizing and fertile, 'a place where knowledge arises' ('Slowly' 8). Morton highlights further the risks associated with such radical openness, theorizing that this type of interconnectedness 'produces a mental openness far more disturbing than outer space' (*The Ecological Thought* 80), and as these films and my analysis will indicate, profound disturbance may be an essential element of ethical responsibility, as well as a logical consequence. In different ways, these films enact degrees of openness to the more-than-human alterity of their environments, openness to time and duration, and openness to contingency and the possibility of death. As they do so, the way of imagining disaster that they insinuate becomes pertinent, perhaps even instructive, for our broader contexts of the Anthropocene, though none of them overtly engage with climate change thematically or narratively.

Despite being produced in different nations and cultural contexts, at different moments during recent decades and in distinct proximities to the historical disasters they represent and refract, these films all operate within overlapping theorizations and classifications of cinema that descend from post-war realist thought, connecting with notions of modernism, auteurism, world cinema, national cinema and slow cinema. Emerging from Iran, Europe and the Philippines, these films by Kiarostami, Haneke and Diaz nonetheless share industrial and critical contexts, attaining global circulation via the festival circuit (*And Life Goes On* and *Time of the Wolf* premiered at Cannes) and due to the reputations of their directors. All three belong to what Bill Nichols calls an 'international fraternity of auteurs' who 'partake in distinctive national culture-work that remains distinct from Hollywood-based norms' ('Discovering Form, Inferring Meaning' 16). This fraternity, for Elsaesser, has 'more in common with each other than with directors of their respective national cinemas', giving rise to 'an international art cinema which communicates similar concerns across a wide spectrum of settings, but within an identifiably stylistic repertoire' (*European Cinema* 18). In the three films discussed here, this stylistic repertoire is bent towards the imagination of disaster.

This is indeed a fraternity, and an overwhelming masculinity is attached to these films. All are directed by men and prominently feature male characters (though as my analysis shall demonstrate, the masculinity they demonstrate is crucially differentiated from that elaborated in Chapter 1). Following the *Cahiers du Cinéma* critics, auteurism as a critical category, and in particular, auteurs' perceived capacity for visionary style and voice, is thoroughly associated with masculinity. As Diana Holmes elaborates, auteurism imagines a director 'as a solitary hero, in Oedipal revolt against his filmic fathers... . no mere skilled director working as part of a team, but a heroic figure whose singular vision found innovative formal expression regardless of the constraints of the film industry' (157–8).

Discourses on auteurism that elevate directors' unique ways of perceiving the world and making social commentary also highlight the way Kiarostami, Diaz and Haneke look to neorealist attitudes with these films. Historically, Bazin praises the socio-political disposition of neorealist directors by highlighting the 'fundamental humanism' of their films and connecting them to a 'revolutionary flavour' (*What Is Cinema?* II.22). More recently, a 'myth of independent creativity' with 'aesthetic and political modernism as its core evaluative taste' (4) is central to Seung-hoon Jeong and Jeremi Szaniawski's formulation of *The Global Auteur* in a useful book that nevertheless does not include a single chapter focusing on a non-male director. Auteurs, in this formulation, are 'agents who carry philosophical concepts or even philosophers in their own right' (5), capable of sustaining 'critically meaningful or artistically transformative stances' (6). Auteurs wield film style to set in motion ideas and arguments that are critically significant and, more importantly, socially or philosophically transformative. As auteurist visions, *Death in the Land of Encantos*, *And Life Goes On* and *Time of the Wolf* invoke a shared cinematic consciousness of disaster honed from the same glimpse as 'the ease and sure eye of Rossellini, Lattuada, Vergano, and de Santis' (Bazin, *What Is Cinema?* II.32).

Though there is a risk, in analysing these diverse films, of homogenizing them due to their thematic unity (Martin-Jones 51), my analysis of each film attempts to be attentive to both their contexts and the nuanced specificities of their shared formal recourses. Across their global contexts, they are united especially by elements of camera style, specifically the long take, which is deployed in each film to convey a concrete understanding of environment that is open to movement and the passage of time; by their insistence on diegetic sound; and by the subjective dispositions of their characters who, in the wake of irreparable disasters, welcome risk, strife and the possibility or inevitability of death.

Auteurism and response-ability

Understanding the nature of the power attributed to auteurs as creatively minded figures whose films distil and express political or philosophical stances allows for these three post-disaster films to be framed as situated ethical responses to historical disasters. Different kinds of auteurs exist, according to Elsaesser: while 'a classic auteur welcomes the external constraints of genre', being aligned with Hollywood (John Ford makes Westerns; Roland Emmerich makes disaster movies), the 'romantic auteur' and the 'European auteur' are outsiders whose authorship is 'celebrated by defining it as that of the creative exception, giving expression to his or her vision' ('The Global Author' 32). European auteurs also come to be 'regarded as representative of their particular "national cinema" and even their nation' (33), suggesting that their philosophical stance emerges from their cultural and geographical situation. A contemporary auteur's public image can also function 'like a "genre"' (34), certain characteristics recurring in their films, leading to expectations for viewers. Unlike post-war European auteurs who were allowed a degree of autonomy, contemporary auteurs who are more globally dispersed face financial constraints and are thus 'obliged to craft a self-image' and 'invent for themselves forms of resistance or paranoia' (34), seeking social or political friction as the grounds on which to express their artistic vision. This schematization of auteurs fits with Lucia Nagib's position that 'different cinemas of the world can generate their own theories' (*World Cinema and the Ethics of Realism* 1), and also Roberto Rossellini's remarks on neorealist auteurs that 'everyone possesses his own realism and everyone thinks that his own is best' (qtd in Armes, *Patterns of Realism* 183). But contemporary authorship also, for Jeong and Szaniawski, 'constitutes a genuine philosophical and political matrix which exceeds the work of the individuals' (9).

Kiarostami, Haneke and Diaz embody all these notions of auteurism in different ways. Between individual genius, geographical contexts, social constraints and philosophical fraternity; and in relation to historical European realisms as well as Hollywood genre conventions, *And Life Goes On*, *Time of the Wolf* and *Death in the Land of Encantos* advance theories of disaster that collectively constitute a philosophy of ethical openness and 'response-ability' (Haraway 35) to disaster.

Haneke is often understood as European rather than as representative of his native Austria, or of France where many of his films have been produced. He casts himself as 'the "last modernist"' and is accordingly compared to auteurs from across Europe: Bergman, Antonioni, Tarkovsky and the like (Frey 'Michael Haneke'). This frames him as a kind of historical holdout, the last of a dying breed of rebellious filmmakers. Szaniawski argues that Haneke 'revives the cinematic modernist idiom (long take, anomie, solitude…)' ('Of Intruders (and Guests)' 135), and *Time of the Wolf* operates thusly. But Haneke also works with genre, and *Time of the Wolf* 'follows the standard-issue presentation structure for post-apocalyptic cinema' (Torner 537). Haneke contends that he *uses* genre, particularly thriller, but asserts a realist tendency, trying to make films that are 'filled with the world' and 'steeped in a verifiable reality' (qtd in Horwath, 'Michael Haneke Interview: Uncut'). His films are geared towards authentically representing the lives of wealthy Western Europeans, and this involves exposing the hypocrisy of bourgeois attitudes via the mimicry and subversion of familiar genre techniques (Grundmann 8).

Kiarostami and Diaz are regarded as representative of Iran and the Philippines, respectively, but critically aligned with European directors. For example, Laura Mulvey describes Kiarostami's films as 'the Iranian reworking of a realist aesthetic' (*Death 24× a Second* 130), and Nichols writes this of encountering Iranian films, including Kiarostami's: that they 'exude a certain austerity ... much closer to the work of Chantal Akerman or Robert Bresson than a Bertolucci or Greenaway' ('Discovering Form, Inferring Meaning' 21). Geography and landscape figure in Nichols' categorization, as he describes how Iranian films 'usher us into a world of wind, sand, and dust ... unusual tempos and foreign rhythms' (17). Similarly, May Adadol Ingawanij locates Diaz in a Philippines paradigm connected to 'an international genealogy of Third World revolutionary art' ('Long Walk to Life' 105). She argues that his 'aesthetics blend the national-popular praxis of the Bandung era with the realist film ethics of French theorist André Bazin' (106), and his films 'construct a symbolic map of the Philippine archipelago' (109). Much analysis of Diaz's films focuses on their extreme duration, aligning him with slow cinema. This label, also attached to Kiarostami (de Luca and Jorge 1), is associated with rejection of 'tropes of conventional mainstream cinema' (Brown, '*Melancholia*: The Long, Slow Cinema of Lav Diaz' 113). An ethic of realism inheres in this rejection because a slow film 'attests to a rehabilitation of the tenets historically associated with cinematic realism as envisioned by its most illustrious proponent, French film critic André Bazin' (de Luca and Jorge 7). The outlook and style of both Diaz and Kiarostami are thus aligned with European neorealism while also connected with specificities of their own nations.

Locating Haneke, Kiarostami and Diaz in these ways, their post-disaster films can be understood as responses to specific historical exigencies. *Death in the Land of Encantos* is 'situated in a definite time and place' (Campos 370). It was shot in the aftermath of typhoon Durian (called Reming locally) which struck the Bicol region in November 2006 following the eruption of the Mayon volcano, causing deadly mudslides. Diaz himself offers testimony: 'It was hell. The smell of death was everywhere. All you could see was utter disarray, devastation, destruction, insanity, pain, sadness, unbearable suffering. Villages were gone, hundreds of people buried alive, hundreds missing' (qtd in Mai, *The Aesthetics of Absence and Duration* 176).

The film, Nadin Mai explains, evolved from footage that Diaz shot in the aftermath, desiring to record with minimal authorial influence: 'Diaz wanted to be a mere observer, and intended to be "journalistic"' (175). It contains ample observational footage that has this documentary function, making viewers bear witness to the devastated landscape and pervasion of death, and Mai draws parallels between Diaz's film and neorealism with respect for how documented landscape can speak of history and trauma (174, 179). Locals also attest to the devastation in documentary interview scenes that include an off-screen voice (probably Diaz). The film's fictional componentry is equally situated in a Philippines context, its narrative revolving around the return of the exiled poet Benjamin Agusan (Hamin), from Russia. Hamin is not only confronted by the disaster, but also his familial history of mental illness, and the reprisal of his persecution for having spoken out against the government. In Diaz's vision of disaster, Hamin wanders through distinct temporalities, interacting with ghosts as the film's nine hours chronicle his descent into madness. Multiple scales of trauma – ecological, emotional and political – play out across a mud-wracked landscape.

Diaz, Mai explains, was 'personally affected' by the Reming disaster because areas he had used as settings for prior films were destroyed (176). A similar scenario underlies Kiarostami's *And Life Goes On*, which was shot following a magnitude 7.4 earthquake in Northern Iran. Kiarostami interpolates himself into the film, as the protagonist is a director who travels with his young son towards the village of Koker seeking two brothers who acted in his previous film (Kiarostami shot *Where Is the Friend's Home?* (1987), featuring local children, in Koker). The film has a documentary function, too, as its long takes record the effects of the earthquake and the cracked landscape the director journeys through.

As with many of Kiarostami's films, a car is the main setting, and this informs the film's style. Viewers see the dusty environment as if becoming passengers, travelling through wrecked villages and witnessing survivors through an open window. Mulvey calls this Kiarostami's 'aesthetics of digression' (125), and Pedram Dibazar describes it as an 'embodied cinema of everyday interaction' (319), both intimating how the film's realism is connected to the car's movement and the encounters that propel and frustrate the director's search as obstacles prompt halting distractions and diversions, but the camera's persistent mobility becomes a destination itself. More than any other film considered in this book, *And Life Goes On* is about material existence or, in Kracauer's words, '"what is just there"' (*Theory of Film* vii) which is, as the title suggests, enduring life. Where Diaz's realism rests on history, Kiarostami's is more existential. Critical descriptions of his film style often centre on poetic qualities, emphasizing a 'type of ambiguous, epiphanic image' (Chaudhuri and Finn 38). This understanding manifests Kracauer's evocations of film's capacity to reveal the world anew to viewers, and here the persistence of movement and of the film itself appears as a unique way of coming to terms with an environment transformed by disaster and suffused with death and loss.

Twice in Kiarostami's film the earthquake is described as an ungodly wolf, hungry to devour lives. Haneke's *Time of the Wolf* is set in an unspecified area of Europe after a disaster has precipitated resource scarcity and societal breakdown. The French-speaking family it follows – Anne, the mother, and her children Eva and Benny – travel along train tracks, eventually joining a group of survivors who wait at a disused station for a train that may or may not arrive. The film doesn't overtly reference historical events but its production can be located amid the same contexts that fuelled Hollywood's 1990s disaster cycle. Haneke explicitly positions his films as oppositional to Hollywood, and *Time of the Wolf* clearly opposes disaster movies. A quote is reproduced on the DVD sleeve: 'my films are intended as polemical statements against American "barrel down" cinema and its disempowerment of the spectator' and in a special features interview, he states 'I did not want my film to fall into the disaster movie category'. Echoing Haneke's sentiment, Torner describes it as 'a film that deliberately denies the viewer any escapism' (532) and 'eschews commercial cinema's aesthetics of spectacle' (533). However, as Catherine Wheatley notes, it still partakes in wider traditions of science fiction (138) and especially resembles post-nuclear television films of the 1980s (139). Oliver Speck locates the film amidst 'traditional auteur-genres' (178), explaining that Haneke invokes 'generic frames' only to 'disappoint viewers' expectations' (179). The father's murder is an example of this, subverting genre tropes and disappointing expectations that masculinist heroism will triumph.

Mapping modern Europe as a slow-burning disaster of alienation, hypocrisy and violence, Haneke's bare realism resists spectacle and sentimentality by withholding narrative information but presenting cruelty with excruciating detail. His style is associated with the notion of 'glaciation' which, as Grundmann writes, refers to affluent European society's 'broad-based descent into indifference, isolation, and lethal coldness' (6). Haneke's first three films (*The Seventh Continent* (1989), *Benny's Video* (1992) and *71 Fragments of a Chronology of Chance* (1994)) are widely known as the glaciation trilogy, and further indulging an auteur approach, Philippe Met even refers to Haneke as 'the iceman', bearing 'frigid chunks of cinematic truth' ('The Iceman Cometh (to a Theater Near You)' 176). Glaciation connotes slowness and there is an unhurried certainty to the way Haneke's films chart the sliding into oblivion and self-annihilation of bourgeois characters. Though his films focus on human problems, the regular appearance of animals suggests a disjuncture between human and non-human worlds that is constituent in the cruelty he critiques, real animal deaths often highlighting characters' indifference to life. *Time of the Wolf* partakes in this broad critique of Western European values, and the displacement it details recalls the Bosnian civil war when the affluent family react fearfully to an Eastern European boy who is scavenging for survival just like them (Torner 359). The film is relentlessly stark, characterized by long sequences that are barely lit so the environment becomes imperceptible to viewers. The rhythm of day and night continues, but it is as if the sun has set on humanity and a 'silent apocalypse' has taken hold in which glaciated cruelty has become, as Berardi writes of Fukushima's radiation, the 'framework of social expectation for daily life' (10).

Haneke, as Speck notes, 'addresses all of Bazin's notions of realism' (182). Here, alongside Diaz's and Kiarostami's films, *Time of the Wolf* constitutes the final full analytical arc of this book's search for a contemporary realism that can face up to disaster. Although distinct in their conjuring of the realist possibilities articulated by Bazin in the aftermath of the Second World War, in the alignment of these auteurs' visions a way of imagining disaster coalesces that is instructive for the juncture of the Anthropocene proposal. It takes the form of a deliberate, questing optics, epitomized by the long take, which directly keys in to ethical concerns.

The long take: Opening the environment

Long takes are used in these films to represent the environment, rendering concrete impressions of geographical place and material presence. With documentary capacity, each film creates a distinct sense of a space transformed by disaster. Post-typhoon Bicol in *Death in the Land of Encantos* is a cloudy zone shown in black and white. The volcano looms over open spaces and destroyed buildings coexist with rocks and trees. The post-earthquake environment of *And Life Goes On* is similarly composed of mountains of scree, cracked dirt and damaged structures but it is shown in sunny colour, bright dust blowing from rubble. Contrastingly, much of *Time of the Wolf* takes place in nearly absolute darkness of night and enclosed spaces. In all these environments, fragments of life from before the disaster are evident and quotidian life continues.

Beyond simply showing these post-disaster environments, these films establish logics of travelling and persistent movement through space. This institutes a shared viewing position that connotes an active sort of looking: searching, probing or questing. In *Death in the Land of Encantos*, extraordinarily long takes show the slow progress of characters moving through the environment in real time. In *And Life Goes On*, tracking shots that look outward from car windows establish a viewpoint aligned with the protagonists' frustrated progression. *Time of the Wolf*, insisting on trains and tracks as figures in setting and narrative, highlights futile attempts at passage. For Bazin, as cinema records reality, it documents objects but also 'makes an imprint of the duration of the object' (*What Is Cinema?* I.97). By staging passage through post-disaster scenarios, these films open up the duration of their worlds, including the disastrous forces that shape them, allowing viewers to encounter them, and perhaps reflect on their impositions, by temporally passing through them. This lends an additional dimension to the way encounter is staged and ethical responsibility conceptualized.

Death in the Land of Encantos begins with a series of long takes that introduce viewers to the devastated landscape. The first, a fixed frame shot, shows a stream running from the centre of the frame into the foreground. In the background, a mountain is shrouded in cloud. This is almost a pastoral scene but occasionally there is a deathly rumbling – a storm? The stirring volcano? Another shot shows boulders strewn among gnarled trees, confirming something chaotic has happened. Next, the camera is moving, a first-person handheld view of someone walking across the same terrain. It turns, surveying the broken landscape. After a cut this same perspective shows a sleeping woman, and a rooster can be heard crowing. This is Hamin's perspective, in another time, looking at his lover. Layers of liminality compound: in the wake of the disaster, a memory of early morning. Throughout the remainder of the film, handheld shots generally show Hamin's subjective viewpoint while fixed shots document the landscape.

Long takes in this film function foremostly to impress the materiality of the post-disaster environment, and though the environment and the film's characters are interrelated, the 'milieu' of the film is more central to its realism (Campos 370). The fixed frame long takes are always askew such that the horizon line is never perfectly horizontal, and Mai suggests the Dutch angles 'visually reinforce the characters' inner struggles' (177) as 'bleak empty landscapes' mirror characters' degraded 'mental states' (178). A more immediate effect takes hold in the opening shots, though, before viewers learn of Hamin's mental trauma. Their duration (each at least a minute and a half) combined with the strange, almost alien nature of the environment when seen at a tilted angle makes it seem as though the film offers the first-person perspective of someone who was just woken up in an unknown place and is working to orient themselves. This happens repeatedly as the extreme duration of Diaz's long takes often show viewers environments for many minutes before they are filled with human action. In the shot that follows this drawn-out introduction, for example, viewers see Hamin walk from the background into the foreground and sit down, weeping amidst the wreckage of a home, before he is joined by another character, Teodoro. His passage into the foreground takes almost ten minutes. Showing characters walking into frame is key to the slowness and sense of movement through space that the film generates, and to Diaz's realism more generally. Ingawanij, in an article on Diaz titled 'Long Walk to Life', observes that 'Diaz's mise-en-scene displays the materiality of the physical environment; he stages movement as powerless human bodies traversing through immense space' (106). Marco Grosoli describes this in specific detail: 'Typically, in Diaz's shots characters appear in the far back of the frame, walk toward the camera, carry out some action and/or dialogue, and laterally exit the frame (long) before the cut. If a space needs "x" minutes to be traversed by a character, then the shot lasts "x" minutes, as long as it takes' (309).

Ingawanij cites Nagib's notion of physical realism (106) to describe Diaz's style, referencing the exertion of actors and emphasizing the 'physicality of engagement on the part of the film cast and crew with the material environment' (106). Use of fixed frames in this manner is evident in the 'poetic postneorealism' of Antonioni and Pasolini described by Shohini Chaudhuri and Howard Finn, who assert that 'fixed shots as characters enter and exit the frame' help films to 'document social reality' (44). In *Death in the Land of Encantos*, such shots document the environmental aftermath of disaster, their regularity emphasizing that the real wrecked environment exists prior to the film's fictional social interactions. The sheer devastation of Bicol's post-disaster landscape means that it takes precedence over human characters, and even as Mai's discussion focuses on Hamin's mental state, she de-emphasizes the significance of human presence in this film, referring to distant characters as 'dots' (188). While viewers wait for these dots to appear, our attention is necessarily drawn to the wrack of dark boulders and lahar dirt, a layer of death that covers everything.

This film reaches for ethics in the manner that Bazin observes in William Wyler's post-war work, seeking an adequate way of looking at a world reconstituted by the eruption of death (*Bazin at Work* 5). A form of ethical encounter is at work here beyond the fictional one staged between Hamin and the elemental forces of disaster that devastate Bicol: the duration of the shot means that before viewers see Hamin walking into the frame, we are made to encounter the wreckage for ourselves, bearing witness to the chaos of boulders and dirt. The camera opens Diaz's own desire to bear witness onto the audience, functioning in the manner that Giuliana Minghelli observes in Rossellini's *Paisan* wherein the post-war landscape is 'allied with the camera eye' which 'becomes a silent witness' (*Landscape and Memory in Post-Fascist Italian Film* 44). Diaz's camera asks viewers to witness with him, dwelling in the long take and being responsive to the passage of time. A character, Claro, who moves between the fictional narrative and the documentary componentry and attests to both Hamin's downfall and the historical devastation of Bicol, seems to confirm this. Mai describes how Claro speaks to other characters, telling them to be aware of the dead – 'listen carefully. You will hear the wailing of all those buried underneath' – but his words are equally directed to viewers as he adds, 'observe closely' (195). Diaz's realism asserts the irreducible materiality of disaster, going beyond staging it as a force encountered by protagonists to also push viewers into encounter with it, conveying ethical potential in this imperative, delivered bluntly by Claro but conveyed assiduously in the film's form, to simply look. In this sense, the film realizes the manner that, as Sarah Cooper describes, for Levinas, 'Death is rethought on the basis of time, not as an end, but as an encounter with uncertainty, with a future' ('Emmanuel Levinas' 97). Time, or more precisely duration, is key to the possibility for this cinematic encounter with post-disaster Bicol to create an opening for spectatorial responsibility. Elaborating Levinas's relevance to cinema, Cooper connects his thought with Bergsonian duration and cites Levinas's position that 'duration becomes the fact that a man can appeal to the interiority of the other man' ('Emmanuel Levinas' 96). In Diaz's cinematic time, within which human characters are so often reduced to dots, it is the bare landscape, rearranged by the typhoon and volcano and bearing the traces of human death alongside the more-than-human force of disaster, that appeals to viewers. The film's form thus creates conditions for viewers to be propelled into responsibility by the relation it creates for us, in time, to the cinematic alterity of the disaster.

And Life Goes On incorporates and complicates the type of first-person subjective shot that Diaz associates with Hamin's perspective, showing a view from the protagonist's car to posit a direct experience of the post-disaster environment in Iran. The mobile perspective in many of Kiarostami's films is associated with cars, and this is true of *And Life Goes On* where side windows especially are connected to the viewpoints of the director, who drives, and his son. In a scene at the beginning of the film, the son lies across the back seats and gazes towards the window, holding his hands to his eyes to make a rectangular shape that alludes to the framing of a shot. A cut shows his perspective, the car's frame filling the edges of the shot. Trees pass by in the foreground while hills appear static in the background. Later, this same perspective shows crowds of survivors and brief encounters with strangers. In one shot the director talks to a man whose face is not visible: viewers see only his torso, framed by the window, and his broken arm in a sling. This travelling perspective conveys a sense of documentary observation of the real environment. As Mulvey observes, 'the film pauses to register and record these scenes of complete devastation' (*Death 24× a Second* 127).

In other moments the film goes even farther as, Dibazar contends, as it 'complicates the process of visual identification by inserting shots that cannot be realistically associated with any of the characters' points of view' (310), generating an uncertainty that frees viewers from identification with characters (311). One shot, for example, extends to a duration impossible for the director/driver, 'who cannot possibly be looking sideways whilst driving for such an extended period' (Dibazar 310). Such shots, connected with the car's movement but also 'completely severed from specific subjective positions' (Dibazar 312), recur throughout the film and contribute to its realism by offering a more objective perspective firmly situated in the post-disaster environment. Shots showing a straight-on view as if looking forward from the car, the road spooling towards the bottom of the frame, convey the impression of moving through space actively, searching or seeking rather than being a passive observer, while also attesting to film's capacity to record movement and time. Viewers also frequently see the car in long shots from a distance that detaches our perspective from the travelling characters. In one shot, we see it motor across a hillside, the sky almost absent from view, above gouges in the landscape that block the road – the visible evidence of the quake.

These shots make the car appear like a dot, emphasizing the elemental force of the disaster, its scale and its power over humans. Such poetic images – separated from subjective viewpoints, highlighting the environment, but interlaced with personal journeys or processes – are linked with a specific notion, an ethics, of openness that courses through Kiarostami's oeuvre. This openness is brought to attention by Chaudhuri and Finn who describe 'epiphanic' imagery that is grounded in diegesis but 'cannot be straightforwardly deciphered as a revelation of either a character's psychological state or that of the filmmaker' conjuring, rather, an '"other" perspective' which is 'felt to reside in the camera itself' (40). In views such as these, as in Diaz's film, the camera itself seems to open the material reality and elemental power of the post-disaster world up to viewers.

As with Diaz, neorealism is a clear precedent to Kiarostami's documenting of a real post-disaster scenario. Mulvey's writing on Kiarostami in *Death 24× a Second* follows a chapter on Rossellini. She connects the two auteurs, citing the way that neorealism 'reflected the shock left by the war and the need for a new cinematic way of thinking about the world' (129) and noting that similarly, 'the shock of the earthquake ... redirected Kiarostami's realism towards the difficult question of a reality that challenged adequate representation' (130). Citing Deleuze, Mulvey describes a 'cinema of record, observation and delay' in the films of both Rossellini and Kiarostami where 'the past in the form of traces and ruins fills the content of the image' (129). Minghelli notes that neorealism relies on 'documentary style filming of post-war ruins', emphasizing the poetic quality of their 'dusty streets drenched in the anonymous light of the everyday' (2) and indeed, both Kiarostami and Rossellini mine the capacity of film to authentically render real environments, showing ruins and wreckage in their fullness. Meanwhile, Diaz's emphasis on landscape and environment over characters is also evidentiary, for Mai, of the geographical and cultural situatedness of his vision, the 'predominance' of nature being 'reminiscent of pre-Hispanic Malay belief in the importance and role of nature' (190). For Diaz and Kiarostami, then, the use of real settings conveys the specific shocks of historically, culturally and geographically situated disasters, and their aesthetics of duration founded on long takes and travelling perspectives imparts an ethical dimension to the representation of these shocks, offering to transmit some of it to viewers.

Time of the Wolf does not document the aftermath of a historical disaster. Nevertheless, it frequently emphasizes the dense materiality of the world it depicts and opens out onto historical reality, pushing viewers into a feeling of encounter with disaster. The film is full of literal darkness that frequently makes it difficult to discern events and, while it is one of Haneke's least written about, this darkness is often discussed. Torner cites a press release in which Haneke claims it is 'one of the darkest films in cinema history', and posits the 'virtually pitch-black night shots' place the film in contrast to the 'visually arresting' landscapes of other post-apocalyptic films (533). Wheatley summarizes the disorienting effect the darkness has for viewers watching the characters' attempts to keep moving: 'As they wander about in the increasingly impenetrable darkness, suspense builds, as the spectator tries to establish the nature of the onscreen events. Why are things so strange? What is happening? What has happened?' (138).

This visuality is certainly frustrating, but it also brings a kind of clarity, illuminating the starkness of events. Several important moments occur at night, lit by firelight. When Ann and the children pass through a village, appealing for help, scraps of electrical light emit from the houses of others who turn them away. They then encounter a bonfire in the street. Viewers first see their flickering reactions – Benny hides his face in his jacket – but as they walk, the camera moves with them to reveal what Torner describes as a 'burning pile of garbage and horse corpses'; the villagers' refusal of Anne and her children thus leads to 'one of the most apocalyptic images in the film' (537). The family later journey to a barn where they shelter and build a funerary altar for Benny's deceased pet bird (more animal death), but in the night Benny disappears and Anne and Eva, fumbling, search for him. Anne lights a fire for Eva before leaving to look further afield, and the film confounds viewers by cutting between external mid-range shots and closer shots of Anne's terrified face illuminated by shreds of burning hay. Finally, at the end of the film, Benny prepares to immolate himself in a fire built in the middle of train tracks. In an unhinged mental state, he believes that sacrificing himself will lead to the others' redemption and, while earlier he had refused to look at the burning horses, here viewers see him stand and encounter blazing flames as if face to face. Silhouetted in the centre of the frame, he takes off his clothes, embracing an intensified bodily vulnerability, an openness towards the elemental force of the fire and the fullness of night. The darkness in these scenes is real and disorienting, compounding Haneke's refusal to divulge narrative information about the disaster but heightening our understanding that it has inaugurated a dire world.

Benny is saved by a night watchman who consoles him in the dark, his attempt at self-sacrifice leading not to transcendental salvation (as it might in Hollywood) but to an interpersonal moment of tenderness, a kind of redemption after all. While the extremity of darkness is notable, the film's primal firelight is equally significant. Isabelle Huppert, who plays Anne, notes in a special features interview the paradoxical coexistence of dark and light in the frame, intimating a higher meaning: 'It is a dark film that sheds light, in every sense of the word … There is a sense of prophecy … like all prophecy it is created in darkness or doubt.' This precisely echoes Maurice Blanchot's ambiguous assertion, reflecting on the Holocaust, that *'it is dark disaster that brings the light'* (7). In near total darkness and in lieu of a spectacular resolution for the characters, the watchman's actions signal an acceptance consistent with the disaster-consciousness mooted by Haytham El-Wardany – 'it is impossible to search for a solution to disaster' – and also resonates with Kiarostami's belief that 'the cinema's role is not to express a solution to problems but to express the problems themselves' (qtd in Nichols, 'Discovering Form, Inferring Meaning' 24).

Shooting in the darkness of night with elemental illumination refutes Hollywood's spectacular aesthetics, but it also reiterates the type of materiality evoked by neorealism's documentary camera style. Not unlike Diaz's and Kiarostami's films, the long take enables a feeling of cinematic encounter for viewers with the fullness of an environment. Although it lacks an obvious historical referent, *Time of the Wolf*'s long take exposure to post-disaster darkness configures for viewers a powerfully ambient encounter with disaster as a nocturnal presence. In Levinasian thought, night can be understood as a substantial, phenomenological force. Alphonso Lingis, for example, writes in his introduction to Levinas's *Collected Philosophical Papers*: 'In the night, where the contours and gradated tones of things and of the spaces between things fade out, we are left not adrift in void but in plenitude, a spatiality without planes nor separations but full and oppressive' (xvii–xviii).

Tom Sparrow expands on this, positing that for Levinas, night 'has a concrete modality' (17). As viewers' eyes work to perceive action in each dark shot, Haneke's film immerses viewers further into this modality, the camera opening them up to the plenitude of night. In a cinematic context, Martin-Jones elaborates the power of on-screen darkness in Apichatpong Weerasethakul's *Uncle Boonmee Who Can Recall His Past Lives* (2010) to constitute a totalizing non-human alterity, describing how in scenes of extreme darkness 'the Earth appears to speak, through the darkness, of its ability to store the stories of human and nonhuman lives alike' (106). Cinematic darkness intimates scale beyond the human and, attesting to Earth's archiving function, hints at a future in which humanity remains only as geological traces. Sparrow intimates the magnitude of encounter with 'nocturnal space' when noting it can be enjoyable or horrific (16) but in Haneke's film as darkness becomes a thick presence, a force of disaster itself, viewers are immersed in a rather quotidian bleakness while characters attempt to continue their everyday existence. Darkness consolidates itself as if in response to human cruelty, especially that of bourgeois social life, and humanity, including possibilities for human responsibility, registers only as fading flickers of firelight.

This may seem ambiguous, but when Haneke's film posits the post-disaster world as relentless night, it conjures Europe's 'heritage of catastrophe' (Walker, *Trauma Cinema* xv), and thus my analysis returns once more to the context of the Second World War. Elaborating Levinasian night, Sparrow cites Blanchot who writes of night as a 'nocturnal mass' that immerses everything (*Thomas the Obscure* 60) alongside Elie Wiesel's Holocaust memoir *Night*, in which Wiesel describes a dark train journey en-route to a death camp. Night becomes synonymous with mass death. By staging much of *Time of the Wolf* in utter darkness, Haneke, a European filmmaker with avowed links to post-war realism, evokes the Holocaust rather than referencing or documenting a specific, recent historical disaster. Refusal to provide narrative detail allows for the Holocaust to resonate in the film's darkness, for the full weight and ambiguity of modern Europe's disastrous heritage to be felt. In cinema, darkness dissolves forms. *Time of the Wolf*'s train station, crowded with refugees who sleep in one shared space, resembles Wiesel's description of life as a captive transported by train (23), emphasizing closeness and scarcity as indistinguishable bodies wait endlessly. When Benny prepares to immolate himself, his silhouetted frame joins with the blackness of the background, his shape meshing with the dark of the environment. For Wiesel, the immersion into dark night en-route to Auschwitz is consonant with the death of God, perhaps the ultimate pervasion of death into life, the paramount disaster.

A sense of movement through an environment is also apparent in Haneke's film and, though it is more frustrated than in *Death in the Land of Encantos* and *Life Goes On*, eventually it opens out onto the world in a highly ambiguous, poetic manner. At the beginning of the film, the family travel in a car – an echo, perhaps, of Kiarostami's style. After the father is murdered, Anne and the children are reduced to walking and pushing a bicycle; the clicking freewheel animating their journey along train tracks until they arrive at the station where stasis sets in. There is no train for the film's characters but, in the final shot, one arrives for viewers. Following the watchman's interruption of Benny's attempted sacrifice, the camera pulls away slowly so that blackness fills most of the frame and then, after an abrupt cut, viewers are shown a bright world as if from a moving train. The camera's steady tracking alerts us to the mode of transportation as the train passes through trees and a verdant country view opens up. The film's setting and narrative, the movement of its protagonists, suggest a desire to pass from dark into light. This final long take, and the cut from the black of night to the daylight of the train's passage, allows for meaning to flow into Huppert's and Blanchot's paradoxical invocations of dark and light. It immediately appears almost utopian, and Torner describes it as 'one of the most optimistic shots within the director's career', suggesting that it signals safe passage towards a better future (544). It is tempting to perceive the cut from dark to light thusly, as a kind of dawning salvation, an allusion to happy resolution.

I propose another, bleaker meaning for this shot though, as the presence of the train recalls Wiesel's *Night* once more. Wiesel writes that on his train journey, 'the days resembled the nights, and the nights left in our souls the dregs of their darkness' (100), and for Sparrow, this is illustrative of Levinas's position 'that daylight is not exempt from the horror of night' (17). The promise of a train teases viewers, just as it teases characters throughout the film, but nothing confirms this is the train everyone has been waiting for. This shot should not be understood as belonging to the film's narrative, which has already received a conclusion (the most utopian moment is the watchman's embrace of Benny). An optimistic reading relies on the position that the shot makes viewers share the viewpoint of the characters, but the absence of a windowpane of guardrail in the frame might lead us to question the perspective it posits. Like Kiarostami's tracking long takes, this shot is severed from the specificities it depicts, having a distinct, dream-like quality that invokes how, as Michel de Certeau writes, the persistently mobile view of train travel 'makes our memories speak or draws out of the shadows the dreams of our secrets' (112). It is best understood as a coda in the manner that Richard Rushton, referencing Chaudhuri and Finn, locates in Kiarostami's films: an ending that 'throws the entire rest of the film into some sort of relief, which resets the dimensions and expectations we had been building throughout the entire film' (153). Chaudhuri and Finn describe open images: 'closing scenes which try not to close down a narrative but rather open it out to the viewer's consideration, to "live on" after the film itself has finished' (52). Their description of the final scene of Kiarostami's *Taste of Cherry* (1997) fits astoundingly well with Haneke's imagery here, attesting further to the fraternity between the two directors: 'the switch from night and death to day and life, far from resolving the narrative, creates ambiguity, an openness, as if we are now watching images of life after death' (52). Haneke's vision of disaster thus echoes Kiarostami's oeuvre. The shot lasts a full two minutes but its brightness does not erase or ease the memory of the darkness viewers have just witnessed, and we are bereft by disaster of a happy ending.

In this way, disaster cannot be overcome. The long take realism of *Time of the Wolf*, like *Life, and Nothing More* and *Death in the Land of Encantos*, evinces how disaster relentlessly transforms environments. Passage through these environments functions to open post-disaster worlds up to viewers in their material specificity, but also their interminable uncertainty. Death, rather than threatening to intrude into the frame, constitutes the matter of the frame in entirety and cannot be turned away from. To look at these three films as a viewer is thus to look openly, and for some time, at disaster, contemplating encounter with its presence and its ultimate alterity.

Silence and responsibility

In these films, sound generally helps to open the material environment up to viewers, establishing an intimacy with the large-scale forces of disaster at hand. All three use music in restricted ways, preferring ambient soundscapes that bolster their documentary capacities. In keeping with their neorealist inheritance, they feature sparse dialogue and almost no non-diegetic music. Summarizing realist style, Ian Aitken posits that film is 'a non-verbal medium which generates feeling that is invoked' ('Introduction' 34), and in these films, ambient sound functions to heighten our awareness of the environment that is visually represented, deepening a feeling of encounter with disaster. Their aurality is thus geared towards silence. Not literal silence, as they all contain loudness (Anne's screaming when searching for Benny, for example), but silence in the sense suggested by Lisa Coulthard, writing about Haneke's films, wherein cinematic silence is 'rarely total' (18): Citing Jean-Luc Nancy's *Listening*, Coulthard posits that 'silence is the essence rather than the absence of sound', and it begins and ends with the subject (19).

Such an understanding of cinematic silence emphasizes the act of listening for viewers and connotes an ethical position linked with imperatives for responsibility in the face of Anthropocene catastrophe. Geographers A. Kanngieser and Nicholas Beuret pose the political potential of silence in the Anthropocene as 'a means for becoming attentive to, and making space for, more-than-human forms of life' and, further, as 'conjunctive absence and presence, excess and lack, activity and passivity' ('Refusing the World' 365). Silence allows for resonance, and therefore connection, facilitating a process of intersubjective encounter. Kanngieser further elaborates the potential of sound in this manner: 'Sound is not just about hearing and responding, or communicating. It is about becoming aware of registers that are unfamiliar, inaccessible, and maybe even monstrous: registers that are wholly indifferent to the play of human drama' ('Geopolitics and the Anthropocene' 81).

Kanngieser and Beuret are interested in encounters between human listeners and non-human volumes in which silence 'works as a mode of active listening, one designed to draw the more-than-human "background" into the foreground of thought' (370). This understanding is readily appropriate for the context of realist cinema in which silence or quietness, and especially the absence of non-diegetic music, helps to acclimate viewers to the experiences of environment and time that films assert.

Listening to these auteurist post-disaster films compels viewers towards ethical responsibility by immersing them more deeply in the unsettling elements of the worlds they see. Coulthard, writing about Haneke's films, theorizes a 'haptic aurality' for viewership that stresses 'the inherently and emphatically tactile nature of hearing' (18). Listening accentuates 'the tactile and experiential', suggesting an intensified, physical awareness wherein to listen is to 'open oneself up to "the resonance of being, or being as resonance"' (16). In the extreme darkness of *Time of the Wolf*, sound becomes a crucial way for viewers to receive information, but primarily functions to further substantiate the deathly presence of dark night. Long passages of the film are extremely quiet and without dialogue, and at times, characters' faces are out of shot or shrouded in darkness but their voices are audible. Haneke's extended darkness functions, for Coulthard, to 'focus our attention and enjoin us to listen carefully' (21). It also asks viewers to listen more environmentally, more expansively. When a dead child is buried at dusk, viewers see only the feet of those gathered to mourn, standing on the earth into which the body has been lowered, while they hear the mother wail. Her individual grief is withheld outside the frame, but viewers encounter a larger feeling of approaching night and encroaching disaster.

Corroborating my observations of the ending of *Time of the Wolf*, Coulthard argues that Haneke's film style demands 'a kind of resonant listening, one aimed not at full understanding, but rather unsettling openness' (17). At the film's conclusion, the crackle of fire is replaced, in the cut, with the mechanical rush of the train, reverberations of metal on metal. Elemental nature gives way to crashing human industry. Following this, however, the film returns to darkness and the credits roll in absolute silence. Credits are, for Coulthard, 'a privileged space for authorial signature' that in Haneke's films generally signal how 'it is as if the film has now finished and transfers its responsibilities to us the listeners' (24). In *Time of the Wolf*, the absolute dark and silence offer Haneke a final opportunity to enact his vision of disaster, opening his film further out towards viewers, enjoining our responsibility.

The cut from the soft crackle of burning wood to the train's loudness at the conclusion of *Time of the Wolf* signals an oscillation also present in *And Life Goes On*: between sounds of modernity – especially machinery and vehicles, which connote motion and acceleration – and sounds associated with nature such as wind and rustling leaves. The largest aural presence in *And Life Goes On* is the car's engine, and Jean-Luc Nancy references 'the heavy noises of cars, trucks, machinery and helicopters' in his observations of the film ('On Evidence' 184). Babak Tabarraee, characterizing Kiarostami's cinema as 'a cinema of silence', configures an understanding of silence similar to Couldhard's: 'an enriched lack, a half-charged space' ('Abbas Kiarostami: A Cinema of Silence' 6). The charge, or the push towards ethics, of *And Life Goes On*'s heavy background noise lies in its attestation to the broad pervasion of death in modernity, as in its context of isolated crisis, it sets in motion larger ideas, prevalent throughout Anthropocene discourse: of technology and industry in hazardous, precarious juxtaposition with nature and the non-human.

In distinction from Hollywood, and the independent films and documentaries considered in this book, none of these films utilize purely non-diegetic music. Music is deployed by these auteurs sparingly and carefully, is always contextualized within the narrative and functions to invoke specific atmospheres. *Time of the Wolf* features Beethoven's 'Violin Sonata No. 5', the Spring Sonata, when a man at the train station plays a cassette and rewinds the tape manually to conserve battery power. This is, for Torner, a moment in the film when a sort of society is consolidated amongst the survivors: 'the social world has realigned along many of its old lines of pleasure and prejudice' (540). In the post-disaster world, pleasure is scarce, particularly for those accustomed to classical music as entertainment. This rendition carries greater significance, as the credits inform viewers the recording is played by Yehudi Menuhin, a violinist who visited Germany immediately after the Second World War to play for survivors, still living in death camps. Menuhin writes of this experience: 'I had to impress upon my mind an actuality beyond imagination and to offer the living victims the sorrow, the repentance, the solidarity of the unharmed' (178). In the film, Menuhin's playing offers both simple pleasure and sorrowful consolation amidst the ruins of society, but the man's conservation of the device's battery suggests that the reach of disaster outlasts any possibility for redemption or solidarity. Haneke's use of this particular recording of the Spring Sonata also further strengthens the resonance of the Holocaust in the film as the refugees, waiting endlessly, come to resemble the death camp survivors described by Menuhin as 'desperately haggard' (179).

And Life Goes On does use non-diegetic music, but in a limited, contextualized way that opens it outward onto reality. Early in the film, the director is stuck in a line of traffic while Vivaldi's 'Concerto for Two Horns' plays on the car radio. The tempo and baroque lightness jars with roadside scenes of burial and a man telling the director of the pain and suffering he has seen. The radio DJ discusses distinctions between Southern European music and Iranian folk music, alerting viewers to a potential cultural incongruity, but the inclusion of Vivaldi here, Steve Choe posits, helps to alleviate 'the weight of death' (133). Later in the film, Vivaldi's concerto returns non-diegetically at several points, including in the final shot where it plays as a slow zoom out shows a view of the landscape, the car rolling out of view, and becomes prominent when the credits roll. For Choe, Kiarostami's choice of music functions to establish universality through 'shared sensitivity to the precariousness of life', and he quotes Kiarostami who says that Vivaldi 'like much of Western classical music ... "belongs to the world"' (133), thus transcending the film's cultural and geographical situation. Especially in the authorial space of the credits, then, the film is opened up to viewers beyond its Iranian context. Nancy suggests that in Kiarostami's film, 'we have to wait for the right moment for music to become possible' (84), as though there are limited uses for music in a post-disaster context where death is everywhere. Choe writes more poetically of the interrelation between life and death and the commencement of music, positing that Kiarostami 'brings death into the scope of life in a kind of rhythm and manner that allows mournful wailing to almost seamlessly flow into the Western harmonies of Vivaldi' (134). Indeed, the apparent opposition between the lightness of Vivaldi and the weight of death generally carried by the film functions to heighten our attention to both. As the title suggests, life goes on, even in the face of onrushing catastrophe and overwhelming death. In both Haneke's and Kiarostami's realist visions of disaster, then, music is integrated into the diegesis in such a way that it more deeply connects the diegetic worlds of their films to historical reality, corroborating the realism of the films and making viewers more keenly aware of the ways that, after disaster, death intrudes into life.

Death in the Land of Encantos, however, makes no use of music, and unlike Kiarostami's and Haneke's films, there is no aural juxtaposition of modern machinery with non-human nature. In the extreme long takes of Diaz's film, listening orients viewers more to the environment than it does to the circumstances of characters. It is the most literally quiet of these three films, and its silence is equated with the complete pervasion of death into the environment: the inability of life to go on. In Mai's analysis of the first scene of interaction between Hamin and Teodoro, she suggests that its muted sound evidences only death: 'The only audible sound, except for the characters' voices, is the wind that is a remnant of the passing typhoon' that 'sounds as though the region has been emptied of life' (184). To further describe the presence of death in the sound of Diaz's film, Mai cites the observations of Otto Dov Kulka, a survivor of Auschwitz-Birkenau, upon returning to the site of the death camp. Kulka writes of 'Landscapes of Silence and Desolation from Horizon to Horizon', noting 'an overwhelming silence. Not even the sound of a bird was heard there' (184). The ending of the film is composed of two extended long takes that are prefaced by a shorter shot that pictures Mount Mayon in the distance, with the lahar's devastation reaching into the foreground. While the final two shots are each marked with distinctive sounds (the chirping of bugs and Hamin's desperate exhalations), the near total silence accompanying this image of the mountain resonates throughout them. The volcano silently towers over the destruction it has wrought, a resonant cinematic presence, a harbinger of death and an agent of disaster.

Silence is, as Kanngeiser and Beuret posit, a 'commoning practice' (376), a means of bringing diverse presences into encounter (sound is, before anything else, a physical encounter: a reverberation). In these auteurist visions of disaster, silence functions to help bring viewers into closer spectatorial encounter with disaster, which necessarily involves attuning viewers to the presence of death. As viewers witness post-disaster environments, the sounds we hear make us conscious of the effects of traumatic disaster that, as El-Wardany notes, 'can become invisible': the persistence of life, and also the pervasiveness of death.

Seers of disaster

Heightened awareness of the environment is apparent in the quiet, long take style of Kiarostami's, Diaz's and Haneke's films, and critical in the way that they address their imagination of disaster to viewers. But modes of attentiveness are also built into the logics of these films on another level, being structured into the subjective dispositions of characters who encounter forces of disaster first-hand. While, as I have argued in Chapter 1, Hollywood disaster movies feature protagonists who act heroically to overcome disaster, protagonists of these auteurist disaster films are restricted from action but keenly attentive to the post-disaster environments they move through. Together, they model a mode of subjectivity and a subjective response to disaster centred on an ability to observe and become attuned to post-disaster environments.

My discussion of sound and silence provides a starting point for understanding these films' characters as ethical subjects. Coulthard and Kanngiesser and Beuret raise possibilities for notions of intersubjectivity connected to silence and listening, which are understood as methods of opening oneself up to the forces of the world. For Kanngieser and Beuret, silence is a way of troubling or refusing heroic calls to action that problematically characterize Anthropocene discourse (364) (the call to viewers at the conclusion of *An Inconvenient Truth*, for example). They posit that in the face of 'mass extinctions, runaway climate change, disappearing ice sheets, and rising sea levels' (376) silence is a more pragmatic, useful response than heroic action because it 'holds space for the more-than-human' and 'creates the grounds for *particular* expanded notions of community or alliance, bound to specific ecological processes and more-than-human agents' (377, italic in the original). Bringing forces and presences together in encounter, silence facilitates a space for ethics. Coulthard references Nancy's notion of the 'resonant subject', describing 'one who is philosophically, epistemologically and sensorially active, who is persistently approaching meaning but not complacently arriving at it' (16). A resonant subject is attentive to their environment, tuning into it in a sustained search for meaning rather than rushing towards resolution.

The structure and pacing of these films demand aural attentiveness from viewers, but they approach these ideas of silence and resonance primarily in visual terms. Their protagonists spend a lot of time listening, but are more clearly shown to be looking, searching and observing. Declining heroic action, they simply look at post-disaster landscapes, attuning themselves to their surroundings and to the resounding presence of death, reckoning with their entanglements in disastrous worlds. Sensorial and philosophical engagement becomes evident in their acts of looking. They practice attentiveness not as the resonant subjects referenced by Coulthard, but as *seeing* subjects, and their acts of seeing connect my discussion once more to the ethical imperative to confront disaster, to 'look disaster in the eye' (El-Wardany).

Further evidencing these filmmakers' links to post-war realist style, characters in all of these films clearly resemble the characters that Gilles Deleuze, theorizing cinema after the 'break' of the horrific shock of the Second World War, calls 'seers': 'a new race of characters' who *see* rather than *act* (xi). Deleuze describes characters in neorealist films who, faced with overwhelming situations, become viewers themselves: 'The character has become a kind of viewer. He shifts, runs and becomes animated in vain, the situation he is in outstrips his motor capacities on all sides … . He records rather than reacts. He is prey to a vision, pursued by it or pursuing it, rather than engaged in action' (3).

Deleuze's seers 'find themselves condemned to wander about or go off on a trip' (39), and this correlates to the way that, as I have discussed, characters in these more recent post-disaster films are consigned to movement and travel. Characters in Haneke's, Kiarostami's and Diaz's films can thus be understood as descendants of characters discussed by Deleuze throughout *Cinema 2* such as Karin in Rossellini's *Stromboli* (1950) who 'cannot react in a way that softens or compensates for the violence of what she sees' when exposed to the harshness of life on the titular volcanic island (2). In this manner, characters in *Time of the Wolf*, *Life, and Nothing More* and *Death in the Land of Encantos* are stunned by the shock of disaster, overwhelmed by death's eruption into their lives, unable to manage and incapacitated such that they cannot act. Hamin, the director, and Benny especially are reduced to simply witnessing the world around them. They figure El-Wardany's invocation of a disaster-consciousness that 'does not seek to flee from disaster, nor to manage it like a crisis, but instead strives to set it in plain sight', their restraint or incapacitation from acting and their straightforward observation of the devastated landscapes they travel through making them seers of disaster. In their response to disaster, they come to embody, in distinct ways, an openness to the decentring of the self in ethical encounter articulated in Levinas's ethics and honed more recently by theorists of post-anthropocentric thought that has helped guide this book's trajectory away from Hollywood. Their role as seers takes on ethical implications that similarly cause the formal innovations of post-war neorealism to resonate at our contemporary moment of environmental upheaval.

Inability to act is most apparent in Diaz's Hamin, who is also the closest to death of these characters. Past traumas recur for Hamin when he returns to Bicol, compounding the loss and devastation he experiences in the post-disaster landscape. Firstly, he is threatened by a government agent who has been tracking him because of his dissident poetry. The agent threatens to kill Hamin, reminding him that he has tortured him in the past. Viewers learn this torture involved the transgression of Hamin's body as Hamin tells his torturer, 'I hope you feel the pain I felt when you electrocuted my penis. I wish you feel the pain of having a tube jammed up your ass … . I wish you experience the same agony [as] when you injected acid into my brain'. Secondly, Hamin recalls his mother whose mental illness led to her death, and as he is increasingly traumatized by disaster, his experience bears resemblance to hers. Hamin's torturer uses this to ridicule him, reminding him (and informing viewers) that he was institutionalized in Russia following the stillbirth of a son: 'You went nuts just like your mother'. These traumas combine to prompt an extreme diminishment of agency and emasculation, expressed as an inability to act. Far from exhibiting heroic qualities, Hamin resembles what Raya Morag terms 'defeated masculinity', located in post-traumatic American cinema: 'Profound loss of self, incoherence at the gendered core of masculine identity, the failure to conform to the heteronormative mythical model, loss or shattering of traditional affiliations … tortured body, and shattering of sexuality – demasculinization' ('Defeated Masculinity' 190).

As Hamin's return to Bicol coincides with the return of traumatic events from his past, the subjective response to disaster that he embodies involves the perforation of physical, psychic and temporal boundaries, almost the opposite of the reification of the masculinist heroics performed by Hollywood disaster movies. As death flows from the volcano to cover the environment, it also flows over Hamin who, fully exposed, has no choice but to succumb.

Diaz belongs to the cohort of mostly Asian and European 'festival authors' in whose films Elsaesser locates his 'new realism' of 'ontological unrest', and Hamin becomes an archetypal 'post-mortem protagonist' ('World Cinema' 9–10). Through him, *Death in the Land of Encantos* engages a subjective point of view marked by intense trauma and proximity to death. Hamin ultimately becomes paranoid, believing he is being followed by government agents who intend to kill him, and looking for them everywhere he goes. Claro tells viewers he suspects

Hamin, like his mother, is suffering a psychotic break. Before the film's final scenes, Hamin dies off-camera. His body, hidden among rocks that the volcanic eruptions and mudslide have strewn across the landscape, is found by other characters, and the true nature of his death remains unknown to viewers. Mai describes the ending of the film as 'a succession of speculations' about whether his throat is cut in murder or suicide (223), suggesting that in this final section of the film, Hamin becomes a ghost, joining with his dead family members (223). Indeed, a familial connection to some kind of life after death is prefigured in earlier scenes that make use of the shaking first-person camera style to show Hamin's perspective in another time, following his mother, working in the family's garden. The penultimate shot of the film shows Hamin in this same garden, alone, looking around and examining things as though he has followed his mother into a different realm resembling his childhood. As Ingawanij observes, 'the cartographic acts of Diaz's films mesh the world of the living with the spaces and temporalities of those who have died but whose presence endures' (109). Hamin, following his mother, exits the world of the living. As in other films I have discussed, a shaky, unstable camera style corroborates subjective trauma associated with disaster, but here it also intimates a returnal resolution through defeat as disaster occasions trauma that links mother to son.

Throughout *Time of the Wolf*, Benny exhibits a similar form of emasculated futility, being completely unable to act except in seemingly unhelpful ways. His final, failed attempt at self-sacrifice seems to indicate a total lack of power and agency. Indeed, his passivity is so extreme he burdens Anne's and Eva's attempts to act. At the beginning of the film he is unable to even look at disaster, hiding from the burning horse corpses, and his face is often hidden as he appears to shy away from the world: a fringe covers his eyes and he lowers his gaze when others look at him. He is also unable to speak; Anne's attempts to engage him being met with silence. This creates an impression that he is paralysed by disaster, unable to confront situations head-on, unwilling to face up to events.

When Benny does act, his actions seem strange, unhelpful abreactions of a traumatized child. His night-time disappearance, for example, apparently worsens things for Anne and Eva and frustrates viewers. But Benny embodies a more complex form of agency than viewer expectations ordinarily cater for. Andrew Tracy hints at this when he writes, echoing Deleuze, that 'Haneke's survivors are witnesses rather than actors, denying their agency even as they exercise it' ('Time of the Wolf'). When Benny returns at dawn, apparently captured by another boy who becomes an ally of sorts and helps the family keep moving, viewers realize that his disappearance actually facilitates the continued progression of the family and the film. Similarly, his attempt at self-immolation enables the most tender moment of the film when he is rescued from the flames. Benny repeatedly goes into the black of night to seek out encounter with disaster. He seems to indulge negative passivity, but his own suffering is furthered so other characters progress and form generative, redemptive relationships.

Benny's final gesture of sacrifice is an attempt to answer for the needs of others, setting his own aside, and his response to disaster is evidential of a kind of passivity articulated by Blanchot in *The Writing of the Disaster*. When Blanchot formulates responsibility in Levinas's ethical terms, writing that '*My responsibility for the Other presupposes an overturning such that it can only be marked by a change in the status of "me", a change in time and perhaps language*' (25, italic in the original), he goes on to add: 'passivity is a task – but in a different language' (27). Benny's muteness attests to his view of the world being markedly different to those around him. It appears as a loss of agency, perhaps even a loss of self. But as a post-mortem protagonist, he is 'marked by limits' on his faculties that actually 'turn out to be enabling conditions' (Elsaesser, 'World Cinema' 9). His traumatization is a restriction that prevents him from speaking and acting pragmatically or heroically, at least in a conventional sense. But he seeks confrontation with forces of disaster and his insistent vulnerability makes the redemption of others possible.

Benny's passivity is augmented by his family, as Anne's efforts are continually frustrated by the petty stubbornness and prejudices of other survivors, while Eva retreats to solitude, seeking consolation by writing letters to her dead father. With this bereaved family at its centre, Haneke's film, in keeping with the director's assertion that his film must avoid the disaster movie category, refutes the masculinist heroism of Hollywood. Indeed, the descents into violence and psychic obliteration that Haneke's characters often undertake are an obvious counterpoint to the way that Hollywood protagonists ascend to heroism, and the way that the father, Georges, is swiftly executed after foolishly attempting to bargain with the invaders of his holiday home seems to ridicule aspirations towards heroism of the sort showcased in Hollywood.

The director in *And Life Goes On* refrains from acting heroically but does not suffer the trauma-induced incapacitation that marks Hamin and Benny. He nevertheless becomes exemplary of Deleuze's notion of the seer, as his seeing is connected to the film's mobile camera style, framed in a more dynamic way that emphasizes looking as an act in its own right. The character is described by Nancy as 'the gaze that moves through the film, the gaze that constitutes the film in the double sense of being its subject and object' ('On Evidence' 79). The film elaborately stages the act of looking, as when the son, looking out the car window, creates a frame with his hands. This framing of a gaze returns later in the film when viewers see the director look at things in order to apprehend the transformed environment and, perhaps, come to terms with the disaster. He wanders amidst a village, having stopped to talk with an actor who played an old man in *Where Is the Friend's Home?*, Kiarostami's previous film. Patterned reverse shots show him appraising wrecked buildings, his eyes resting on frames and openings in the cracked structures. In one opening, an oil lamp appears and a woman tells a child to hurry up and fetch it; life going on amidst ruins. Moments later, the director spies olive trees in the distance through a doorframe and the camera zooms towards them as Vivaldi begins to play, foreshadowing Kiarostami's subsequent film *Through the Olive Trees* (1994) (cinema, too, goes on). He walks towards the doorframe to look through it himself but first steps back to examine a picture of an old man, described thusly by Nancy: 'A kind of old, poor-quality color print affixed to the wall of a partially destroyed house. A crack in the wall crosses the image, tears it without undoing it' (79). The content of the image is unimportant, but the director's seeing it is significant, as Nancy writes, 'the absence of commentary is filled only by the gaze of the filmmaker (actor) who looks at this image' (79). Gazing into the torn image, the director perceives the loss incurred in disaster, the intrusion of death into life. In the openings and frames of the wrecked buildings, he witnesses villagers finding ways to continue their lives. Elaborately staging these acts of viewing, the film attests to the capacity of ordinary, mundane life to resist death, even as it erupts powerfully.

The director's gaze remains consistent throughout the film, conveying persistence even (or especially) in its apparent passivity and futility. His search for the young brothers is unsuccessful as his attempts to reach their town are derailed by grieving victims, a traffic jam, a damaged road. In each attempt, Mulvey suggests, 'chaos and devastation delays the journey, breaking it up into episodes and short encounters' (131). In this way, Kiarostami's film conforms with Bazin's impressions of Rossellini, whose style he argues 'maintains a succession of events, but these do not mesh like a chain with the sprockets of a wheel' and 'the mind has to leap from one event to the other as one leaps from stone to stone in crossing a river' (*What Is Cinema?* II.35). Amidst the film's indirectness, narrative ellipses and poetic gaps in the continuity of its visual perspective, the continual gaze of the director maintains a coherency, flow and focus that become tantamount to an insistence on looking disaster in the eye. The director wears glasses and his brow is frequently furrowed. When he talks to others, he often seems distracted, his gaze set on something else. As regularly as Kiarostami's film shows viewers the force of the earthquake, evident in broken buildings and blocked roads, it also shows the face of the director. Viewers see him looking in close-up where he gazes at specific scenes or objects and in mid shots where his eyes chart the road, seeking the direction of his progression. Even as the disaster dissuades and distracts him, he toils to confront it.

Stripped of their capacity to act, and especially to act heroically, all three of these characters become open to post-disaster environments. In some ways they are similar to the confused, traumatized protagonists of the independent films discussed in Chapter 2, but while seeing remains vexed for those characters (evidenced by the wounding of eyes in *Donnie Darko* and *Southland Tales* and Donnie's and Carol's gazing into mirrors), these protagonists of realist style exhibit a clarity of vision. Their ability to observe, to become acutely aware of how disaster transforms their worlds, constitutes a capacity for ethical encounter. These encounters dislodge them from themselves in different ways: for Hamin, encounter means certain death, and for Benny, it means willingness to die, while for Kiarostami's director, it means a certainty that life will go on, differently, in the face of death. The subjective response to disaster that Kiarostami's protagonist embodies is particularly potent: viewers learn little of his identity or personality and there is no specific, individual trauma that befalls him beyond the earthquake. He is characterized principally by his searching, becoming a figure of pure vision. For Deleuze's seers, 'vision is no longer even a presupposition added to action … it occupies all the room and takes the place of action' (124), and from this subjective position, unable to act, there is no option but to look at what disaster has wrought. In these seers of disaster, and across these films, viewers thus find something akin to an ethical subject in the sense that this book has pursued: as Levinas repeats, 'ethics is an optics' (*Totality and Infinity* 23), a way of looking, and these characters have no option but to look towards disaster, to face up to its deathly alterity.

The ethical dynamics of Deleuze's writing on cinema are understood to tend towards possibility, emphasizing potentiality and difference, and these films are extremely generative in their positing of ethical potentials, especially when counterposed with Hollywood's dominant disaster imaginaries. Rodowick writes that for Deleuze, as opposed to morality, ethics 'evaluates expression according to the immanent mode of existence or possibilities of life it implies' and choosing ethics involves affirming and harnessing powers of change 'in ways that value life and its openness to change' over 'fealty to moral absolutes' ('The World, Time' 101). Bending a similar sentiment more overtly towards cinema, and according with the qualities of perception and insight critically attributed to auteurs, Bogue posits that where cinema 'serves a privileged function for philosophical thought' ('To Choose to Choose – to Believe in This World' 115), for directors 'the first task of thinking differently in images is to … dissolve the links of habitual association that tie images to one another' (122). Where, as Chapter 1 has established, Hollywood's disaster tradition represents the habitual reification of traditionally masculinist powers, elaborated via remarkably unbending narrative formulas that impose moral hierarchies, these films are avenues out of such traditions, avenues for thinking differently about encounter with disaster. Diaz's and Kiarostami's films can be critically positioned as rebuttals to Hollywood's disaster tradition, but Hanneke's film more elaborately engages with and dismantles the tropes and formulas underlying Hollywood disaster movies. Despite (or perhaps because of) their affinities for death, all three films parse ways that, faced with disaster, there are ways to act beyond and apart from the regressive vanity of macho heroism. In lieu of clear-cut narrative resolution, for their seer characters embracing vulnerability and death thus leads directly or alludes to complex notions of resolution: resolution not as conclusion but, rather, as commitment or resolve. In looking towards disaster and accepting the changes it brings, their responsibility to life beyond themselves is made clear.

Realist style for the Anthropocene

Arranging this chapter by discussion of specific formal features intimates how my analysis of these films aspires to more than a survey. Many auteurs have recently been making films about the types of disaster and environmental crises bound up in the Anthropocene (e.g. Lars von Trier's *Melancholia* (2011), Darren Aronofsky's *Mother!* (2017) and Paul Schrader's *First Reformed* (2017) – in auteur cinema, as in Hollywood, disaster persists as a masculine fascination beyond the films I have selected for analysis in this chapter). Grouping these films by Kiarostami, Haneke and Diaz, from disparate moments in recent history and diverse geographical locations, together attests to a possibility for dispersed traditions of realist style to offer a consolidated outlook on the crises of Earth's current historical juncture. Taking stock of the formal features consistent across these three films, I posit that together they constitute an architecture for a contemporary realism of disaster capable of substantively engaging with the ethical situation prompted by the Anthropocene, wherein humans are become newly aware of how they come into encounter with the wider world and are intertwined with non-human forces.

There are productive tensions and resonances between the philosophical outlooks of Haneke, Diaz and Kiarostami expressed in their distinctive versions of realist style and apparent in these visions of disaster. Haneke shares a stylistic solidarity with Kiarostami, but where Kiarostami's films can be whimsical or light in tone – exemplified by his use of Vivaldi – Haneke's are brutally dark and cold, with only brief moments in *Time of the Wolf* hinting at the tenderness that vulnerability can make possible. The extreme duration of Diaz's film and its long takes sets his realist style apart from Kiarostami's and Haneke's. However, Diaz and Kiarostami are united by their timely response to historical natural disasters, and their post-disaster films are documentary-like records. Haneke's film, meanwhile, is distinct in that it intimates the history of disaster in Europe, alluding to the Holocaust experience while operating as post-apocalyptic fiction. The philosophical outlook that arises from viewing these three films as a group centres on the act of looking. But more than looking, a probing movement that is a gradual and seemingly futile movement across devastated terrain: the laboured walking of *Death in the Land of Encantos*, the interrupted automobile momentum of *And Life Goes On* and the promise of an arriving train in *Time of the Wolf*. This movement is undertaken by traumatized subjects who nevertheless work to orient themselves, questioning how they should look at the world, and asking what ways of looking might suffice.

Haneke's ciphering of the Holocaust allows a return to Levinas's ethics, and to the way that Levinasian ethics of encounter resonate at the juncture of the Anthropocene proposal, as diverse scholars and theorists posit a need to find newly adequate ways of looking at others in a contemporary situation increasingly constituted by the eruption of death. Further than encouraging the mode of noticing described by Swanson et al. as 'slowing down to listen to the world' (8) that I have associated with *There Once Was an Island*'s contemplative style in Chapter 4, the slow, deliberate way of looking posited by these films forms an ideal medium for representing what Kim Fortun has described as 'the *longue durée* in which environmental problems become manifest' (311) or what Rob Nixon has termed, with reference to environmental injustice, slow violence: 'a violence that is neither spectacular nor instantaneous, but rather incremental and accretive, its calamitous repercussions playing out across a range of temporal scales' (2). As these films' pairing of post-disaster environments and characters who can only look transcends their auteur directors, offering an interpretation of realist style for the Anthropocene, their cinematic imagination of disaster is in step with the incremental, irrevocable eruption of death.

The post-disaster environments of these films provoke viewers to imagine something that, to Rosi Braidotti, is unthinkable for the narcissistic human subject: that life would go on without it. Braidotti remarks, echoing the title of Kiarostami's film, that even without humans 'life does go on, relentlessly nonhuman in the vital force that animates it' (*The Posthuman* 137). In this sense, disaster is the continuation of life and change, even as it spells death and destruction for some. This apparently contradictory contention is made clear in many of the long takes of these films that render dynamic environments emptied out of potentially heroic human action: the churning energy of Mayon looming over Bicol, dust blowing across ruined villages in the north of Iran and the rustle of trees somewhere along a dark railway line in Western Europe. These environments, constituted by death but still enduring, appeal to viewers as alterity. The inability of these films' protagonists to act (and these films' refusal of action more generally) marks their ethical responsibility: they stand in for a humanity that could be, in Blanchot's words, 'marked by a change in the status of "me", a change in time and perhaps in language' (*The Writing of the Disaster* 25), a change provoked by looking at the world around them.

Coda: 'The fall of the regular fall of the beat, the disaster again'

The quiet city

In 2020, a decade after the first earthquake in Christchurch, I found myself in another, different disaster zone as a new set of expectations for daily life were inaugurated across the world by the Covid-19 pandemic. Attempting to account for the significance of the way this disaster seemed to change things, Richard Hil, Kristen Lyons and Fern Thompsett write in 2022 of how 'the global disruption sparked by the COVID-19 pandemic since early 2020 – to economies, communities, and everyday life – has challenged many of our sensibilities and assumptions. The great shibboleths of Enlightenment-inspired modernity like permanence, progress, certainty and growth have been dramatically and irrevocably fractured' (1).

Taking the place of these shibboleths, they posit, has been a condition of unknowing and apprehension, notably including 'dire predictions of chaos and collapse spurred by the climate crisis' (1). Forces of disruption and death gripped the world in ways both familiar and new, as this global disaster posed an apparently peremptory challenge to the ideals of rational humanity and the march of modernity. In my day-to-day experience, as lockdowns were instituted to stop the virus spreading, anomie took hold and life was characterized for many months by drifting oscillations between a sense of severe trauma and feelings of overwhelming boredom. During multiple extended periods of lockdown in Melbourne, Australia, many of which included curfews and limitations on even local travel, I refreshed and scrolled various livestreams and newsfeeds tracking statistics like daily counts of infection and death in an attempt to understand the disaster's magnitude. I video called friends and colleagues to share stories and commiserate. I walked daily in my neighbourhood, keeping my distance from others, becoming accustomed to degrees of isolation.

I did not feel it with the certainty that I experienced after seeing the earthquake, but nevertheless all of this seemed somehow familiar. Desperate for banal distraction, I endlessly watched YouTube videos and returned regularly to several uploaded in April 2020 by filmmaker, vlogger and cyclist Terry B titled *ExtendedCut – New York City Lock Down*, *Times Square Is Deserted* and *Empty Brooklyn Bridge*. These videos, documenting New York City and presenting an on the ground perspective of the Covid-19 pandemic that both complemented and contrasted the sober quantification of disaster offered in news feeds and broadcasts, refract much of what this book has dealt with. Terry B contextualizes *ExtendedCut – New York City Lock Down* by speaking directly to viewers, though his face is never visible: 'What's up? It's Terry B with another cycling-related video. We're in the middle of a, uh, stay at home order in New York – this is day five – with the exception of the ability to go out and exercise, and ride your bike, so that's what I'm doing.'

Resembling a derive, Terry B's videos share his perspective in real time as he rides his bicycle through the seemingly near-deserted city. The camera, attached to his body, is in a constant and mostly consistent state of motion, delivering a mobile representation of the largely empty streets. *ExtendedCut – New York City Lock Down* is the length of a feature film, being one hour and twenty-five minutes long (*Times Square Is Deserted* and *Empty Brooklyn Bridge* are much shorter), during which Terry B tours many Manhattan landmarks. When he passes One World Trade Center, he invokes 9/11, remarking indifferently 'the uh ... what's it called? Freedom Tower is right over here. ... This is where the Twin Towers were.' Terry B tilts the camera slightly so the massive glass tower momentarily becomes partly visible and asks viewers, 'Can you see that, up there?'

After some time and repeated viewing of online videos like these, I developed an understanding of how this time of Covid-19 also seemed like a movie. Roughly the first third of the Hollywood post-apocalyptic action thriller *I Am Legend* (2007) depicts the film's hero, US army virologist Robert Neville roving New York City three years after a disastrous event. Neville is apparently the only human left alive, and the sunny, empty city becomes his playground as he drives a red sports car at dangerous speed, swerving among abandoned skyscrapers through intersections overgrown with grass and shrubs. When he practices his golf swing from the wing of a Lockheed A-12 Blackbird jet perched atop an aircraft carrier, the Brooklyn Bridge and the Manhattan Bridge, visible in the background, lie smashed into the East River. Viewers may intuit this is a result of efforts to isolate Manhattan, as the preceding disaster stems from a virus that turns humans into nocturnal vampiric mutants, whom Neville encounters later. *I Am Legend* shares many characterizing features of the Hollywood disaster genre outlined in Chapter 1. It is a textual recursion, being the third filmic adaptation of Richard Matheson's 1954 novel of the same name, following *The Last Man on Earth* (1964) and *The Omega Man*, starring Charlton Heston. It raises questions of complicity and anxieties around technology as its virus is a mutated form of measles developed by scientists to cure cancer. A form of resolution comes when Neville, an army man and a scientist played by *Independence Day*'s Will Smith, clearly fitting the mould of a disaster movie hero, develops a cure. The film goes some way towards delivering a vision of Rosi Braidotti's promise of a world without humans, and might even be understood as staging a conflict, a struggle between the Hollywood disaster hero and the ongoing of life that exceeds them, 'the generative force of *zoe*, the great animal-machine of the universe, beyond personal individual death' (*The Posthuman* 136). Writing in the journal *Clinical Infectious Diseases* in 2003, a group of infectious disease experts conclude that 'most depictions of aspects of infectious diseases in cinema are inaccurate' (Pappas et al. 942) but nevertheless, during repeated Covid-19 lockdowns when I wandered my suburban neighbourhood and sometimes glimpsed Melbourne's skyline in the distance, livestreamed press conferences with politicians and scientists, and idly procrastinated on YouTube, *I Am Legend* functioned to structure my imagination of what a viral disaster could look and feel like, animating my experience of the global disruption described by Hil, Lyons and Thompsett.

Robert Yeates, in *American Cities in Post-Apocalyptic Science Fiction*, explains that New York City is a 'repeat victim' of apocalypse (27). In many ways *ExtendedCut – New York City Lock Down* mirrors *I Am Legend* and other similar Hollywood genre movies, partaking in the spectacular cinematic imagination of disaster enacted by many of the films I have analysed and discussed in this book as it figures Manhattan as the epicentre of an imperilled humanity. Its street-level perspective, framed by skyscrapers on either side, calls forth memories of scenes from *Independence Day* and other films where New Yorkers take to the streets fleeing explosions, tidal waves and the like. The quietness and lack of expected busyness recalls *The Day After Tomorrow* where, after a massive flood and a brutal storm, New York becomes a frozen wasteland, still and silent. Its protagonist and narrator, while not really a hero, is a solitary male explorer, a man of action embracing risk to catalogue monuments at risk of abandonment. But *ExtendedCut – New York City Lock Down* also recoups many of the aspects of realist style I have highlighted in Chapter 5. It includes only a few cuts, mostly delivering a durational, long take perspective. Its mobile camera reflects the experience of a body in motion in the world, and the persistent forward momentum of the motion it exhibits very clearly echoes Kiarostami's car in *And Life Goes On*. Viewers become quickly attuned to the inherent danger – the exposure – of riding a bicycle in traffic, but there is a relative calmness to its perspective. Where the spectacle of New York and other cities in disaster movies, especially after 9/11, tends towards hectic imagery of exploding, collapsing skyscrapers, shards of glass and metal calving off to fall below, here the material city remains spookily intact as human life within it is exploded, both socially and biologically.

ExtendedCut – New York City Lock Down also demonstrates, crucially, that the cinematic imagination of disaster is no longer limited to films, but that the contours of film form, genre and realism that this book has traced remain broadly, perhaps increasingly, relevant. During Covid-19 lockdowns, cinemas were off-limits, and this has perhaps helped to hasten the advent of what some theorists, such as William Brown, refer to as 'a post-cinematic age' involving 'home viewing, smart television, online videos and more' (*Non-cinema* 1–2). In this age, Brown posits, 'it nonetheless is the techniques developed in the cinema (framing, lighting, cutting, make-up and so on) that proliferate on the near-ubiquitous screens of modernity' (2). As much as disaster remains a particular preoccupation of feature filmmaking, a powerful genre in Hollywood, and as climate crisis continues to worsen, the imagination of disaster also proliferates via video games, music videos, advertisements and other media. As disaster recurs in these media, the cinematic capacities and disinclinations for ethical response to the exigencies of history that I have highlighted continue to exert their powers, and Hollywood remains a dominant cultural referent, a touchstone for re-asserting the mastery of humans over both nature and technology. Meanwhile, pointing towards the continued possibilities of the formal sensibilities and ethics teased out via realist theory (and making a case for the ongoing relevance of film theory in evolving landscapes of media and media theory), Tom Gunning posits, 'I firmly believe Bazin would view the ongoing development of new media not as the end of cinema but as a stage in its continuing invention. ... far from an outmoded idealist conservative, it may be that Bazin himself has not yet been invented' ('The World in Its Own Image' 125). How might a Bazinian realism, seeking percipient responsiveness to history that resonates with Donna Haraway's call for 'response-ability' at Earth's current disastrous juncture, being 'present in and to onrushing catastrophe' (35), persist beyond cinema?

Disintegration Loop 1.1 and the disaster again

Near the beginning of *The Writing of the Disaster*, Maurice Blanchot writes: 'To want to write: what an absurdity. Writing is the decay of the will, just as it is the loss of power, and the fall of the regular fall of the beat, the disaster again' (17).

Obliquely, Blanchot refers to the way the Holocaust continually reverberates in the lives of survivors, and perhaps to the difficulty or impossibility of seeking to recollect or record that immensely traumatic disaster. His words also signal the etymological considerations for disaster raised at the beginning of this book: *dis astro*, fallen star, fallen world. Perhaps something biblical or eschatological, the fall of man, is at hand.

Disintegration Loop 1.1 can perhaps be categorized as a music video. It is the visual accompaniment to American avant-garde composer William Basinski's *dlp 1.1*, the first track from his album *The Disintegration Loops*. *dlp 1.1* resembles the fall of the regular fall of the beat in an almost literal way. It is composed of a recording of an old tape loop that, salvaged by Basinski in 2001 for archiving and then played for an extended duration, begins to deteriorate; to literally, materially, fall apart. Over its roughly one-hour duration, listeners hear velvety horns that slow down, becoming dejected and a percussive brush that decays into a scrape. *dlp 1.1* evokes a chopped and screwed or digitally corrupted version of the Twentieth Century Fox fanfare that plays at the beginning of so many films, famously accompanying an animated sequence that presents the Hollywood studio's logo as the centre of a magnificent, modern cityscape. When 9/11 happened shortly after Basinski digitized this decaying loop, he filmed the Manhattan skyline from a rooftop in Brooklyn. The resulting video, *Disintegration Loop 1.1*, is a static long take that captures the city skyline for an hour during twilight on the day of the terror attacks and the fall of the Twin Towers, showing smoke billowing across buildings, which are silhouetted as dusk takes hold, and then the black of night.

Yusuf Sayed suggests *Disintegration Loop 1.1* is '*the* establishing shot of the twenty-first century' ('Of Mourning and Evening'). This intimates how the video's plaintive, poetic documentation of this disastrous moment in American and global history seems to capture but also exceed its indexical referent, gesturing towards a great fall and a greater decay, and resonating with subsequent experience of disaster as both a sudden, rupturing event, but also a force that institutes ongoing conditions for everyday life. The video can be understood to have a documentary function as a record of a major historical event, and may also be understood as fulfilling the criteria of conventional, long take realist aesthetics, as it opens up an experience of time to viewers. But *Disintegration Loop 1.1* also elides the social world of the disaster, at least in a literal sense, showing nothing at ground level and including no human subjects. It is partial, fragmentary. As a memento of 9/11, it includes nothing of how, as E. Ann Kaplan details, 'response to 9/11 is added onto normal New York life' (9), from 'memorials in Union Square' and 'posters stuck all over the streets' showing 'rows of images of lost people' to 'National Guard soldiers in their khakis stood at the barriers' at Ground Zero (7), and 'flag-flying' as 'a newly engaged patriotism' but also a new, collective understanding among strangers: 'On the subway too, we looked at each other as if understanding what we all were facing' (9). Joanna Demers describes how as viewers 'we see nothing from the street, of course; no places, no people jumping from the towers', and this means, therefore, that 'it's easy to be metaphorical and read the events of that day, as well as the image of those collapsed buildings, as symbols of the decay of the American empire' (82).

Disintegration Loop 1.1's vision of Manhattan seemingly emptied out of people prefigures the New York City of both *I Am Legend* and *ExtendedCut – New York City Lock Down*. A synergy is overtly engaged between 9/11 and the Covid-19 pandemic as Basinski's major work is also recuperated in a documentary film created during 2020 titled *Disintegration Loops* (2021) that narrates his creation of *dlp1.1* and how it became an elegy to 9/11. Shot during lockdown, this film re-deploys *dlp1.1* as the soundtrack to several black and white shots of New York City that centre monuments and widely familiar locations like Brooklyn Bridge and Central Park, mostly devoid of people. The 9/11 of Basinski's original video thus perdures, as *Disintegration Loop 1.1* succeeds not only in representing the disastrous historical event it indexes, but also in creating a concrete, poetic impression of disaster that persists beyond that event.

'The phenomenon of 9/11', notes Kaplan, 'was perhaps the supreme example of a catastrophe that was experienced globally via digital technologies (Internet, cell phone) as well as by television and radio' (2). When the first plane struck the World Trade Center on 9/11, it was very early in the morning in Aotearoa New Zealand. I was a teenager, and I remember my mother waking me up much earlier than usual to watch TV news reports while I ate breakfast. When I arrived at school, my teacher wheeled a TV into the classroom so, again and again that morning, I watched the Twin Towers fall. I had never been to

New York or America but I knew the skyline and those buildings from films, TV and media: 1990s disaster movies including *Independence Day*, *Deep Impact* and *Godzilla*, but also *Late Night with David Letterman*, *Friends* and *Seinfeld*, music videos for songs like *Rollin'* by Limp Bizkit and *Heart of Glass* by Blondie. To me, they were certainly emblems of America, and especially of American culture and the allure of American entertainment. Watching 9/11 from afar did not seem so much like a movie but, rather, like a movie gone wrong. When I encountered *Disintegration Loop 1.1* years later, I felt that as it deals in the passage of time, repetition and decay, it fixes the significance of that transformative moment in plain sight. As the video presents New York City, and the City in general, as a wounded, languishing, hollowed out symbol for the progress of rational humanity, *Disintegration Loop 1.1* resembles and represents not only 9/11 but the way that, as Deborah Bird Rose writes, in modernity and at the advent of the Anthropocene, 'the work of the moment is disaster piled upon disaster' (*Wild Dog Dreaming* 89).

At the start of this book I posited that as we humans seem to find ourselves befalling disaster after disaster, in large part due to worsening climate crisis, and are also increasingly compelled to recognize our own constituency in perpetuating those disasters, reckoning with the unevenly distributed role of human enterprise in writing the fate of the Earth, it is pertinent to ask how one might imagine life in a disaster zone. Writing about experience of 9/11 in terms of trauma's capacity to shape and reshape experience of the world for New Yorkers, Kaplan describes how 'history, memory, time and space collapsed in to one present time' and therefore 'produced a new subjectivity' (4). If *Disintegration Loop 1.1* is an establishing shot for a post-9/11 world of climate change and anthropogenic disaster, rather than a final curtain-fall, it prompts viewers to wonder how things will unfold: what, or whom, will we see after the first cut? As films and media like not only *Disintegration Loop 1.1*, but also *San Andreas*, *Donnie Darko* and others condense, reflect, work through and elsewise represent recent history, they implicitly respond to the cascading disasters of our time, perhaps hastening our recognition of subjective experiences of disaster. I have tried to highlight here how some films have posited some ideas about how humanity can see itself intertwining with and perhaps taking responsibility for a world that is increasingly awry. I have suggested that different kinds of films do this in many different ways, with different political, philosophical and ethical connotations, and that realism might be understood as the means by which they enact these responses. In particular, I have been attentive to how films might spur on or recuperate the formation of subjects, presenting protagonists who dwell in disaster zones and are shaped by their encounters with disaster.

I have contended that Hollywood's disaster movie genre does not seek to articulate the type of ethical response signalled as crucial in the face of the widespread disasters that inhere in the Anthropocene proposal by Rose and others, including Haraway, who work towards post-anthropocentric ethics. The spectacularly rendered disaster scenarios of these films, rather, evade ethical responsibility, reifying extant social hierarchies and especially patriarchal knowledges. They stage encounters with disaster in which heroes who are mostly male, white and uniformed emerge to dominate all forms of alterity, from earthquakes to aliens. Their generic formulas constitute a realism of action, a form of masculine melodrama that addresses the threat of death by re-asserting the status quo, doubling down on the strategies of ostensible progress that have provoked many present disasters. These films work to perpetually allay anxieties about mass death rather than confront it as a possibility and, in this sense, they turn away from the inexorable onrushing catastrophe that presently confronts the Earth.

In the shadow of Hollywood's 1990s disaster movie cycle, I have observed an extended subgenre of independent films that refracts the looming presence of eco-catastrophe in oblique ways, and described it as being concerned with strange disaster. Films like *Safe*, *Donnie Darko* and *Southland Tales* imagine disaster as a covert presence that precipitates death from within the fabric of everyday life. They respond specifically to the world of the North American suburban middle class at the historical moment of the millennial turn, a time of dawning popular awareness of climate change. Indexing this world and its denizens, the realism that these films share hinges on different techniques of fragmentation and omission, as they disrupt and invert familiar formal tendencies from Hollywood. This realism is tied to protagonists who meander towards dissolution, being displaced from positions of primacy and confronted by ambiguous, treacherous forces of disaster. Unsure of their place in the world and pushed towards death, they glimpse possibilities for other modes of existing. Imagining life in the zones of strange disaster evoked by these films is a question of embracing uncertainty, accommodating alterity and abiding displacement.

Turning to documentary, I have noted two possibilities for documentary representation of disaster in contexts of climate change that are linked to two different positions on documentary's capacities for realism, describing these with reference to Donna Haraway's 'Situated Knowledges' as the view from above and the view from a body. In the former, I have traced a resonance with Hollywood in large-scale, paradigmatic climate change documentaries, apparent in spectacular aerial visuality and masculinist figures of cosmopolitanism and authority. Emphasizing a detached objectivity, posing discourses of science and capital as primary means for knowing and encountering the world, the realism of these documentaries takes the form of a conquering logic that can echo and reinforce disasters of colonialism. Elsewise, the view from a body resonates in many ways with understandings of realist film style, and I have observed it in *There Once Was an Island* and *On an Unknown Beach*, which are characterized by impressionistic camera techniques that are influenced by and reflect the churn of the material world, and the inclusion of multiple subjective viewpoints. The view from a body connotes a corporeal encounter, and the ideas of documentary realism that it is associated with emphasize embedded perspectives and lived experience. These duelling views suggest divergent ways of imagining disaster. Imagining disaster from above involves distance, conceiving of events like sea level rise as phenomena that remain elsewhere, happening to other people, that might be mitigated by prescribed action and technological innovation. Imagining disaster from the body, meanwhile, involves intimacy and specificity, positing disaster as an event experienced by bodies in space, an event that ruptures selfhood, family, cultures and tradition as it destroys environments. As the documentary films that I have examined imagine anthropogenic oceanic disaster, my attention to how they imagine the South Pacific as a disaster zone has helped to drive this book's thesis beyond the Northern Hemisphere contexts that are the domain of Hollywood, and that also frequently dominate Anthropocene discourse.

Dispersed in different locations across the world, I have described an auteurist-realist tendency for the cinematic representation of disaster: in three films by directors who reflect their situations in Iran, Europe and the Philippines while being clearly influenced by the neorealism of post-war Italian directors. As distinct visions of disaster, *And Life Goes On*, *Time of the Wolf* and *Death in the Land of Encantos* all nonetheless exhibit a slow, observational camera style that centres around the capacity of the long take to render disastrous environments in a documentary-like manner, atmospheric sound and minimal use of music that augments these environmental renderings and enhances a feeling of exposure for viewers, and characters who are incapacitated or refrain from heroic action but instead observe keenly, becoming seers. Life in the disaster zones that they posit is imagined as a process of adjustment, a necessary acclimation to reconstituted environments and new formations of selfhood that have been imposed by forces that exceed the human.

Beyond the fault lines traced in this book, there are certainly other ways that films can prompt viewers to imagine disaster. It has not been my task to provide an exhaustive catalogue of disaster films, but opening up some paths beyond Hollywood and beyond genre, I have sought to create a sense of the abundant power of film's capacity to respond to the demands of a history of disaster, and in particular to the history of environmental disaster and climate crisis that we presently inherit. Ostensibly isolated historical disasters can teach us much as we seek to orient ourselves in the wider atmosphere of disaster that the notion of the Anthropocene connotes, and my recourse to Bazin and Levinas indicates how the events of the Second World War continue to loom large as aesthetic and philosophical responses to the unprecedented eruptions of death that it entailed remain instructive. But this is also true of 9/11, and 3.11, and the earthquake in Iran in 1990, and dawning awareness in suburbia of global warming, and the flooding of Nukutoa, where disaster has provoked new and different ways of looking at and being in the world. Beyond Hollywood's disaster imaginary, with its ever-increasing spectacular hypothetical scenarios, films emerge in the wake of disasters such as these, seeking to reckon with them. If we pay attention to such films, they might engender ethical ways of being in the world and bearing with the presence of disaster.

Bibliography

Agarwal, Anil, and Sunita Narain. *Global Warming in an Unequal World: A Case of Environmental Colonialism*. New Delhi: Centre for Science and Environment, 1991.
Aitken, Ian. 'The European Realist Tradition', *Studies in European Cinema*, vol. 3, no. 3, 2007, pp. 175–88.
Aitken, Ian. 'Introduction'. In *The Major Realist Film Theorists: A Critical Anthology*, edited by Ian Aitken. Edinburgh: Edinburgh University Press, 2016, pp. 1–40.
Alaimo, Stacy. *Bodily Natures: Science, Environment, and the Material Self*. Bloomington: Indiana University Press, 2010.
Alaimo, Stacy. *Exposed: Environmental Politics and Pleasures in Posthuman Times*. Minneapolis: University of Minnesota Press, 2016.
Altman, Rick. *Film/Genre*. London: British Film Institute, 1999.
Andrew, Dudley. 'An Atlas of World Cinema', *Framework: The Journal of Cinema and Media*, vol. 45, no. 2, 2004, pp. 9–23.
Andrew, Dudley. *What Cinema Is! Bazin's Quest and Its Charge*. Chichester: Wiley-Blackwell, 2010.
Anson, April. '"Master Metaphor": Environmental Apocalypse and the Settler States of Emergency', *Resilience: A Journal of the Environmental Humanities*, vol. 8, no. 1, 2020, pp. 60–81.
Armes, Roy. *Patterns of Realism*. New York: A.S. Barnes, 1971.
Balsom, Erika. *An Oceanic Feeling: Cinema and the Sea*. New Plymouth, Aotearoa New Zealand: Govett-Brewster Art Gallery, 2018.
Batalibasi, Amie. '"Aeasi" 360 Virtual Reality Documentary Premieres in Canada and Australia'. 2018. Accessed 10 September 2022. https://amiebatalibasi.com/aeasi-360-virtual-reality-documentary-premieres-in-canada-and-australia/.
Bazin, André. *Bazin at Work: Major Essays and Reviews from the Forties and Fifties*. Translated by Alain Piette and Bert Cardullo, edited by Cardullo. New York: Routledge, 1997.
Bazin, André. *What Is Cinema?* Volume I. Translated by Hugh Gray. Berkeley: University of California Press, 1967.
Bazin, André. *What Is Cinema?* Volume II. Translated by Hugh Gray. Berkeley: University of California Press, 1972.
Bennett, Jane. 'Systems and Things: A Response to Graham Harman and Timothy Morton', *New Literary History*, vol. 43, no. 2, 2012, pp. 225–33.
Bennett, Jane. *Vibrant Matter*. Durham, NC: Duke University Press, 2010.

Berardi, Franco. *The Uprising: On Poetry and Finance*. Los Angeles, CA: Semiotext(e), 2012.

Birks, Chelsea. *Limit Cinema: Transgression and the Nonhuman in Contemporary Global Film*. New York: Bloomsbury Academic, 2021.

Blanchot, Maurice. *Thomas the Obscure*. Barrytown, NY: Station Hill Press, 1988.

Blanchot, Maurice. *The Writing of the Disaster*. Lincoln: University of Nebraska Press, 1995.

Bogue, Ronald. 'To Choose to Choose – To Believe in This World'. In *Afterimages of Gilles Deleuze's Film Philosophy*, edited by D. N. Rodowick. Minneapolis: University of Minnesota Press, 2010, pp. 115–32.

Bonilla, Yarimar. 'The Coloniality of Disaster: Race, Empire, and the Temporal Logics of Emergency in Puerto Rico, USA', *Political Geography*, vol. 78, 2020, p. 102181.

Bordwell, David. 'Part One: The Classical Hollywood Style, 1917–60'. In *The Classical Hollywood Cinema: Film Style and Mode of Production to 1960*, by Bordwell, Janet Staiger and Kristin Thompson. London: Routledge, 1999, pp. 1–95.

Bould, Mark. *The Anthropocene Unconscious: Climate Catastrophe Culture*. London: Verso, 2021.

Braidotti, Rosi. *The Posthuman*. Cambridge: Polity Press, 2013.

Braidotti, Rosi. *Posthuman Knowledge*. Cambridge: Polity Press, 2019.

Brown, William. '*Melancholia*: The Long, Slow Cinema of Lav Diaz'. In *Slow Cinema*, edited by Tiago de Luca and Nuno Barradas Jorge. Edinburgh: Edinburgh University Press, 2015, pp. 112–22.

Brown, William. *Non-Cinema: Global Digital Film-Making and the Multitude*. New York: Bloomsbury, 2018.

Campos, Patrick F. *The End of National Cinema: Filipino Film at the Turn of the Century*. Quezon City: University of the Philippines Press, 2016.

Carson, Rachel. *Silent Spring*. Boston, MA: Mariner Books, 2002.

Caruth, Cathy. *Unclaimed Experience: Trauma, Narrative, and History*. Baltimore, MD: Johns Hopkins University Press, 1996.

Chaudhuri, Shohini, and Howard Finn. 'The Open Image: Poetic Realism and the New Iranian Cinema', *Screen*, vol. 44, no. 1, 2003, pp. 38–57.

Choe, Steve. 'The Just Distance: Abbas Kiarostami and the Aftermath of Devastation'. In *Film on the Faultline*, edited by Alan Wright. Bristol, UK: Intellect Books, 2015, pp. 125–46.

Code, Lorraine. *Ecological Thinking: The Politics of Epistemic Location*. Oxford: Oxford University Press, 2006.

*Cohen, Richard A. (Ed.). *Face to Face with Levinas*. Albany: State University of New York Press, 1986.

Cooper, Sarah. 'Emmanuel Levinas', In *Film, Theory and Philosophy: The Key Thinkers*, edited by Felicity Colman. Montréal: McGill-Queens University Press, 2009, pp. 91–9.

Cooper, Sarah. 'Introduction: The Occluded Relation: Levinas and Cinema', *Film-Philosophy*, vol. 11, no. 2, 2007, pp. i–vii.
Cooper, Sarah. *Selfless Cinema? Ethics and French Documentary*. England: Legenda, 2006.
Corlett, David. *Stormy Weather: The Challenge of Climate Change and Displacement*. Sydney: University of New South Wales Press, 2008.
Coulthard, Lisa. 'Haptic Aurality: Listening to the Films of Michael Haneke', *Film-Philosophy*, vol. 16, no. 1, 2012, pp. 16–29.
Cubitt, Sean. 'Everybody Knows This Is Nowhere: Date Visualization and Ecocriticism'. In *Ecocinema Theory and Practice*, edited by Sean Cubitt, Salma Monani and Stephen Rust. New York: Routledge, 2012, pp. 277–96.
Davy, Barbara Jane. 'An Other Face of Ethics in Levinas', *Ethics and the Environment*, vol. 12, no. 1, 2007, pp. 39–65.
de Certeau, Michel. *The Practice of Everyday Life*. Berkeley: University of California Press, 1988.
de Luca, Tiago, and Nuno Barradas Jorge. 'Introduction: From Slow Cinema to Slow Cinemas'. In *Slow Cinema*, edited by Tiago de Luca and Nuno Barradas Jorge. Edinburgh: Edinburgh University Press, 2015, pp. 1–21.
Deamer, David. *Deleuze, Japanese Cinema, and the Atom Bomb: The Spectre of Impossibility*. New York: Bloomsbury, 2014.
Deleuze, Gilles. *Cinema 2: The Time Image*. London: Continuum, 2005.
DeLillo, Don. *White Noise*. New York: Penguin, 1984.
DeLoughrey, Elizabeth. *Allegories of the Anthropocene*. Durham, NC: Duke University Press, 2019.
DeLoughrey, Elizabeth. 'Submarine Futures of the Anthropocene', *Comparative Literature*, vol. 69, no. 1, 2017, pp. 32–44.
DeLoughrey, Elizabeth. 'The Sea is rising: Visualising climate change in the Pacific islands', *Pacific Dynamics: Journal of Interdisciplinary Research*, vol. 2, no. 2, pp. 186–97.
Demers, Joanna. *Drone and Apocalypse: An Exhibit Catalog for the End of the World*. Hants: Zero Books, 2015.
Demos, T. J. *Against the Anthropocene: Visual Culture and Environment Today*. Berlin: Sternberg Press, 2017.
Dibazar, Pedram. 'Wandering Cars and Extended Presence: Abbas Kiarostami's Embodied Cinema of Everyday Mobility', *New Review of Film and Television Studies*, vol. 15, no. 3, 2017, pp. 299–326.
DiCaprio, Leonardo. 'Leonardo DiCaprio at the UN: "Climate Change Is Not Hysteria – It's a Fact"', *The Guardian*, 23 September 2014. Accessed 10 October 2022. www.theguardian.com/environment/2014/sep/23/leonarodo-dicaprio-un-climate-change-speech-new-york.

Doane, Mary Ann. 'Pathos and Pathology: The Cinema of Todd Haynes', *Todd Haynes: A Magnificent Obsession*, special issue of *Camera Obscura: Feminism, Culture, and Media Studies*, vol. 19, no. 3(57), 2004, pp. 1–21. edited by Amelie Hastie. Durham, NC: Duke University Press.

Doyle, Julie. 'Communicating Climate Change in *Don't Look Up*', *Journal of Science Communication*, vol. 21, no. 5, 2022, pp. 1–7.

Drabinski, John E. *Levinas and the Postcolonial: Race, Nation, Other*. Edinburgh: Edinburgh University Press, 2011.

Dyer, Richard. 'Double Indemnity: Todd Haynes/Edward Hopper: Todd Haynes with Richard Dyer', *Tate Modern*, 2004. Online audio recording. Accessed 23 August 2018. www.tate.org.uk/context-comment/video/double-indemnity-todd-haynesedward-hopper-todd-haynes-richard-dyer.

Eells, Josh. 'Dwayne Johnson: The Pain and the Passion that Fuel the Rock', *Rolling Stone*, April 2018. Accessed 8 February 2021. https://www.rollingstone.com/movies/movie-features/dwayne-johnson-the-pain-and-the-passion-that-fuel-the-rock-630076/.

Elsaesser, Thomas. *European Cinema: Face to Face with Hollywood*. Amsterdam: Amsterdam University Press, 2005.

Elsaesser, Thomas. 'The Global Author: Control, Creative Constraints, and Performative Self-contradiction'. In *The Global Auteur: The Politics of Authorship in 21st Century Cinema*, edited by Seung-hoon Jeong and Jeremi Szaniawski. New York: Bloomsbury, 2016, pp. 21–41.

Elsaesser, Thomas. 'World Cinema: Realism, Evidence, Presence'. In *Realism and the Audiovisual Media*, edited by Lucia Nagib and Cecilia Mello. Basingstoke: Palgrave Macmillan, 2009, pp. 3–19.

El-Wardany, Haytham. 'Notes on Disaster', *ArteEast Quarterly*, Winter 2015. Accessed 26 August 2021. arteeast.org/quarterly/notes-on-disaster/.

Farbotko, Carol. 'Wishful Sinking: Disappearing Islands, Climate Refugees and Cosmopolitan Experimentation', *Asia Pacific Viewpoint*, vol. 51, no. 1, 2010, pp. 47–60.

Fay, Jennifer. *Inhospitable World: Cinema in the Time of the Anthropocene*. New York: Oxford University Press, 2018.

Fisher, Mark. *Capitalist Realism: Is There No Alternative?* Portland, OR: Zero Books, 2009.

Fisher, Mark. *Ghosts of My Life: Writings on Depression, Hauntology and Lost Futures*. Winchester: Zero Books, 2014.

Fisher, Mark. *The Weird and the Eerie*. London: Repeater, 2017.

Fortun, Kim. 'From Latour to Late Industrialism', *HAU: Journal of Ethnographic Theory*, vol. 4, no. 1, 2014, pp. 309–29.

Frey, Mattias. 'Michael Haneke', *Senses of Cinema*, no. 57, December 2010. Accessed 10 October 2022. Sensesofcinema.com/2010/great-directors/ichael-haneke/.

Gablik, Suzi. *The Reenchantment of Art*. London: Thames & Hudson, 1992.
Gates, James, and Adam Luxton. 'Interview: Adam Luxton and *On an Unknown Beach*', *Pantograph Punch*. July 2016. Accessed 10 October 2022. Pantographpunch.com/post/Adam-Luxton-Unknown-Beach.
Gazi, Jeeshan. 'Redeeming Kracauer's Theory of Film: An Examination of the Importance of Material Aesthetics', *SubStance*, vol. 45, no. 1, 2016, pp. 66–80.
Girgus, Sam B. *Levinas and the Cinema of Redemption: Time, Ethics, and the Feminine*. New York: Columbia University Press, 2010.
Gray-Sharp, Katarina. *My Responsibility in the Face of Mass Extinction*. University of Waikato, New Zealand, PhD thesis, 2021. https://hdl.handle.net/10289/14209.
Grosoli, Marco. 'Space and Time in the Land of the End of History'. In *The Global Auteur: The Politics of Authorship in 21st Century Cinema*, edited by Seung-hoon Jeong and Jeremi Szaniawski. London: Bloomsbury, 2016, pp. 303–22.
Grundmann, Roy. 'Auteur de Force: Michael Haneke's "Cinema of Glaciation"', *Cineaste*, vol. 32, no. 2, 2007, pp. 6–14.
Gunning, Tom. 'The World in Its Own Image: The Myth of Total Cinema'. In *Opening Bazin: Powtwar Film Theory and Its Afterlife*, edited by Dudley Andrew with Hervé Joubert-Laurencin. New York: Oxford University Press, 2011, pp. 119–26.
Gyllenhaal, Jake. 'How We Made Donnie Darko', *The Guardian*, 13 December 2016. Accessed 10 October 2022. https://www.theguardian.com/film/2016/dec/12/how-we-made-donnie-darko-jake-gyllenhaal.
Hall, Nina. 'Climate Change, Refugees and Migration'. In *Fair Borders? Migration Policy in the Twenty-First Century*, edited by David Hall. Wellington: Bridget Williams Books, 2017, pp. 150–71.
Hamilton Faris, Jaimey. 'Gestures of Survivance: Angela Tiatia's *Lick* and Feminist Environmental Performance Art in Oceania', *Pacific Arts*, vol. 20, no. 1, 2020, pp. 6–22.
Haraway, Donna. 'Situated Knowledges: The Science Question in Feminism and the Privilege of Partial Perspective', *Feminist Studies*, vol. 14, no. 3, 1988, pp. 575–99.
Haraway, Donna. *Staying with the Trouble: Making Kin in the Chthulucene*. Durham, NC: Duke University Press, 2016.
Heise, Ursula. 'Journeys through the Offset World: Global Travel Narratives and Environmental Crisis', *Substance*, vol. 41, no. 1, 2012, pp. 61–76.
Hil, Richard, Kristen Lyons and Fern Thompsett. *Transforming Universities in the Midst of Global Crisis: A University for the Common Good*. Abingdon: Routledge, 2022.
Hilton, Nick. 'From *Infinity War* to *Okja*: Why Overpopulation Is Cinema's Crisis du Jour', *The Guardian*, 15 May 2018. Accessed 17 August 2021. https://www.theguardian.com/film/2018/may/15/infinity-war-okja-overpopulation-cinema-ready-player-one-downsizing.
Hoberman, J. 'Nashville Contra Jaws: Or "The Imagination of Disaster" Revisited'. In *The Last Great American Picture Show: New Hollywood Cinema in the 1970s*, edited

by Thomas Elsaesser, Alexander Horwath and Noel King. Amsterdam: Amsterdam University Press, 2004, pp. 195–222.

Holmes, Diana. 'Sex, Gender and Auteurism: The French New Wave and Hollywood'. In *World Cinema's 'Dialogues' with Hollywood*, edited by Paul Cook. London: Palgrave Macmillan, 2007, pp. 154–71.

Horn, Eva. *The Future as Catastrophe: Imagining Disaster in the Modern Age*. New York: Columbia University Press, 2018.

Hornblower, Margot. 'Have Gun, will Travel', *Time*, vol. 152, 1998, p. 44.

Horne, Gerald. *The Apocalypse of Settler Colonialism: The Roots of Slavery, White Supremacy, and Capitalism in 17th Century North America and the Caribbean*. New York: Monthly Review Press, 2017.

Horwath, Alexander. 'Michael Haneke Interview: Uncut', *Film Comment*. November–December 2009. Accessed 10 October 2022. www.filmcomment.com/article/michael-haneke-interview/.

Hughes, Helen. *Green Documentary: Environmental Documentary in the Twenty-First Century*. Bristol: Intellect Books, 2014.

Ingawanij, May Adadol. 'Long Walk to Life: The Films of Lav Diaz', *Afterall*, vol. 40, 2015, pp. 102–15.

Ingram, David. 'The Aesthetics and Ethics of Eco-Film Criticism'. In *Ecocinema Theory and Practice*, edited by Sean Cubitt, Salma Monani and Stephen Rust. New York: Routledge, 2012, pp. 43–61.

Ivakhiv, Adrian. *Ecologies of the Moving Image: Cinema, Affect, Nature*. Waterloo, Canada: Wilfred Laurier University Press, 2013.

Ivakhiv, Adrian. *Shadowing the Anthropocene: Eco-Realism for Turbulent Times*. Santa Barbara, CA: Punctum Books, 2018.

Jeong, Seung-hoon, and Jeremi Szaniawski. 'Introduction'. In *The Global Auteur: The Politics of Authorship in 21st Century Cinema*, edited by Seung-hoon Jeong and Jeremi Szaniawski. London: Bloomsbury, 2016, pp. 1–19.

Jolly, Margaret. 'Engendering the Anthropocene in Oceania: Fatalism, Resilience, Resistance', *Cultural Studies Review*, vol. 25, no. 1, 2019, pp. 172–95.

Kakoudaki, Despina. 'Representing Politics in Disaster Films', *International Journal of Media and Cultural Politics*, vol. 7, no. 3, 2011, pp. 349–56.

Kakoudaki, Despina. 'Spectacles of History: Race Relations, Melodrama, and the Science Fiction/Disaster Film', *Camera Obscura*, vol. 17, no. 2 (50), 2002, pp. 108–53.

Kanngieser, Anja. 'Geopolitics and the Anthropocene: Five Propositions for Sound', *GeoHumanities*, vol. 1, no. 1, 2015, pp. 80–5.

Kanngieser, Anja, and Nicholas Beuret. 'Refusing the World: Silence, Commoning, and the Anthropocene', *The South Atlantic Quarterly*, vol. 116, no. 2, 2017, pp. 363–80.

Kaplan, E. Ann. *Trauma Culture: The Politics of Terror and Loss in Media and Literature*. New Brunswick, NJ: Rutgers University Press, 2005.

Kara, Selmin. 'Anthropocenema: Cinema in the Age of Mass Extinctions'. In *Post-Cinema: Theorizing 21st Century Film*, edited by Shane Denson and Julia Leyda. Sussex: Reframe Books, 2016. http://reframe.sussex.ac.uk/post-cinema/.

Keane, Stephen. *Disaster Movies: The Cinema of Catastrophe*. London: Wallflower Press, 2001.

King, Geoff. *Donnie Darko*. London: Wallflower Press, 2007.

Kracauer, Siegfried. *Theory of Film: The Redemption of Physical Reality*. Introduction by Miriam Hansen. Princeton, NJ: Princeton University Press, 1997.

Kulka, Otto Dov. *Landscapes of the Metropolis of Death: Reflections on Memory and Imagination*. Cambridge, MA: Harvard University Press, 2013.

Levinas, Emmanuel. *Collected Philosophical Papers*. Translated by Alphonso Lingis, introduction by Alphonso Lingis. Leiden, the Netherlands: Martinus Nijhoff, 1987.

Levinas, Emmanuel. *The Levinas Reader*, edited by Seán Hand. West Sussex: Basil Blackwell, 1989.

Levinas, Emmanuel. *Totality and Infinity: An Essay on Exteriority*. Translated by Alphonso Lingis. Leiden, the Netherlands: Martinus Nijhoff and Duquesne University Press, 1979.

Levinas, Emmanuel, and Richard Kearney. 'Dialogue with Emmanuel Levinas'. In *Face to Face with Levinas*, edited by Richard A. Cohen. Albany: State University of New York Press, 1986.

Lippit, Akira Mizuta. *Atomic Light (Shadow Optics)*. Minneapolis: University of Minnesota Press, 2005.

Lippit, Akira Mizuta. 'Between Disaster, Medium 3.11', *Mechademia*, vol. 10, 2015, pp. 2–25.

Lorimer, Jamie. 'The Anthropo-scene: A Guide for the Perplexed', *Social Studies of Science*, vol. 47, no. 1, 2017, pp. 117–42.

Lynas, Mark. *High Tide: News from a Warming World*. London: Flamingo, 2004.

Mai, Nadin. *The Aesthetics of Absence and Duration in the Post-Trauma Cinema of Lav Diaz*. University of Stirling, Scotland, PhD thesis, 2015. STORRE: Stirling Online Research Repository, dspace.stir.ac.uk/handle/1893/22990#.W-0todUza70.

Martin-Jones, David. *Cinema against Doublethink: Ethical Encounters with the Losts Pasts of World History*. Abingdon: Routledge, 2019.

Menuhin, Yehudi. *Unfinished Journey*. New York: Knopf, 1977.

Met, Philippe. 'The Iceman Cometh (to a Theatre Near You): Michael Haneke's Glaciation Trilogy'. In *Film Trilogies: New Critical Approaches*, edited by Claire Perkins and Constantine Verevis. Basingstoke: Palgrave Macmillan, 2012, pp. 164–78.

Minghelli, Giuliana. *Landscape and Memory in Post-Fascist Italian Film: Cinema Year Zero*. New York: Routledge, 2013.

Mitman, Gregg. *Reel Nature: America's Romance with Wildlife on Film*. Seattle: University of Washington Press, 2009.

Morag, Raya. 'Defeated Masculinity: Post-Traumatic Cinema in the Aftermath of the Vietnam War', *The Communication Review*, vol. 9, no. 3, 2006, pp. 189–219.

Morgan, Daniel. 'Rethinking Bazin: Ontology and Realist Aesthetics', *Critical Inquiry*, vol. 32, no. 3, 2006, pp. 443–81.

Morrison, James. *The Cinema of Todd Haynes: All That Heaven Allows*. London: Wallflower Press, 2007.

Morton, Timothy, *Dark Ecology: For a Logic of Future Coexistence*. New York: Columbia University Press, 2016.

Morton, Timothy. *The Ecological Thought*. Cambridge, MA: Harvard University Press, 2010.

Morton, Timothy. *Hyperobjects: Philosophy and Ecology after the End of the World*. Minneapolis: University of Minnesota Press, 2013.

Mulvey, Laura. *Death 24× a Second: Stillness and the Moving Image*. London: Reaktion Books, 2006.

Mulvogue, Jessica Siobhan. 'Catastrophe Aesthetics: The Moving Image and the Mattering of the World', *Transformations*, vol. 30, 2017, pp. 39–55.

Nagib, Lucia. *Realist Cinema as World Cinema*. Amsterdam: Amsterdam University Press, 2020.

Nagib, Lucia. *World Cinema and the Ethics of Realism*. London: Continuum, 2011.

Nancy, Jean-Luc. *Listening*. New York: Fordham University Press, 2007.

Nancy, Jean-Luc. 'On Evidence: "Life and Nothing More" by Abbas Kiarostami', *Discourse*, vol. 21, no. 1, 1999, pp. 77–88.

Narine, Anil. 'Introduction: Eco-Trauma Cinema'. In *Eco-Trauma Cinema*, edited by Anil Narine. Abingdon: Routledge, 2014, pp. 1–24.

Nash, Kate. 'Documentary-for-the-Other: Relationships, Ethics and (Observational) Documentary', *Journal of Mass Media Ethics*, vol. 26, no. 3, 2011, pp. 224–39.

Nash, Kate. 'Telling Stories: the Narrative Study of Documentary Ethics', *New Review of Film and Television Studies*, vol. 10, no. 3, 2012, pp. 318–31.

Nash, Kate. 'Virtual Reality Witness: Exploring the Ethics of Mediated Presence', *Studies in Documentary Film*, vol. 12, no. 2, 2018, pp. 119–31.

Neilson, Toby. 'Different Death Stars and Devastated Earths: Contemporary SF Cinema's Imagination of Disaster in the Anthropocene', *Science Fiction Film and Television*, vol. 12, no. 2, 2019, pp. 241–58.

Neimanis, Astrida. *Bodies of Water: Posthuman Feminist Phenomenology*. London: Bloomsbury, 2017.

Nichols, Bill. 'Discovering Form, Inferring Meaning: New Cinemas and the Film Festival Circuit', *Film Quarterly*, vol. 47, no. 3, 1994, pp. 16–30.

Nichols, Bill. '"Getting to Know You": Knowledge, Power, and the Body'. In *Theorizing Documentary*, edited by Michael Renov. London: Routledge, 1993, pp. 174–192.

Nichols, Bill. *Representing Reality: Issues and Concepts in Documentary*. Bloomington: Indiana University Press, 1991.

Nixon, Rob. *Slow Violence and the Environmentalism of the Poor*. Cambridge, MA: Harvard University Press, 2011.
North, Dan. *Performing Illusions: Cinema, Special Effects and the Virtual Actor*. London: Wallflower Press, 2008.
Ortner, Sherry. 'Against Hollywood: American Independent Film as a Critical Cultural Movement', *HAU: Journal of Ethnographic Theory*, vol. 2, no. 2, 2012, pp. 1–21.
Pappas, Georgios, Savvas Seitaridis, Nikolaos Akritidis and Epimanondas Tsianos. 'Infectious Diseases in Cinema: Virus Hunters and Killer Microbes', *Clinical Infectious Diseases*, vol. 37, no. 7, 2003, pp. 939–42.
Pearl, Monica B. 'AIDS and New Queer Cinema'. In *New Queer Cinema: A Critical Reader*, edited by Michele Aaron. Edinburgh: Edinburgh University Press, 2004, pp. 23–35.
Perkins, Claire. *American Smart Cinema*. Edinburgh: Edinburgh University Press, 2012.
Pickles, Katie. *Christchurch Ruptures*. Wellington: Bridget Williams Books, 2016.
Porter, Caroline. 'Nonhuman Subjectivity: Agnes Varda's *The Beaches of Agnes* and *The Gleaners and I*', *Film International*, vol. 16, no. 2, 2018, pp. 93–102.
Potter, Susan. 'Dangerous Spaces: *Safe*', *Todd Haynes: A Magnificent Obsession*, special issue of *Camera Obscura: Feminism, Culture, and Media Studies*, vol. 19, no. 3(57), 2004, pp. 125–55, edited by Amelie Hastie. Durham, NC: Duke University Press.
Prentice, Chris. '"On the Beach?": The Question of the Local in Aotearoa/New Zealand Cultural Studies'. In *On Display: New Essays in Cultural Studies*, edited by Anna Smith and Lydia Weavers. Wellington, New Zealand: Victoria University Press, 2004, pp. 111–29.
Prentice, Chris. 'The Shaking of New Zealanders', *Journal of New Zealand Literature*, vol. 31, no. 2, 2013, pp. 3–73.
Randell, Karen. '"It Was Like a Movie", Take 2: *Age of Ultron* and a 9/11 Aesthetic', *Cinema Journal*, vol. 56, no. 1, 2016, pp. 137–41.
Raymond, Emilie. *From My Cold, Dead Hands: Charlton Heston and American Politics*. Lexington: University Press of Kentucky, 2006.
Reid, Roddey. 'UnSafe at Any Distance: Todd Haynes' Visual Culture of Health and Risk. For Steven Shaviro', *Film Quarterly*, vol. 51, no. 3, 1998, pp. 32–44.
Renov, Michael. 'Introduction: The Truth about Non-fiction'. In *Theorizing Documentary*, edited by Michael Renov London: Routledge, 1993, pp. 1–11.
Renov, Michael. *The Subject of Documentary*. Minneapolis: University of Minnesota Press, 2004.
Roddick, Nick. 'Only Stars Survive: Disaster Movies in the Seventies'. In *Performance and Politics in Popular Drama: Aspects of Popular Entertainment in Theatre, Film and Television 1800–1976*, edited by David Bradby, Louis James and Bernard Sharratt. Cambridge: Cambridge University Press, 1980, pp. 243–270.

Rodowick, D. N. 'The World, Time'. In *Afterimages of Gilles Deleuze's Film Philosophy*, edited by D. N. Rodowick. Minneapolis: University of Minnesota Press, 2010, pp. 97–114.

Rogers, Anna Backman. 'Imaging Grief and Loss: Laura Mulvey's *Death 24× a Second* as Film-philosophy', *de arte*, vol. 50, no. 92, 2015, pp. 11–18.

Ross, Andrew. *Strange Weather: Culture, Science, and Technology in the Age of Limits*. London: Verso, 1991.

Rose, Deborah Bird. *Shimmer: Flying Fox Exuberance in Worlds of Peril*. Edinburgh: Edinburgh University Press, 2022.

Rose, Deborah Bird. 'Shimmer: When All You Love Is Being Trashed'. In *Arts of Living on a Damaged Planet: Ghosts of the Anthropocene*, edited by Anna Tsing, Heather Swanson, Elaine Gan and Nils Bubant. Minneapolis: University of Minnesota Press, 2017, pp. 51–63.

Rose, Deborah Bird. 'Slowly – Writing into the Anthropocene', *TEXT* 20, October 2013. Accessed 26 August 2021. www.textjournal.com.au/speciss/issue20/Rose.pdf.

Rose, Deborah Bird. *Wild Dog Dreaming: Love and Extinction*. Charlottesville: University of Virginia Press, 2011.

Rothberg, Michael. *Traumatic Realism: The Demands of Holocaust Representation*. Minneapolis: University of Minnesota Press, 2000.

Rushton, Richard. *Cinema after Deleuze*. London: Continuum, 2012.

Russell, Bruce. 'What True Project Has Been Lost?': Towards a Social Ontology of Improvised Sound Work. RMIT University, Melbourne, PhD thesis. RMIT Research Repository. https://researchrepository.rmit.edu.au/esploro/outputs/doctoral/What-true-project-has-been-lost-Towards-a-social-ontology-of-improvised-sound-work/9921863623301341.

Rust, Stephen. 'Hollywood and Climate Change'. In *Ecocinema Theory and Practice*, edited by Sean Cubitt, Salma Monani and Stephen Rust. New York: Routledge, 2012, pp. 191–211.

Ryan, Michael, and Douglas Kellner. *Camera Politica: The Politics and Ideology of Contemporary Hollywood Film*. Bloomington: Indiana University Press, 1988.

Saxton, Libby. 'Blinding Visions: Levinas, Ethics, Faciality'. In *Film and Ethics: Foreclosed Encounters*, edited by Lisa Downing and Libby Saxton. Abingdon: Routledge, 2010, pp. 95–106.

Sayed, Yusuf. 'Of Mourning and Evening: William Basinski's "Disintegration Loop 1.1"', *Mubi Notebook*. Accessed 20 August 2022. https://mubi.com/notebook/posts/of-mourning-and-evening-william-basinski-s-disintegration-loop-1-1.

Schrader, Astrid. 'Abyssal Intimacies and Temporalities of Care: How (Not) to Care about Deformed Leaf Bugs in the Aftermath of Chernobyl', *Social Studies of Science*, vol. 45, no. 5, 2015, pp. 665–90.

Seymour, Nicole. *Strange Natures: Futurity, Empathy, and the Queer Ecological Imagination*. Urbana: University of Illinois Press, 2013.

Shaviro, Steven. *Post Cinematic Affect*. Portland, OR: Zero Books, 2010.
Shaviro, Steven. 'Southland Tales', *The Pinocchio Theory*, 10 December 2007. Accessed 29 October 2018. www.shaviro.com/Blog/?p=611.
Shohat, Ella, and Robert Stam. *Unthinking Eurocentrism: Multiculturalism and the Media*. London: Routledge, 2014.
Smaill, Belinda. *The Documentary: Politics, Emotion, Culture*. London: Palgrave Macmillan, 2010.
Smaill, Belinda. *Regarding Life: Animals and the Documentary Moving Image*. Albany: State University of New York Press, 2016.
Smith, Linda Tuhiwai. *Decolonizing Methodologies: Research and Indigenous Peoples*. London: Zed Books, 2021.
Solnit, Rebecca. *A Paradise in Hell: The Extraordinary Communities That Arise in Disaster*. New York: Penguin Books, 2010.
Sontag, Susan. *Against Interpretation and Other Essays*. London: Penguin, 2009.
Sparrow, Tom. *Levinas Unhinged*. Portland, OR: Zero Books, 2013.
Speck, Oliver. *Funny Frames: The Filmic Concepts of Michael Hanneke*. London: Continuum, 2010.
Stadler, Jane. *Pulling Focus: Intersubjective Experience, Narrative Film, and Ethics*. New York: Continuum, 2008.
Staehler, Tanja. 'Images and Shadows: Levinas and the Ambiguity of the Aesthetic', *Estetika: The Central European Journal of Aesthetics*, vol. 47, no. 2, 2010, pp. 123–43.
Steinberg, Philip, and Kimberly Peters. 'Wet Ontologies, Fluid Spaces: Giving Depth to Volume through Oceanic Thinking', *Environment and Planning D: Society and Space*, vol. 33, 2015, pp. 247–64.
Stern, Lesley. '"Paths that Wind through the Thicket of Things"', *Critical Inquiry*, vol. 28, no. 1, 2001, pp. 317–54.
Stern, Lesley. *The Scorsese Connection*. Bloomington: Indiana University Press, 1995.
Stern, Lesley, and Tracy Cox-Stanton. 'Interview: The Cine-Files speaks with Lesley Stern About Her work's Abiding Interest in Cinematic Affect', *The Cine-Files*, no. 10, 2016. Accessed 14 September 2021. https://www.thecine-files.com/interview-lesley-stern/.
Steyerl, Hito. *The Wretched of the Screen*. London: Sternberg Press, 2012.
Sultana, Farhana. 'The Unbearable Heaviness of Climate Coloniality', *Political Geography*, vol. 99, 2022, p. 102638.
Swanson, Heather, Anna Tsing, Nils Bubant and Elaine Gan. 'Introduction: Bodies Tumbled into Bodies'. In *Arts of Living on a Damaged Planet: Monsters of the Anthropocene*, edited by Anna Tsing, Heather Swanson, Elaine Gan and Nils Bubant. Minneapolis: University of Minnesota Press, 2017, pp. 1–12.
Szaniawski, Jeremi. 'Of Intruders (and Guests): The films of Michael Haneke and Aleksey Balabanov'. In *The Global Auteur: The Politics of Authorship in*

21st Century Cinema, edited by Seung-hoon Jeong and Jeremi Szaniawski. New York: Bloomsbury, 2016, pp. 133–48.

Tabarraee, Babak. 'Abbas Kiarostami: A Cinema of Silence', *Soundtrack*, vol. 5, no. 1, 2012, pp. 5–13.

Te Punga Somerville, Alice. 'The Great Pacific Garbage Patch as Metaphor: The (American) Pacific You Can't See'. In *Archipelagic American Studies*, edited by Brian Russell Roberts and Michelle Ann Stephens. Durham, NC: Duke University Press, 2017, pp. 320–338.

Torner, Evan. 'Civilization's Endless Shadow: Haneke's *Time of the Wolf*'. In *A Companion to Michael Haneke*, edited by Roy Grundmann. Chichester: Wiley-Blackwell, 2010, pp. 532–50.

Tracy, Andrew. 'Time of the Wolf', *Reverse Shot*, 24 June 2004. Accessed 10 October 2022. reverseshot.org/reviews/entry/1494/time_wolf.

Trinh, T. Minh-Ha. 'The Totalizing Quest of Meaning'. In *Theorizing Documentary*, edited by Michael Renov. New York: Routledge, 1993, pp. 90–107.

Tzoumakis, Yannis. *American Independent Cinema: An Introduction*. Edinburgh: Edinburgh University Press, 2006.

Virilio, Paul. *Politics of the Very Worst*. Los Angeles, CA: Semiotext(e), 1999.

von Mossner, Alexa Weik. 'Slow Violence on the Beach: Documenting Disappearance in *There Once Was an Island*'. In *The Beach in Anglophone Literatures and Cultures: Reading Littoral Space*, edited by Ursula Kluwick and Virginia Richter. Farnham: Ashgate, 2015, pp. 175–91.

Wakefield, Stephanie. 'Man in the Anthropocene (as Portrayed by the Film *Gravity*)', *May*, no. 13, October 2014. Accessed 29 August 2021. www.mayrevue.com/en/lhomme-de-lanthropocene-tel-que-depeint-dans-le-film-gravity/.

Walker, Janet. 'Projecting Sea Level Rise: Documentary Film and Other Geolocative Technologies'. In *A Companion to Contemporary Documentary Film*, edited by Alexandra Juhasz and Alisa Lebow. Chichester: Wiley Blackwell, 2015, pp. 61–85.

Walker, Janet. *Trauma Cinema: Documenting Incest and the Holocaust*. Berkeley: University of California Press, 2005.

Wark, McKenzie. 'Anthropo{mise-en-s}cene', *Public Seminar*. 10 December 2014. Accessed 26 August 2021. www.publicseminar.org/2014/12/anthropomise-en-scene/#.WZOUz1UjG70.

Weatherill, Charlotte Kate. 'Sinking Paradise? Climate Change Vulnerability and Pacific Island Extinction Narratives', *Geoforum*, vol. 145, 2022, p. 103566.

Weaver, Caity. 'Dwayne Johnson for President!', *GQ*, 10 May 2017. Accessed 26 August 2021. www.gq.com/story/dwayne-johnson-for-president-cover.

Wheatley, Catherine. *Michael Haneke's Cinema: The Ethic of the Image*. Oxford: Berghahn Books, 2009.

White, Rob. *Todd Haynes*. Champaign: University of Illinois Press, 2013.

Wickman, Forrest. 'Hollywood Has Found a Surprising New Way to Destroy City Skylines', *Slate*, 5 July 2016. Accessed 26 August 2021. www.slate.com/blogs/browbeat/2016/07/05/independence_day_resurgence_x_men_apocalypse_and_hollywood_s_newest_favorite.html.

Wiesel, Elie. *Night*. New York: Hill & Wang, 2006.

Williams, Linda. 'Introduction'. In *Viewing Positions: Ways of Seeing Film*, edited by Linda Williams. New Brunswick, NJ: Rutgers University Press, 1994, pp. 1–20.

Williams, Linda. 'Melodrama Revised'. In *Refiguring American Film Genres: History and Theory*, edited by Nick Browne. Berkeley: University of California Press, 1998, pp. 42–88.

Wilson, D. Harlan. 'Technomasculine Bodies and Vehicles of Desire: The Erotic Delirium of Michael Bay's *Transformers*', *Extrapolation*, vol. 53, no. 3, 2012, pp. 347–64.

Yacowar, Maurice. 'The Bug in the Rug: Notes on the Disaster Genre'. In *Film Genre Reader IV*, edited by Barry Kieth Grant. Austin: University of Texas Press, 2012, pp. 313–331.

Yeates, Robert. *American Cities in Post-Apocalyptic Science Fiction*. London: UCL Press, 2021.

Zalasiewicz, Jan, Mark Williams, Will Steffen and Paul Crutzen. 'The New World of the Anthropocene', *Environmental Science and Technology*, vol. 44, no. 7, 2010, pp. 2228–31.

Zylinska, Joanna. *The End of Man: A Feminist Counterapocalypse*. Minneapolis: University of Minnesota Press, 2018.

Zylinska, Joanna. *Minimal Ethics for the Anthropocene*. London: Open Humanities Press, 2014.

Zylinska, Joanna. *Nonhuman Photography*. Cambridge, MA: MIT Press, 2017.

Filmography

2012. Dir. Roland Emmerich. Centropolis Entertainment, 2009.
28 Days Later. Dir. Danny Boyle. DNA Films and UK Film Council, 2002.
Aeasi – As Far as the Eye Can See Above the Sea. Dir. Amie Batalibasi. 2018.
After Earth. Dir. M. Night Shyamalan. Sony Pictures, 2013.
Airport. Dir. George Seaton. Universal Pictures, 1970.
An Inconvenient Truth. Dir. Davis Guggenheim. Lawrence Bender Productions and Participant Productions, 2006.
And Life Goes On. Dir. Abbas Kiarostami. The Institute for the Intellectual Development of Children & Young Adults, 1992.
Annihilation. Dir. Alex Garland. Skydance Films, DNA Films and Scott Rudin Productions, 2018.
Antichrist. Dir. Lars von Trier. Zentropa Entertainments, arte France Cinema and Canal+, 2009.
Armageddon. Dir. Michael Bay. Touchstone Pictures, Jerry Bruckheimer Films and Valhalla Motion Pictures, 1998.
Arrival. Dir. Denis Villeneuve. FilmNation Entertainment, Lava Bear Films and 21 Laps Entertainment, 2016.
Avengers: Age of Ultron. Dir. Joss Whedon. Marvel Studios, 2015.
Avengers: Infinity War. Dirs. Anthony Russo and Joe Russo. Marvel Studios, 2018.
Beasts of the Southern Wild. Dir. Benh Zeitlin. Cinereach, Court 13 and Journeyman Pictures, 2013.
Before the Flood. Dir. Fisher Stevens. Appian Way, RatPac Documentary Films, Insurgent Docs, Mandarin Film Productions and National Geographic Documentary Films, 2016.
Death in the Land of Encantos. Dir. Lav Diaz. Sine Olivia Pilipinas and Hubert Bals Fund, 2007.
Deep Impact. Dir. Mimi Leder. The Manhattan Project, Zanuck/Brown Productions and DreamWorks Pictures, 1998.
Disintegration Loop 1.1. Dir. William Basinski. 2001.
Disintegration Loops. Dir. David Wexler. Cinema 59 Productions, 2021.
Donnie Darko. Dir. Richard Kelly. Pandora Cinema and Newmarket Films, 2001. Metrodome Distribution DVD, 2003.
Earthquake. Dir. Mark Robson. Universal Pictures, 1974. Universal Studios Home Entertainment DVD, 2006.
Edge of Tomorrow. Dir. Doug Liman. Village Roadshow Pictures, 2014.

Empty Brooklyn Bridge. Dir. Terry Barentsen. YouTube, 2020. https://www.youtube.com/watch?v=lOrPviPnZc8&ab_channel=TerryB.

End of Days. Dir. Peter Hyams. Beacon Pictures and Universal Pictures, 1999.

ExtendedCut – New York City Lock Down. Dir. Terry Barentsen. YouTube, 2020. https://www.youtube.com/watch?v=psXUQzHFhgk&t=1742s&ab_channel=TerryB.

Geostorm. Dir. Dean Devlin. Warner Bros. Pictures, Skydance Media and Electric Entertainment, 2017.

Godzilla. Dir. Roland Emmerich. Centropolis Entertainment, Fried Films and TriStar Pictures, 1998.

Gravity. Dir. Alfonso Cuarón. Heyday Films, Esperanto Filmoj and Warner Bros. Pictures, 2013.

Holding On. Angela Tiatia. Sullivan and Strumpf, 2015.

I Am Legend. Dir. Francis Lawrence. Village Roadshow Pictures, 2007.

Independence Day. Dir. Roland Emmerich. Centropolis Entertainment and 20th Century Fox, 1996. 20th Century Fox Home Entertainment DVD, 2001.

L'Arrivée d'un train en gare de La Ciotat. Dirs. August Lumière and Louis Lumière. Société Lumière, 1896.

Lick. Angela Tiatia. Museum of Contemporary Art Australia, 2015.

Magnolia. Dir. Paul Thomas Anderson. Ghoulardi Film Production and JoAnne Sellar Productions, 1999.

Moonfall. Dir. Roland Emmerich. Summit Entertainment, UK Moonfall LLP, Huayi Brothers, Tencent, Centropolis Entertainment, 2022.

On an Unknown Beach. Dirs. Adam Luxton and Summer Agnew. Ponzi Pictures, 2016.

Rogue One: A Star Wars Story. Dir. Gareth Edwards. Lucasfilm Ltd., 2016.

Safe. Dir. Todd Haynes. American Playhouse, Channel Four Films and Good Machine, 1995.

San Andreas. Dir. Brad Peyton. New Line Cinema and Village Roadshow Productions, 2015.

Short Cuts. Dir. Robert Altman. Spelling Pictures International, Cary Brokaw Productions and Avenue Productions, 1993.

Snowpiercer. Dir. Bong Joon-ho. Moho Film, Opus Pictures, and Stillking Films, 2013.

Southland Tales. Dir. Richard Kelly. Darko Entertainment, Persistent Entertainment and Cherry Road Films, 2006.

Soylent Green. Dir. Richard Fleischer. Metro-Goldwyn-Mayer, 1973.

Speed. Dir. Jan de Bont. Mark Gordon Productions and 20th Century Fox, 1994.

Star Wars: The Force Awakens. Dir. J. J. Abrams. Lucasfilm Ltd. and Bad Robot Productions, 2015.

Teeth. Dir. Mitchell Lichtenstein. Pierpoline Films, 2007.

The Day After Tomorrow. Dir. Roland Emmerich. Centropolis Entertainment, Lionsgate Films, Mark Gordon Company and 20th Century Fox, 2004.

The Fly. Dir. Kurt Neumann. 20th Century Fox, 1958.

The Host. Dir. Bong Joon-ho. Chungeorahm Film and Sego Entertainment, 2006.
The Poseidon Adventure. Dir. Ronald Neame. Kent Productions Ltd., 1972.
The Quiet Earth. Dir. Geoff Murphy. Cinepro, Pilsbury Productions and Mr. Yellowbeard Productions Ltd., 1985.
The Thing. Dir. Matthijs van Heijningen Jr. Strike Entertainment and Morgan Creek Productions. 2011.
The Towering Inferno. Dir. John Guillermin. Irwin Allen Productions and United Films, 1974.
The 400 Blows. Dir. François Truffaut. Les Films du Carrosse, 1959.
There Once Was an Island: Te Henua e Nnoho. Dir. Briar March. On the Level Productions, New Zealand Film Commission and Creative New Zealand, 2010.
Time of the Wolf. Dir. Michael Haneke. Arte France Cinema, Bavaria Film, Canal+, Centre National de la Cinématographie, Eurimages, France 3 Cinema, Les Films du Losange and Wega Film, 2003.
Times Square Is Deserted. Dir. Terry Barentsen. YouTube, 2020. https://www.youtube.com/watch?v=ywN9oaTbwQ0&t=9s&ab_channel=TerryB.
Titanic. Dir. James Cameron. 20th Century Fox, Paramount Pictures and Lightstorm Entertainment, 1997.
Waterworld. Dir. Kevin Reynolds. Gordon Company, Davis Entertainment and Licht/Muller Film Corporation, 2005.

Index

Aeasi (Batalibasi, Amie) 129
aerial view 41, 88, 99, 104–5, 107, 110, 115, 118, 123, 134
After Earth (Shyamalan, M. Night) 51
Agnew, Summer 99
Airport (Seaton, George) 41, 80
Airport 1975 (Smight, Jack) 43
Aitken, Ian 21, 26, 120, 158
Alaimo, Stacy 15, 16, 78, 100, 110
aliens, in disaster movies 2, 5, 8, 14, 45
Altman, Rick 48
Altman, Robert 67
American Beauty (Mendes, Sam) 69, 72
American independent cinema 67, 87, 95
Anderson, Paul Thomas 67
Andrew, Dudley 22
Annihilation (Garland, Alex) 54–5
Anote's Ark (Rytz, Matthieu) 102
Anson, April 44
Anthropocene 2–3, 5, 66, 68, 99, 100, 101, 108, 113, 121, 123, 127, 142, 158, 163, 179, 180, 182
  catastrophic conditions of 11, 158
  and climate change 29, 37
  death-connoting effects of 8–9
  global ecological crises 47–8
  in movies after 1990s 45–52
  non-anthropocentric ethics for 15
  realist style for 170–2
'Anthropocenema' 50–1
Antichrist (von Trier, Lars) 50
Aotearoa, *see* New Zealand
Arctic Tale (Ravetchand Robertson) 102
Armageddon (Bay, Michael) 45, 48, 49, 51, 82
Aronofsky, Darren 170
Arrival (Villeneuve, Denis) 54–5
Atomic Light (*Shadow Optics*) (book) 30
Attack of the Puppet People (Gordon, Bert I.) 38

Australia 15–16, 125, 173
  see also Oceania
auteur cinema 30, 142–8, 170
Avatar (Cameron, James) 107
Avengers: Age of Ultron (Marvel Cinematic Universe) (Whedon, Joss) 56–60
Avengers: Infinity War (Russo and Russo) 59

Balsom, Erika 108
Batalibasi, Amie 129
Bay, Michael 49
Bazin, André 4, 6, 19–21, 24, 27, 90, 103, 131
  about realism 4–5, 23
Beasts of the Southern Wild (Zeitlin, Benh) 51
Beethoven 160
Before the Flood (Stevens, Fisher) 29–30, 99, 101, 111–18, 119, 121, 128, 135, 137
Bennett, Jane 11
Berardi, Franco 3–4, 148
Beuret, Nicholas 158, 163
Bicycle Thieves (De Sica, Vittoria) 19–20
Birks, Chelsea 30
Blanchot, Maurice 5, 7, 11, 87, 91, 110, 117, 155, 167, 172, 177
  ethics of 16
  and responsibility 11, 87, 117
blockbusters 28, 29, 35–6, 49, 50, 52, 53, 54, 56, 59, 60, 62, 65, 66, 68, 92, 141
  see also individual movies
Blue (Madison, Theron) 102
Bonilla, Yarimar 4
The Book of Eli (Hughes and Hughes) 48
Bosch, Hieronymus 111, 116
Bould, Mark 2–3, 54, 55
Braidotti, Rosi 5, 11, 12–13, 16, 24, 39, 44, 64, 65, 172, 175
The Brain Eaters (Vesota, Bruno) 38
Brown, William 176
Buffy the Vampire Slayer (Rubel, Fran) 92

camera technologies, *see* cinematography
capitalist realism 94
  environmental catastrophe in 96
  Fisher's conception of 95
Carson, Rachel 70
Caruth, Cathy 90–1
Cast Away (Zemeckis, Robert) 48
catastrophe 4, 47, 50, 69, 112, 136, 156, 158, 178
  environmental and climate 9, 95–6
  post-war 74
  visualizing 51
  see also eco-catastrophe
de Certeau, Michel 157
Chaudhuri, Shohini 150, 153, 157
Children of Men (Cuarón, Alfonso) 96
Choe, Steve 161
The Chumscrubber (Posin, Arie) 84
cinematic disaster imaginaries 1, 3, 9
cinematography
  aerial shot 41, 88, 104–5, 107, 110, 115, 123, 125, 134, 181
  close-up shots 136
  documentary style 155
  dutch angle 150
  eye level shot 131
  ground level shot 126
  impressionistic techniques 101, 120, 181
  long take 148–58
  mobility of 26
  observational style 181
  in ocean 123–4
  overhead shot 114
  post-war landscape 151
  reverse angle shot 73
  submerged perspective of 127
  view from a body 119
  in water 122–3, 129–36
  wide angle shot 130
classic auteur 143
climate change 1, 14, 15–16, 22, 29, 37, 45–6, 72, 94, 101–2, 110
  and anthropogenic disaster 29, 99, 119, 179
  and climate disaster 111
  environment and 104
  global warming and 45
  top-down visualizations of 122

Code, Lorraine 79, 80
Cohen, Richard 85
computer generated imagery (CGI) 46, 49, 51, 58, 61, 63, 64, 107, 108, 109, 115
Cooper, Sarah 6, 8, 13, 151
Corlett, David 109
Coulthard, Lisa 158, 159, 160, 163
Covid-19 pandemic 173, 175, 176, 178
  in New York 174
Cuarón, Alfonso 51, 52, 96
Cubitt, Sean 108

Dante's Peak (Donaldson, Roger) 61
Darko, Donnie 28
Davy, Barbara Jane 12
The Day After Tomorrow (Emmerich, Roland) 49, 87, 105, 107–8
Deamer, David 30
Death in the Land of Encantos (Diaz, Lav) 30, 141, 143, 149, 150, 158, 162, 164, 171, 181
Deep Impact (Leder, Mimi) 30, 45, 107–8
Deleuze, Gilles 11, 153, 164
Deleuze, Japanese Cinema, and the Atom Bomb (book) 30
DeLillo, Don 94–5
DeLoughrey, Elizabeth 101, 120, 123
Demers, Joanna 178
Demos, T. J. 108
Diaz, Lav 141, 143, 145, 153, 166, 170
  long takes 162, 171
  neorealism 153
  realism 150, 151
DiCaprio, Leonardo 99, 111–18, 126
Die Hard (McTiernan, John) 62
disaster(s) 163
  cinematic representations of 7–8
  definition of 7
  disaster-consciousness, concept of 10
  in documentary film 99
  'elemental' 16–17, 23, 35, 42, 63, 64
  extra-terrestrial 2, 5, 8, 14, 45
  human and non-human alterity 15–18
  meteor/asteroid 45, 46, 57
  movies, *see* individual movies
  scenes 35, 47, 51, 89, 132
  see also natural disasters; man-made disasters

disaster movie(s) 1, 4, 17, 26, 29, 30, 35, 37, 133
  aliens in 2, 5, 8, 14, 45
  cities in 176
  documentary style 100–2
  1970s cycle of 40–1, 44–5, 48, 57, 60, 65–6
  1990s cycle of 45–52, 63, 82, 179, 180
  realism of 65
  sci-fi movies 44–5, 49, 70
  2010s movies 62
  see also Hollywood disaster movies
disaster-consciousness, concept of 10, 136–7, 155, 164
  see also El-Wardany, Haytham
Disintegration Loop 1.1 (Basinski, William) 177–82
Disintegration Loops (Wexler, David) 178
Doane, Mary Ann 76
documentary 28, 31, 180
  environmental 99, 102–3, 116, 119, 120
  ethics 126
  and fiction film 16
  filmmakers 102
  films 99, 101, 181
  'masculinist bias' in 107
  music in 160
  and narrative cinema 17
  neorealism 155
  non-diegetic music in 160
  observational 121, 125–6, 146, 181
  realism 103, 105, 181
Donnie Darko (Kelly, Richard) 4, 27, 29, 67, 80–7, 89, 92–3, 94, 95, 169, 179, 180
Doyle, Julie 117–18
Drabinski, John E. 12

Earthquake (Robson, Mark) 41, 43, 45, 61
earthquake 3, 7, 8, 14, 16–17, 29, 30, 35, 36, 41, 45, 60–1, 69, 99, 120, 130, 133, 135–6, 146, 147, 169, 173–4, 180, 182
eco-catastrophe 29, 54, 83, 100, 112, 180
  see also catastrophe
ecofeminist theory 78
Ecologies of the Moving Image (book) 30
Edge of Tomorrow (Liman, Doug) 50, 55
elemental disaster 23, 35, 42, 63, 64, 102, 124, 131, 136, 151, 153

Eliot, T. S. 89
Elsaesser, Thomas 38, 142, 143
  new realism 26, 165
  post-mortem protagonists 27, 82, 121
El-Wardany, Haytham 10, 14, 15, 21, 65, 136, 155, 162
Emmerich, Roland 45, 46, 49, 105
environmental disaster 96, 182
Etheridge, Melissa 110, 116
ethics 12, 16, 20
  documentary ethics 126
  of encounter for disastrous epoch 9
  'face to face', encounter 6, 11, 27, 38, 47, 73–80
  Levinasian 5, 6, 8, 13, 21, 110, 126, 171
  and realism 103, 105, 181
  and responsibility 5, 6, 11, 13, 17, 18, 37, 48, 55, 66, 87, 110, 142, 149, 159, 172, 180
Eurocentrism 12–13, 18, 39, 63, 101
European 4, 15, 20, 28, 171, 172
  auteurs 144
  music 161
  neorealism 145
  realisms 144
European auteur 144
extra-terrestrials, *see* aliens, in disaster movies

Farbotko, Carol 109
Faris, Jaimey Hamilton 128
Fay, Jennifer 7, 22, 30
femininity, in movies 53–6
  see also masculinity
film sound 76, 81, 162
  see also music/songs
Finn, Howard 150, 153, 157
fire 70, 71, 93, 154, 160
First Reformed (Schrader, Paul) 170
First World War 39
Fisher, Mark 71, 90
flooding 36, 83, 85, 106, 107, 109, 111, 122, 125, 126, 182
The Fly (Neumann, Kurt) 38–9
The Force Awakens (Abrams, J. J.) 51
Fortun, Kim 171

The 400 Blows (Truffaut, François) 22
Friends (sitcom) 179
Fukushima disaster 3–4

Gablik, Suzi 75
Gazi, Jeeshan 21
Geostorm (Devlin, Dean) 108
global warming 2, 45, 46, 49, 59, 60, 69, 72, 99, 102, 107, 114, 182
Godzilla (Emmerich, Roland) 46, 179
Gore, Al 99, 103–11, 112, 117, 118, 121
Gravity (Cuarón, Alfonso) 36, 50–1, 52–6, 63
Gray Lady Down (Greene, David) 43
Gray-Sharp, Katarina 12
Grosoli, Marco 150
Guggenheim, Davis 99, 111
Gunning, Tom 19, 176
Gyllenhaal, Jake 83

Haeundae (Je-kyoon, Yoon) 35–6
Hall, Nina 109
Haneke, Michael 141, 143, 144, 147–8, 154, 156, 160, 162, 163, 166, 167, 170, 171
Happiness (Solondz, Todd) 84
Haraway, Donna 5, 10, 11, 16, 24, 99–100, 104, 118, 122, 134, 137, 176, 180–1
Haynes, Todd 67, 74, 76
Heart of Glass (Blondie) 179
heroic realism 62–6
  in disaster movies 17, 42–3, 44
Heston, Charlton 42–3, 48, 62, 175
High Tide (Lynas, Mark) 109
Hiroshima and Nagasaki
  bombing of 4
  incineration of 40
Hoberman, J. 43
Holding On (Tiatia, Angela) 128
Hollywood disaster movies 1, 10, 17, 26, 29, 30, 35, 37, 42–3, 44, 65, 68, 83, 87, 90, 92, 101, 102, 105, 163, 165, 170
  and the Anthropocene 45–52
  cinematic disaster imaginaries 16
  and independent cinema 68
  masculinist heroism in 42–5, 55–7
  music in 160
  non-diegetic music in 160
  see also disaster movie(s)

Holmes, Diana 142
Holocaust 11, 141, 155–6, 161, 171
  disaster movies 4, 5–7, 16
  and the Second World War 6
Hopper, Edward 74, 76, 86
Horn, Eva 39
Hornblow, David 120, 131, 134
Horne, Gerald 3
The Host (Joon-ho, Bong) 50
Hughes, Helen 103, 119
The Hungry Tide (Ghosh, Amitav) 102
hypnotherapy 120, 133, 135

I Am Legend (Lawrence, Francis) 40, 48, 50
The Ice Storm (Lee, Ang) 69
An Inconvenient Truth (Guggenheim, Davis) 4, 29, 87, 99, 101, 102–3, 104, 105, 106, 107, 108, 109–19, 121, 127, 135, 137, 163
Independence Day (Emmerich, Roland) 45, 46, 47, 51, 54, 57, 82, 88, 106, 175, 179
Independence Day: Resurgence (Emmerich, Roland) 49, 58, 59
independent films
  and Hollywood cinema 67–8
  music in 160
  non-diegetic music in 160
  in the United States 67–8, 87, 95
'indirect disaster' films (Ivakhiv) 69, 72, 74, 90
Ingawanij, May Adadol 150, 166
Ingram, David 88
Inhospitable World (book) 30
The Inland Sea (Carra, Lucille) 120
Interstellar (Nolan, Christopher) 63
Invasion of the Body Snatchers (Siegel, Don) 38
island
  aerial visualizations of 123
  exposure to disaster 123
  slow motion shots across water 122–3
It Came from Outer Space (Arnold, Jack) 38
Italian films 20, 151, 181
Ivakhiv, Adrian 18, 25, 30, 69, 72, 74, 90

Jefferies, Peter 130, 133
Jeong, Seung-hoon 143

Johnson, Dwayne 62, 92
Jolly, Margaret 128

Kakoudaki, Despina 36, 46–8
Kanngieser, A. 158, 159, 163
Kaplan, E. Ann 178
Kara, Selmin 50–1, 53
Keane, Stephen 36, 45, 46, 48, 53, 64
Kellner, Douglas 36, 43
Kelly, Richard 67, 81, 87
Kiarostami, Abbas 141, 145, 153, 157–8, 161, 162, 164, 168, 169, 170, 171
King Kong (Cooper and Schoedsack) 37
King, Geoff 67, 68, 82, 83
Kracauer, Siegfried 4, 6, 20, 21, 22, 25, 27, 120, 131
  about realism 23
Kulka, Otto Dov 162

The Last Man on Earth (TV series) 175
Late Night with David Letterman (talk show) 179
Leder, Mimi 30
Levinas, Emmanuel 5, 11–12, 14, 56, 68, 72–3, 85, 155
  ethics of 12, 16
  and film 6–8, 17–18, 21, 151
Lick (Tiatia, Angela) 128
Life, and Nothing More (Kiarostami, Abbas) 30, 158, 164
And Life Goes On (Kiarostami, Abbas) 4, 141, 142, 143, 146, 147, 149, 152, 156, 160, 161, 167, 171, 176, 181
Limit Cinema (book) 30
Lippit, Akira Mizuta 7, 30
Listening (Nancy, Jean-Luc) 158
long take(s) 19, 26, 30, 131, 141, 143, 148–58
Lorimer, Jamie 9
Luxton, Adam 99, 135
Lynas, Mark 109

Mad Max: Fury Road (Miller, George) 50, 63
Magnolia (Anderson, Paul Thomas) 67, 69–73, 75, 77, 81, 84, 87, 89, 92, 94, 95
Man of Steel (Snyder, Zack) 49, 59

man-made disasters
  climate crisis 45, 110
  extractivism 2, 3
  First World War 39
  global warming 45, 46, 49, 60
  Holocaust 4, 5–7, 11, 16
  mass death and extinction 2, 48, 50–1, 54, 58
  pollution 2, 73
  Second World War 3, 4–5, 16, 20, 22, 29
  see also disasters; natural disaster
March, Briar 99, 122
Martin-Jones, David 13, 17, 18, 31, 47, 63, 155
'masculinist bias' 107
masculinity 42–3, 44, 53, 63–4, 65
  dominant frameworks of 106
  in 1970s disaster genre films 42–3, 44
  in 1990s disaster films 45–52
  see also feminity, in movies
McKay, Adam 117
McQueen, Steve 42
Melancholia (von Trier, Lars) 170
melodrama movies 47, 64–5, 180
  realism of 65
Menuhin, Yehudi 160–1
meteor/asteroid 45, 46, 57
Minghelli, Giuliana 151, 153
Minimal Ethics for the Anthropocene (book) 5
Modern Life (Depardon, Raymond) 119
modernity 3, 79, 91, 142–4, 160, 173, 179
  ecology and 130
  and industrialization 119
  pressures of 65
  traumatic conditions of 44
Moonfall (Emmerich, Roland) 108
Morgan, Daniel 19
Morning Sun (painting) 74, 76
Morrison, James 75
Morton, Timothy 7, 14, 16, 38, 72, 136
von Mossner, Alexa Weik 122, 126
Mother! (Aronofsky, Darren) 170
Mulvey, Laura 8, 152, 153
Mulvogue, Jessica 21–2
music/songs 71, 88, 116, 119, 120, 124, 133, 158–9, 160, 161, 179, 181
  see also film sound

Musser, Charles 102, 120

Nagib, Lucia 19, 24, 26, 127
Nancy, Jean-Luc 158
Narine, Anil 49
narrative cinema 17
  classical 82
  generic 74
  non-linear narrative 55
  time-loop structure of 50
Nash, Kate 17, 129
national cinema 142, 144
natural disasters
  earthquake 3, 7, 8, 14, 16–17, 29, 30, 35, 36, 41, 45, 60–1
  sea level rise 4, 16
  tidal wave/tsunami 3, 36
  see also disasters; man-made disasters
Neilson, Toby 51
Neimanis, Astrida 108
neorealism 20, 26, 29, 146, 153
  documentary camera style 155
  European 145
  films 19
  post-war 141, 165, 181
neorealist auteur 144
'new realism' (Elsaesser) 26, 27, 165
New Zealand 1, 3, 31, 99, 109, 120, 133, 178
  climate justice or environmental justice 171–2
  colonialism or post-colonialism 101
  ecology 130
Nichols, Bill 103, 125, 142
Nichols, Jeff 13, 28
9/11, New York City terrorist attacks 1, 2, 35, 36, 49, 58, 61, 107, 174, 176, 177–9, 182
1950s sci-fi disaster movies 1, 37–45, 63, 87, 164
1970s disaster movie cycle 35, 63
  disaster genre films 37, 44–5
  masculinity in 42–3
1990s disaster movies cycle 35, 67, 82, 103, 180
  Anthropocene into 45–52
  disaster genre films 45–52
  disasters, proxies for social concerns 47–8
  masculinity in 47–8

Night (book) 156
Nixon, Rob 121
North, Dan 58
Nukutoa island 122–3

Oceania 99
  see also Australia
oceans
  disaster zones 101
  ethics 136–8
The Omega Man (Sagal, Boris) 43, 175
On an Unknown Beach (Luxton and Agnew) 30, 99, 101, 119, 120, 129–30, 132–6, 181
Ortner, Sherry 67

Pacific ocean 3, 101
  submersion in 123
panoramic view 99
A Paradise Built in Hell (Solnit, Rebecca) 4
Pearl, Monica B. 74
perceptual realism 58, 64
The Perfect Storm (Petersen, Wolfgang) 48
Perkins, Claire 83
Peters, Kimberly 123, 131
Pickles, Katie 136
poetic postneorealism 150
point of view 77, 122, 129, 131, 165
pollution 2
Porter, Caroline 136
The Poseidon Adventure (Neame, Ronald) 35, 41, 42, 61, 107
post-anthropocentric
  ethical thinking 16
  theorists 27
post-disaster 48, 50, 62, 112, 124, 133, 149, 171, 172
  landscape 150, 158, 159, 163
'post-mortem protagonists' (Elsaesser) 27, 29, 82, 96, 121, 165, 167
post-war
  European auteur 144
  Italian films 20
  neorealism 141
Potter, Susan 76
Prentice, Chris 16, 132

The Quiet Earth (Murphy, Geoff) 133

Rampage (Peyton, Brad) 62
Randell, Karen 49, 58
Raymond, Emilie 43
  realism 23
realism 5, 18–19, 150, 180
  Bazinian realism 19, 24, 176
  capitalist realism 95–6
  cinematic 129, 145
  and documentary 103–5, 119, 122
  ethics of 20
  film theorists 4–5
  heroic realism 62–6
  Italian neorealism 141
  neorealism 20–1, 23, 26, 29–30, 153, 155, 165, 181
  perceptual realism 58, 64
  post-war realism 141
  theories of 5, 6
realist film theorists 4, 101
  André Bazin 4–5, 131
  Siegfried Kracauer 4–5
Remengesau, Tommy 116
Renov, Michael 107, 121–2
Representing Reality (Nichols, Bill) 103
The Road (Hillcoat, John) 50, 63
Roddick, Nick 36, 41, 43
Rogers, Anna Backman 8
Rogue One (Edwards, Gareth) 51–2
romantic auteur 144
Rome, Open City (Rossellini, Roberto) 19–20
Rose, Deborah Bird 5, 12, 14, 16, 93, 126, 141
Ross, Andrew 69, 94
Rossellini, Roberto 20, 151, 153
Rothberg, Michael 7
Russell, Bruce 56, 120, 133–4, 135, 137
Rust, Stephen 105
Ryan, Michael 36, 43

Safe (Haynes, Todd) 4, 29, 67, 73–80, 86, 90, 92, 93, 95, 96, 180
The Safety of Objects (Troche, Rose) 84
The Saltmen of Tibet (Koch, Ulrike) 120
San Andreas (Peyton, Brad) 35, 36, 49, 52, 60–2, 108, 179
Saxton, Libby 13, 18
Schrader, Astrid 126

Schrader, Paul 170
sci-fi movies 4, 29, 30, 37, 39, 44, 45, 49, 88
Scott, Seann William 92
sea level rise 4, 15–16, 99, 101, 105, 107, 109, 111, 119, 120, 122, 123, 128, 137, 181
Second World War 4, 16, 20, 22, 29, 107
Seinfeld (sitcom) 179
Serres, Richard 131
Seymour, Nicole 74, 80
Shaviro, Steven 89
Shohat, Ella 18
Short Cuts (Altman, Robert) 67, 69–73, 74, 75, 77, 80–1, 84, 87, 89, 92, 94, 95
  earthquake in 69
Skyjacked (Guillermin, John) 43
Skyscraper (Thurber, Rawson Marshall) 62
Sleep Furiously (Koppel, Gideon) 119
slow cinema 30, 142, 145
Smaill, Belinda 102, 121
Smith, Will 175
Snowpiercer (Joon-ho, Bong) 51
Solnit, Rebecca 4
Someplace with a Mountain (Goodall, Steve) 102, 127
Sontag, Susan 1, 4, 36, 38–9, 44, 49, 51, 64, 81, 87, 94
Southland Tales (Kelly, Richard) 67, 81, 87, 88, 89–90, 91, 93–6, 104, 169, 180
Soylent Green (Fleischer, Richard) 43, 50
Sparrow, Tom 12, 155
Speed (de Bont, Jan) 53
Staehler, Tanja 68
Stalker (Tarkovsky, Andrei) 29
Stam, Robert 18
Star Wars films 51
Staying with the Trouble (Haraway, Donna) 10, 15, 24, 66, 134
Steinberg, Philip 123, 131
Stern, Lesley 24
Stevens, Fisher 99, 111
Steyerl, Hito 91
Strange Weather: Culture, Science, and Technology in the Age of Limits (book) 69
Stromboli (Rossellini, Roberto) 164
Sully (Eastwood, Clint) 80
Sultana, Farhana 114

Sun in an Empty Room (painting) 74
superhero comics 29
Swanson, Heather 127, 171
The Sweet Hereafter (Egoyan, Atom) 69
Sweetgrass (Barbash and Castaing-Taylor) 119
Szaniawski, Jeremi 143

Take Shelter (Nichols, Jeff) 13, 28
Te Punga Somerville, Alice 102
Teeth (Lichtenstein, Mitchell) 50
The Terminator (Cameron, James) 57
There Once Was an Island (March, Briar) 30, 99, 101, 119, 122–137, 171, 181
This Island Earth (Newman and Arnold) 38
3/11, Fukushima disaster 1, 2, 3–4, 7, 14, 182
  and climate change 14
  earthquake and tsunami 3–4
Through the Olive Trees (Kiarostami, Abbas) 168
ThuleTuvalu (von Gunten, Matthias) 102
Tiatia, Angela 128
tidal wave/tsunami 3, 35–6
Time of the Wolf (Haneke, Michael) 4, 30, 141–4, 147–9, 153, 155, 156, 158, 159, 160, 164, 166, 171, 181
Titanic (Cameron, James) 111
The Towering Inferno (Guillermin, John) 41, 42, 61, 62
Transformers: Age of Extinction (Bay, Michael) 59
Transformers: Dark Side of the Moon (Bay, Michael) 107
von Trier, Lars 170
Trinh, T. Minh-ha 131
Truffaut, François 22, 28
Twister (de Bont, Jan) 45
2010s disaster movies 28, 35, 36, 48, 49, 59–60, 62

2012 (Emmerich, Roland) 49, 107–8
Tzoumakis, Yannis 67

underwater imagery 128
United States 15–16, 29
Unthinking Eurocentrism (book) 18

da Vinci, Leonardo 44
Virilio, Paul 42
virtual reality (VR) work in movies 129
Vitruvian Man (painting) 44
Volcano (Jackson, Mick) 45

Walker, Janet 105, 127
war, effect on filmmaking 20, 45, 74
The War of the Worlds (book) 39, 45
Wark, McKenzie 50
water 122–9
  slow motion shots across 122–3
  view from a body 122–9
  virtual reality (VR) work 129
Waterworld (Reynolds, Kevin) 46, 50
Weatherill, Charlotte 109–10, 125
Wells, H. G. 39
Where Is the Friend's Home? (Kiarostami, Abbas) 168
White Noise (book) 94–5
White, Rob 74
Why We Fight (Capra, Frank) 21
Wiesel, Elie 156
Williams, Linda 18, 64–5
world cinema 2, 30, 38, 53
The Writing of the Disaster (book) 11, 167
Wyler, William 20, 23, 151

Yacowar, Maurice 7, 8, 36, 42, 43
Yusuf Sayed 177

Žižek, Slavoj 90
Zylinska, Joanna 5, 11, 12, 25, 45, 100

www.ingramcontent.com/pod-product-compliance
Lightning Source LLC
Chambersburg PA
CBHW052042300426
44117CB00012B/1934